MORALITY AND MODERNITY

This book argues that the modern world calls into existence certain conceptions of morality, but also destroys the grounds for taking them seriously. Modernity both needs morality and makes it impossible.

Morality and Modernity has a broader focus than is usual within moral philosophy in that it spells out the social presuppositions of the various conceptions of morality at work in the modern world. This enables it to cast new light on some familar topics in contemporary moral philosophy – utilitarianism, Kantianism, liberalism, rights, virtue, and moral realism, as well as on some less familiar ones – power, gender, nihilism, and nationalism. It also provides a critical account of the most important moral responses to modernity, ranging from Mandeville, Hume, Adam Smith and Kant, through Marx, Nietzsche, and Weber, to Gewirth, Rawls, Habermas, and MacIntyre.

Ross Poole believes that if moral philosophy is to reassert its traditional ambition to stake out a position on the important social issues of the day, it must take seriously its own social content. A moral philosophy is an aspect of social life, and it is only as such that it can be mobilised and brought critically to bear on existing social practices.

Ross Poole is Associate Professor of Philosophy at Macquarie University, Australia

IDEAS
Series Editor:
Jonathan Rée, Middlesex Polytechnic

Original philosophy today is written mainly for advanced academic specialists. Students and the general public make contact with it only through introductions and general guides.

The philosophers are drifting away from their public, and the public has no access to its philosophers.

The IDEAS series is dedicated to changing this situation. It is committed to the idea of philosophy as a constant challenge to intellectual conformism. It aims to link primary philosophy to non-specialist concerns. And it encourages writing which is both simple and adventurous, scrupulous and popular. In these ways it hopes to put contemporary philosophers back in touch with ordinary readers.

Books in the series include:

SOCIAL PHILOSOPHY
Hans Fink

PHILOSOPHY AND THE NEW PHYSICS
Jonathan Powers

THE MAN OF REASON
Genevieve Lloyd

PHILOSOPHICAL TALES
Jonathan Rée

Forthcoming

FREEDOM, TRUTH AND HISTORY
Stephen Houlgate

MORALITY AND MODERNITY

Ross Poole

London and New York

FOR MY MOTHER
AND
IN MEMORY OF MY FATHER

First published 1991
by Routledge
11 New Fetter Lane, London EC4P 4EE

Simultaneously published in the USA and Canada
by Routledge
a division of Routledge, Chapman and Hall, Inc.
29 West 35th Street, New York, NY 10001

Typeset in 10/12pt Bembo by
J&L Composition Ltd, Filey, North Yorkshire
Printed in Great Britain by
Biddles Ltd, Guildford, Surrey

British Library Cataloguing in Publication Data
Poole, Ross
Morality and modernity. — (Ideas)
1. Moral philosophy
I. Title II. Series
170

Library of Congress Cataloging in Publication Data
Poole, Ross.
Morality and modernity/Ross Poole.
p. cm. — (Ideas)
Includes bibliographical references and index.
1. Ethics, Modern. 2. Liberalism. I. Title. II. Series: Ideas (London, England)
BJ301.P66 1991
170'.9'03—dc20 90-39730

ISBN 0-415-03600-3 — ISBN 0-415-03601-1 (pbk.)

CONTENTS

PREFACE

I have been fortunate that friends have been willing to read and criticise various drafts of this book. Genevieve Lloyd, Tony Skillen, Carole Pateman, Paul Redding and Lisabeth During have all made extensive comments on substantial parts of the manuscript. Jonathan Rée has read much of the material several times over, and has always been a sympathetic critic, as well as a meticulous and creative editor. There would have been many more deficiencies in argument, presentation and style if it had not been for the patience, knowledge and critical acumen of these people. In less direct but very real ways, the book contains much that I have learned over the years from the late Bill Bonney, Win Childs, Nicholas During, Ann Game, Ian Lennie, Sandy Lynch, San MacColl, Alexander Poole and Lynne Segal.

A belated conversion to word-processing meant that I was able to prepare most of the manuscript by myself; however, it would be remiss not to mention the generous and efficient secretarial support I have received over many years from Barbara Young. Virginia Calov and Carol Cohn provided crucial assistance in the last stages.

To all these people, many thanks.

I have drawn on material from the following published papers: 'Morality, Masculinity and the Market', *Radical Philosophy*, Spring 1985, No. 39, pp. 16–23; 'Structures of Identity: Gender and Nationalism', in Paul Patton and Ross Poole (eds), *War/Masculinity*, Sydney, Intervention Publications, 1985; 'Modernity, Rationality, and "the Masculine"', in Terry Threadgold and Anne Cranny-Francis (eds), *Feminine/Masculine and Representation*, Sydney, George Allen & Unwin, 1990; and 'Nietzsche: The Subject of Morality', *Radical Philosophy*, Spring 1990, No. 54, pp. 2–9.

Ross Poole
February 1990

INTRODUCTION

The argument of this book is a simple one. It is that the modern world calls into existence certain conceptions of morality, but also destroys the grounds for taking them seriously. Modernity both needs morality, and makes it impossible.

The concept of morality is not, except in a highly abstract and non-specific sense, a universal; every society constructs its own form of morality. So my argument is not that the modern world destroys the ground for believing in certain universal moral principles and values; it is rather that it provides no good reason for believing in its *own* principles and values. Modernity has called into play a dominant conception of what it is to have reason to act; this conception has the consequence that the dictates of morality have little purchase on the motivations of those to whom they are addressed. Modernity has constructed a conception of knowledge which excludes the possibility of moral knowledge; morality becomes, not a matter of rational belief, but subjective opinion. In a world which is antithetical to faith and dogma, morality can only survive as a matter of personal faith or dogmatic conviction. In neither case can morality retain the authority it needs to play its role in social and individual life.

I use the term 'modernity' to cover that form of society which began to come into existence in Western Europe in the seventeenth and eighteenth centuries, found its exemplary manifestation in North America, and has since spread to or impinged on the rest of the world. The term is intended to invoke the idea – which has been around at least since the beginning of this period – that the modern world differs in significant respects from other – 'premodern', 'traditional' – forms of society. But what are the differentiating features of modern society? In the first three chapters I consider several answers to this question. The idea that the spread of market relationships is the key to understanding modern social life was the product of eighteenth century attempts to understand the new 'commercial society' that was then coming into existence. The concept of the market was the great achievement of classical political economy; a version of it continues to dominate mainstream economic theorising. For Marx in the nineteenth century, it was not the market as such but the dynamic of capital accumulation which was central to understanding modernity. At the beginning of the twentieth century, Max Weber gave an account of modernisation in terms of the concept of 'rationalisation'. In more recent years, feminist writers have emphasised the changing form of the distinction between an arena of 'public' life and a presupposed but marginalised realm of 'private' life. This account has placed the issue of gender at the heart of the analysis of modernity.

These accounts have often been developed in critical response to each other. For my purposes, however, it is possible to treat them as complementary: each serves to pick out aspects of social life ignored or downplayed by the others. Each provides a description of a way of life which is characteristic of the modern world; each provides an account of human agency, human relationships and – neither last nor least – a conception of morality. These ways of life, and their associated moralities, exist in varied relationships of complementarity and tension with each other. Part of the moral problem of modernity is that there is no principled way in which disputes between them can be resolved. But this is merely symptomatic of a deeper problem. Modernity supplies no good reason to accept any of the disputing moral positions. Each morality provides an account of what individuals ought to do, but none of them provides a good reason for individuals to take them seriously. Given the conceptions of human agency and reason prevalent in the modern world, a rational individual will reject the claims of morality. As Bernard Mandeville suggested at the beginning of the eighteenth century, morality can only be a system of illusion, whose main justification is that it serves certain social purposes.

In Chapters 4 to 6, I consider three of the more significant moral responses to modernity. Liberalism, in a form derived largely from Kant, continues to dominate discussion of morality in recent philosophy. In Chapter 4, I situate and criticise three different versions of liberalism: that of Alan Gewirth, of John Rawls and of

Jürgen Habermas. In Chapter 5, I discuss a moral ideology which has been of enormous significance in the modern world, but which has not received anything like the attention it deserves from philosophers – the discourse of nationalism. In Chapter 6, I consider Nietzsche's claim that the appropriate response to modernity is to reject morality altogether. For Nietzsche, nihilism is the fate of modernity, and it is a fate which should not merely be accepted, but embraced with joy and enthusiasm. In many respects, Nietzsche's position is the most coherent response to modernity, even though it is – quite literally – mad. I suggest that Nietzsche's own collapse into insanity signals in the strongest sense possible the moral failure of modernity.

The thesis that morality is suspect in the modern world is not a new one. Almost inevitably, it is asserted in nostalgic mode: morality is suspect now in a way in which it was not in premodern societies. Clearly it is well to be sceptical of narratives which tell of a fall from an earlier state of grace; idealising the past is no way to understand the present. We should be as suspicious of stories of decline as we have learned to be suspicious of earlier stories of progress. They tell the same story, but reverse the values. There is no one contrast between modern and premodern societies, and to talk of the transition between them in terms of loss or gain begs almost all the important questions.

My main purpose in this book is to provide a diagnosis of the moral failures of modernity, but in the final chapter I make some tentative suggestions for overcoming these failures. I discuss some of the arguments in Alasdair MacIntyre's influential *After Virtue*, and try to extract what I take to be their rational core from the nostalgic mode in which they are presented, and the reactionary nature of his conclusions. MacIntyre's rejection of modernity is absolute; for him, the only hope for the resurrection of morality lies in those residues of a lost past which continue to exist in the modern world. My own view of modernity is a more nuanced one, and I argue against MacIntyre that if there is hope, it does not lie in the past but in the present: in those elements of modernity which point towards an alternative future.

The book is an essay in moral philosophy. But it takes a wider focus than has been usual within that discipline – at least in the English speaking world. While many of the themes discussed in the following pages – utilitarianism, Kantian moral philosophy, justice, virtue, the objectivity of moral judgements – will be familiar to students of recent moral philosophy, others – nationalism, power, consumption, gender – will not. Even the more familiar topics will be placed in a context which disciplinary boundaries would locate elsewhere than in moral philosophy. But it is part of my argument that positions in moral philosophy are informed by much more general views about the nature of society – and vice versa. We will not get far in understanding any of the major positions which have been taken within moral philosophy, unless we are prepared to look at the conceptions of the human individual, human relationships and ultimately of the nature of society, which inform them. Nor, conversely, will we get far in studying forms of social life unless we accept that conceptions of morality are implicit in every form of human existence.

Moral philosophy has recently begun to reassert its traditional ambition to stake out a position on the important social issues of the day. If it is to be successful in this enterprise, it must take seriously its own social content. Too often, moral philosophers – especially those of a Kantian or utilitarian bent – have sought an external vantage point from which social issues might be assessed. The cost of this enterprise has been vacuity and irrelevance. Morality is an aspect of social life, and it is only as such that it can be mobilised and brought critically to bear on existing social practices. Of course, as aspects of social life, moralities are themselves subject to social criticism and change. The task of moral philosophy is to participate in that process of criticism and to help direct that change. When moral philosophy becomes aware of its own social content, it will become aware of some of its limitations. But it may also come to recognise some of its strengths.

1

THE MARKET AND ITS MORALITIES: UTILITARIANISM, KANTIANISM AND THE LOSS OF VIRTUE

> Supposing virtue had been the road to fortune, either I should have been virtuous or I should have simulated virtue as well as the next man.
>
> (Diderot)[1]

It is hard to overestimate the importance of the eighteenth century in the genesis of modern conceptions of social life. It was in this century that a large number of thinkers came to believe that a fundamentally new kind of society was coming into existence in Western Europe, and undertook the project of making sense of the changes that were taking place. The enterprise was immensely productive, not only of an understanding of the modern world, but also of how that understanding was to be gained. Almost all the disciplines which today define the various areas of social enquiry can trace their origins to the disputes, debates and discoveries of the eighteenth century: economics, sociology, ethnography, history, aesthetics, even philosophy, were all born in this period. The fixity of the divisions between the disciplines was, however, a later development. Though most of the great theorists of the eighteenth century – Hume, Adam Smith, Adam Ferguson, Mandeville, Montesquieu, Diderot, Voltaire – celebrated the division of labour, they did not practise it. (Significantly enough, it was Kant who called for a more intensive application of the division of labour in intellectual life: in practising what he preached, he invented modern philosophy.[2]) In particular, they did not draw a sharp distinction between social understanding and moral debate. They were aware that the issue between tradition and modernity was a choice between different ways of life and the different conceptions of morality associated with those ways of life. Their project was not just to understand but also to participate in the moral debates which accompanied the transition to the modern world. It is necessary for us to understand their enterprise – as they understood it – as 'moral science'. That this term has become, not just an archaism, but a near oxymoron, is a consequence of their work; but it is also a barrier to understanding it.

My concern in this chapter is with one major theme in eighteenth century moral science: the characterisation of modern society as 'commercial society', or – as we would say now – as 'market society'. This concept was given its canonical formulation by Adam Smith, but it can reasonably be considered a collective product. It was one of the great intellectual achievements of the eighteenth century, and it continues to dominate mainstream economic thought. It also, I will argue, informs the dominant conceptions of morality in the modern world. Initially I will present it without some of the nuances and qualifications with which it was presented by Adam Smith and others. Some – though not all – of these will emerge later in the chapter.

'COMMERCIAL SOCIETY'

> Man has almost constant occasion for the help of his brethren, and it is vain for him to expect it from their benevolence only. He will be more likely to prevail if he can interest their self-love in his favour, and show them that it is for their advantage to do for him what he requires of them. Whoever offers to another a bargain of any kind, proposes to do this. Give me that which I want, and you shall have this which you want, is the meaning of every such offer; and it is in this manner that we obtain from one another the far greater part of the good offices that we stand in need of. It is not from the benevolence of the butcher, the brewer, or the baker, that we expect our dinner, but from their regard to their own interest. We address ourselves, not to their humanity but to their self-love, and never talk to them of our necessities but of their advantages.
>
> (Adam Smith)[3]

Many of the characteristic features of commercial society derive from three elements:

(i) a social division of labour, such that the various productive activities through which human wants are satisfied are divided amongst distinct individuals and groups of individuals (thus there are those who grow wheat, others who bake bread, still others who brew beer and so on);
(ii) a legal framework of private property and contract, such that individuals have exclusive rights to the use of those objects which they own, and also the right to transfer these rights to others; and
(iii) an individual propensity for self-interested behaviour.

These conditions did not spring into existence in the sixteenth or seventeenth century; elements of them have been present in almost all societies. What is uniquely characteristic of the modern world is the extent to which they have become central and pervasive features of social life. Historically, the development of the three conditions went more or less hand in hand. It was not until a legal institution of individual property rights was well established that a national and international division of labour came to exist, not just for a few luxury items, but for a wide range of subsistence goods. Alongside these developments was the emergence of a conception of identity and motivation focussed on the independent private property owning individual. For the moment, however, I will not be concerned with the historical actuality of market society, but with its concept – with an 'ideal type' in Max Weber's sense. For this it is convenient to treat the conditions as distinct though related elements.

If we assume that each individual has a variety of wants, then the social division of labour implies a situation of mutual interdependence, with each individual dependent upon the activity of others for the satisfaction of his wants. (We will see in Chapter 3 why the male pronoun is appropriate here.) The institution of private property means that the goods are not directly available to satisfy the wants of those who do not own them. The problem is resolved through the market: individuals exchange goods which they own but do not want for goods they want but do not own. Thus, goods become commodities. Exchange may be direct, as in barter. However, any moderately complex market economy will require the existence of money as a medium of exchange, where money both measures the exchange value of all other commodities and is directly exchangeable with them.

Each individual will strive to maximise the satisfaction of his wants. All things being equal, he will only be able to do this by participating in market relationships, and this will require that he direct his energies towards producing goods which other people want. Thus, the self-interested individual must become socially productive. Each individual will strive to sell his own goods for as much as possible, and purchase those of others for as little as possible. However, so long as there is no interference, each must accept the price determined by the ratio between the supply of similar goods and the effective demand for them. In these circumstances, the best way for an individual to improve his position is to be more efficient than his competitors. So the market puts a premium on productive efficiency. Of course, fluctuations in supply and demand will benefit the fortunate, and penalise the unfortunate. However, such fluctuations will be reflected in the price of commodities, and this will enable those adversely affected to relocate their productive activity away from areas of over-production. Where everyone does this, there will be a tendency for demand and supply to move towards an equilibrium, and thus for those wants which find expression in the market to be satisfied by it. But this tendency will never be fully realised. The diversity of individual wants which is presupposed by the market will be increased by it, goods which were once luxuries will come to be taken for granted, and what were wants will become needs. However, as wants and needs increase, so too will the market provide the means to satisfy them.

These results may be called 'invisible hand theorems' (after Adam Smith). Individuals pursue essentially self-directed goals, but as a consequence of this, a range of other goals are achieved: the wants of others are satisfied, productive efficiency increases, what were luxuries become everyday consumption items and so on.[4] There is a logic to the process, but it is not that of individual intention. The overall social order must be conceived in terms of the unintended consequences of individual action. There is, in other words, a hiatus between the intentional content of individual activity and its overall social significance.

This story presupposes a certain quite specific conception of individual identity. If the operations of the market are going to fall into the beneficent patterns described, the participants must be prepared to exchange their property, move from one area of productive activity to another and give up particular social relationships as market forces dictate. This implies that the individuals concerned have a concept of themselves – an 'identity' as I shall use the term – which is given independently of (in 'abstraction from') specific property holdings, specific kinds of work and specific social relationships. In other social forms, that one owns a particular piece of land, performs particular tasks or stands in particular social relations, has been considered essential to one's identity. They are conceived of, not as subject to choice, but rather as defining the place from which choices are made. Within the market, however, these become not sources of identity, but roles which one might assume better to achieve one's purposes. The individual who assumes these roles, but has an identity independent of them, is the abstract individual of much liberal, political, economic and social theorising.

The goals pursued by these abstract individuals also take on an abstract and indeterminate character. There are a large number of diverse productive activities co-ordinated by the market. Each of these activities has its specific goals and criteria of performance. However, insofar as the individual must be prepared to move from one activity to another, he must be concerned, not so much with the goals which are specific to each activity (e.g. the particular excellence involved in a craft), but with an end which is achievable through certain activities but which may equally be achieved through others. Though the market presupposes a range of different desires, it imposes a certain homogeneity on them. The object of desire is always something beyond the activity which one engages in to achieve it. Indeed, it becomes plausible to suppose that all the desires which find expression in the market have a common goal, a shared end for which the medley of activities in the market is merely a means.

It is a matter of some nicety to specify what that end is. It must be something which is sufficiently non-specific to be produced equally by a wide variety of different activities, but at the same time have sufficient substance to move individuals to action on its behalf. This problem was resolved by early utilitarians by positing pleasure (or happiness) as the ultimate object of all desire, and pain (or unhappiness) as the ultimate object of all aversion, where these were conceived of as measurable psychological states, distinct from the activities which produced them. The relationship of this pleasure/pain continuum to these activities was precisely analogous to the profit and loss which resulted from market transactions;

indeed, on Bentham's customarily blunt account of the matter, one's pain or pleasure is precisely measured by the amount of money one possesses:

> The thermometer is the instrument for measuring the heat of the weather: the barometer for measuring the pressure of the air. Those who are not satisfied with the accuracy of these instruments must find out others that shall be more accurate, or bid *adieu* to Natural Philosophy. Money is the instrument for measuring the quantity of pain or pleasure. Those who are not satisfied with the accuracy of this instrument must find out some other that shall be more accurate, or bid *adieu* to Politics and Morals.[5]

Contemporary utilitarians have sought to avoid the psychological implausibility of Bentham's account by positing, as a kind of metadesire, the desire to satisfy all one's other desires, so that what is finally desired is the satisfaction of all (or as many as possible) of one's desires. This manoeuvre provides an absolutely general way of specifying what it is one wants when one wants something, without being committed to the thesis that there is a substantive object (a psychological state or whatever) which is always wanted. The precise solution is of little importance here. I will occasionally adopt the jargon of individuals seeking to maximise their 'utilities', but do not pretend to have a clear account of what this means. The major point is that however we characterise the final goal of individual behaviour, this must take on a highly abstract and non-specific character; it thus corresponds to the equally abstract character of the goal seeking individual.

Mediating between these two abstractions are the various determinate activities involved in the production and exchange of commodities. These may be characterised as 'work' in the slightly special sense of activities whose *raison d'être* lies outside them: they are primarily conceived of as means to distinct ends. As such, these activities fall within the scope of that form of reason which is required by the market: that of seeking the most efficient means of achieving given ends. The individual who is rational in this instrumental sense is one who minimises the work required for the goal pursued; and unless an individual is rational in this way, he will not participate effectively in market transactions.

This form of reason must also inform the behaviour of individuals with respect to each other. If the invisible hand is to weave its beneficent patterns, each individual must be prepared to treat others solely in terms of their contribution to his own goals. If he is moved by the circumstances of those with whom he is bargaining, he will not enforce the competitive price; if he is touched by the plight of his employees, he will not replace them with more efficient methods of production; and if he is sensitive to the feelings and aspirations of his debtors, he will not enforce bankruptcies. In the long run it is non-altruistic behaviour which produces the most beneficial results; however, that run may be very long indeed, and the suffering of many specific individuals remains uncompensated, except perhaps by the prosperity of others. Widespread sensitivity to the plight of such individuals would mean that the long run tendencies would remain unactualised. It is only to the extent that individuals are ready to act with a certain impersonality, not to say ruthlessness, with respect to each other that the market as a whole will exhibit the beneficent tendencies which have been its glory.

Once the identity of the individual is conceived in abstraction from his relations with others, the assumption of pervasive self-interest becomes almost inescapable. Other individuals occur in the reasoning of such individuals only as means or impediments to ends which are independent of them. Within this structure, it becomes impossible to conceive of activities which are genuinely other-directed, i.e. take the well-being (or the ill-being for that matter) of another as their goal. And whatever the precise content of the individual's final goals, these are sought as *his* goals (his utility, his gratification). The self-directedness which is necessary for optimal market behaviour emerges as part of the very structure of purposive activity.

Reason in an instrumental sense informs the behaviour of the market individual. But reason also exists in another form and with a different function: that of comprehending the workings of commercial society and explaining them to its members. For the market is characterised by a certain opacity: as a whole, it displays certain patterns or regularities, which have something of the appearance of natural laws. However, these laws are not natural, but social: they are the outcome of human actions. But, as we have seen, they are not intended as such; rather they are the unintended consequence of what individuals do. Hence, it is the task of the science of society, with political economy as its first exemplar, to discern the nature of these laws and to explain to those who both make these laws but are subject to them, the secret of their own social behaviour.[6] The cognitive gap between individual intention and social consequence which it is the task of social science to bridge is not merely the result of inattention or social complexity. It is due to a discontinuity between what is intended and what is finally achieved. The individual is concerned solely with his own well-being; nevertheless, the result of what he does is to further the well-being of others with whom he is not concerned. Indeed, he will secure this result much more surely than if he had taken the well-being of others as the direct object of his behaviour.[7] It is part of the logic of the market to sever the conceptual continuity between the intentional content of an individual's action and its overall social meaning. Reason in the form of social science is needed to explain to the individual the meaning of what he does.

In so doing, of course, it also justifies it. Self-interest is validated, not in its own terms, but because it is conducive to social well-being. This argument has important repercussions for conceptions of morality. For it is a crucial presupposition of an ethics of virtue, at least in the form in which this was debated in the late sixteenth and early seventeenth centuries,[8] that there be a continuity between the motivation for an act and its effects, e.g. between the virtuous disposition to seek the public good and the actual furthering of that goal. However, if it is the case – as was gleefully argued by Bernard Mandeville[9] – that an overriding concern with self is a much more effective source of social prosperity and well-being, that 'private vices' are 'public benefits', then that presupposition fails. In which case the 'knight of virtue'[10] must either adopt the quixotic and unattractive stance of clinging to the moral centrality of motivation whatever the consequences, or move towards a more consequentialist evaluation of human acts. This latter is the path towards utilitarianism.

UTILITARIANS AND FREE-RIDERS

It is not surprising that utilitarianism is the morality most readily associated with the market. After all, the glory of the market is the extent to which it maximises production in just those directions in which human wants exist and minimises the effort involved. If the satisfaction of wants counts as happiness and effort as pain, and the excess of happiness over pain is utility, then utility seems to be just what the market provides, and utilitarianism just what it needs.

There are many conceptual, as well as historical, linkages between the theory of the market and modern (i.e. post-Bentham) utilitarianism. First, there is the conception of happiness or utility as something distinct from the various activities which give rise to it. As we have seen, this concept of a final goal is strongly suggested by the account of individual motivation presupposed by the market. It is equally involved in any systematic presentation of utilitarianism. If the general happiness is to be the *summum bonum* of morality, then the various particular happinesses must be conceived as commensurable, perhaps even quantifiable items, so that they may all be combined together as components of this global happiness; they are thus distinct from the qualitatively diverse activities which produce them. Second, both utilitarianism and market theory employ the same concept of rationality: the end is given, and the role of reason is to minimise the costs of achieving that end. Finally, the utilitarian calculus makes no essential reference to such contingencies as friendship and love. These have their instrumental value or disvalue as sources of pleasure or pain, but then so too do other forms of consumption. Utilitarianism strictly enjoins us to count all subjects of happiness and pain as equal, and not to give particular consideration to those near and dear to us. Utilitarian morality is as impersonal as the market in its distribution of rewards and punishments.

Modern critics are no doubt right to argue that psychological hedonism, i.e. the claim that each individual seeks to maximise his own pleasure and minimise his own pain, is logically distinct from the utilitarian moral principle that each individual ought to maximise total pleasure and minimise total pain. However, if the self-interest which is characteristic of market behaviour is conceived to be the way in which pleasure maximising behaviour is translated into the currency of commodities and exchange, then there is a causal relationship between hedonistic behaviour and the utilitarian goal. There may even be a stronger connection. After all, if it is the case that his own happiness is for each individual the only good, then it is a tantalisingly easy move to the claim that the only social good – i.e. the good(s) of all individuals – is the happiness of all individuals. While this is not a decisive argument, it provides a challenge: what *else* could the social good be?

The causal link between self-interested behaviour and overall social well-being is only maintained so long as self-interest operates within the limits set by private property and contract. However, it is not clear that individuals who are ruthlessly self-interested as we have supposed them to be will respect those limits. They will, one would assume, steal or break contracts just as soon as it is in their interests to do so, i.e. when the probability of gain outweighs that of loss. But unless individuals have some assurance that property rights will be respected and contracts kept, they will have no reason to involve themselves in production and exchange. Without some constraints on the operation of self-interest, the market would soon collapse into chaos. So the individual must be supplied with a reason for keeping his actions within the limits necessary to sustain the market. The existence of an effective legal framework is clearly part of the story. We have good instrumental reason not to steal if we know we are likely to be caught. But it does not seem likely that it could be the whole story. Often enough, instrumental reason will suggest that we would get away with breaking the law. The stability of a system of law usually depends on coercion being required only in a few cases, with the majority of those subject to the law obeying it because they think that, in some sense, they 'ought' to. Somewhere along the line, morality enters the picture: we respect the property of others and keep our promises because we think that it is morally right to do so.

Prima facie, utilitarianism seems well suited to provide the appropriate morality. From the assumption that generalised utility is the goal to be achieved, together with the thesis of pervasive self-interest, it is a relatively easy matter to deduce the need for a state and a body of law laying down the various restrictions on individual behaviour which are necessary. (Bentham devoted much of his life to the fine tuning of this enterprise.) Further, if utility is the source of moral value, this derivation is also a justification of these restrictions. Thus, the union between utilitarian morality and the market seems appropriate and felicitous.

There is, however, a crucial problem. A utilitarian morality may successfully specify just those limitations required by the market; but if these are to exist as duties or obligations, they must have some purchase on the motives of those subject to them. If generalised utility is to be the ground of obligation it must provide or locate a reason why those subject to the obligations should act in the ways prescribed. I use the term 'reason' here fairly broadly. It is intended to capture the idea that when one knows what one ought to do one also has, *eo ipso*, some motivation, though not necessarily a sufficient one, so to act. To inform an individual that he ought to do something is, in this broad sense, to provide him with a reason for so acting. Thus, if the account provided by utilitarianism of what is morally obligatory is to be satisfactory, it must provide or link up with an explanation of its purchase on the motivation of those subject to it. Clearly, this generates problems for utilitarianism. The content of utilitarian morality is the general happiness; but the psychological basis for market behaviour is concern for oneself. Is there a place for this other concern which now seems necessary?

There is only one answer to this question which is compatible with the austere account of the market provided so far. If we continue to assume that individuals will act out of a calculated concern for their own well-being, then the only possible restriction on self-interest must be self-interest itself. David Hume was, at least in the *Treatise*, tempted towards a position like this:

> There is no passion ... capable of controlling the interested affection, but the very affection itself, by an alteration of its direction. ... For whether the passion of self-interest be esteemed virtuous or vicious, 'tis all of a case; since it alone restrains it.[11]

Self-interest is generally furthered by preserving the institutions of property and contract, so the required motivation to restrict one's activity comes from rational self-interest. The force of morality is, on this account, that of a reasoned assessment of what is best for the individual, and the apparent conflict between duty and inclination is the conflict between long term and short term self-interest.

As Hume came to recognise, this suggestion fails. While the connection between the well-being of the individual and that of society may hold in general, there are far too many cases where the two come apart for it to be plausible to hold that there is an identity between them. To take only the most striking case: even in a peaceful society, there will be cases where protection of the society from external or internal enemies will require that some individuals be prepared to sacrifice their property and even their lives on its behalf. And there is no way that this can be justified on the basis of individual self-interest, however rational and long term.[12]

A slightly different problem is the case of the 'free-rider'.[13] On any occasion when self-interest prompts an individual to infringe the property rights of another or to renege on a contractually incurred obligation, he may be imagined to reason as follows:

> While it is in my interests that this institution (property, contract) exists, and I can see that its existence depends on people generally respecting it, it is highly unlikely that my not doing so now will make a significant difference. It may be the case that if everyone else reasons as I do and breaches the institution when self-interest prompts it, then the institution on which they and I depend will break down, and I certainly do not want this to happen. But the fact that I reason this way and act upon my reasoning is of negligible relevance to how other people reason and act. Hence, I will breach the institution.

But everyone will reason this way; and so the institutions on which the market depends will collapse.

One response – Hobbes' near enough[14] – to the free-rider's reasoning is to propose a system of coercion which is so efficient, with sanctions which are so terrible, that it will never be rational to argue in this way because the probability and extent of punishment will always outweigh the probability and extent of gain. However, Hobbes' solution merely postpones the problem. The morality in question must also apply to those who must enforce the law and punish breaches of it. But it is easy enough to generate free-rider problems for them, especially when they are called upon to resist the offer of a bribe, or to risk life and limb in the service of the law. The problem cannot, on pain of regress, be resolved in this way.

What the free-rider shows is that the moral disposition necessary to support a utilitarian morality cannot be found in the structure of rational self-interest. But where else can it be found? At this point it is necessary to modify the account of the market provided so far. Some utilitarians have fallen back on an assumption of benevolence.[15] They have postulated, as part of the psychological equipment of those subject to a utilitarian morality, a sentiment of generalised fellow feeling: the capacity to desire the happiness of others and feel an aversion to their sufferings. Given that this sentiment exists, perhaps in a latent form, it will be the function of moral discourse to activate it. However, though feelings of benevolence and fellow feeling are familiar enough, they are of their nature directed towards specifiable and usually familiar others. But the obligations necessary to regulate market behaviour concern unknown others; they come into play just where benevolence is lacking. Further, the account of the market which displays its beneficent tendencies as a whole is such as to preclude beneficence as an active principle in the parts. This is not to say that it requires active animosity. On the contrary, it is antithetical to any non-transferable emotion. It requires a reasoned concern with one's own well-being and a disinterest in the well-being of others.

Adam Smith, who saw this problem more clearly than most, tended to fall back on an assumption of virtue: a readiness to override self-interest in the name of the public good. But the existence of this motivation is as problematic as that of benevolence. As Smith in some moods recognised, and as his compatriot Adam Ferguson argued more strongly, just those aspects of commercial society which were responsible for its glories, would also militate against the practice of virtue. The division of labour would limit the vision and concerns of those subject to it, and the inequalities which were its natural consequence would create envy and hostility. These would all work against the development of a concern for the public well-being.[16]

There is a deeper problem. The kind of identity presupposed by the market is that of an individual whose well-being may well be achieved in ways which detract from the overall social well-being (except insofar as it is a very small part of it). To demand virtue of such an individual is to ask for a quite inexplicable altruism: a sacrifice of everything to which his life is devoted. But worse, such altruism will in crucial cases be, not just mysterious, but irrational. Let us suppose that an individual does, inexplicably, take the general good as an end. In the cases before us, securing that good requires that enough individuals are prepared to forego their own interests on its behalf. The contribution of any given individual will often be very small compared with that well-being which is sacrificed by refraining from theft or from breaking a contract. The rational altruist (the man of virtue) will know that *his* contribution to maintaining the institution will make very little difference to whether others contribute, and that it is highly unlikely to make a difference to whether the institution is maintained or not. It may make a small contribution, though if it is additional to what is required, it may also be wasted surplus. In any event, the contribution will be small compared with the the individual well-being lost. Thus, even the altruist will not contribute to maintaining those institutions which only marginally depend on his contribution, and instead devotes his energies to more immediate causes where his contribution will make a difference. Indeed, if he reasons that his own well-being is a component part of the overall well-being, the cause to which he devotes his energies may be his own, and his behaviour will be indistinguishable from that of his self-interested neighbour.[17]

This problem is, of course, that of the free-rider again. It shows that not even altruism provides a motive which is sufficient to provide a rational support to a utilitarian morality (or, indeed, to provide a number of other socially necessary goods). In this context, it arises from the attempt to rework an ethic of virtue in a situation where the social identity required by that ethic is not available. Thus, according to Aristotle's (no doubt highly idealised) account, the ancient Greek *polis* defined a form of life in which the identity of the (adult, male) individual is that of citizen and is constituted in part by participation in those activities necessary to sustain the *polis*. In which case, the well-being of the individual ('*eudaimonia*') is in part definable by the contribution that the individual makes to the social good. There is, at least in general, no question of sacrificing the one for the other. In this situation, an appropriate morality – indeed, if we are to believe Aristotle, *the* appropriate morality – is one concerned primarily with excellence of character or virtue. Individuals learn how to live well, and in living well they do what they need to do to sustain the social and political order to which they belong.[18] For the civic humanist tradition, as articulated in eighteenth century debates about commercial society,[19] social identity was conferred by a relationship with a certain kind of property, namely land, which linked the individual to the larger social whole. Performance of those activities necessary to sustain the larger whole (e.g. military and civic duties) was not merely a means of achieving that result, but was also an expression of that identity. The link between the individual and the social good was not secured by the contingencies of the market, but by the social identity of the individual.

An identity of this kind is not available within the market. Here, individual identity is constituted by abstraction, and well-being has to do with acquisition and private enjoyment. One's identity is not given by participation in the politics and culture of the *polis*. Land is not a secure bulwark of personal identity, but an exchangeable item with the same external relationship to its owner as any other commodity. In the absence of these or other comparable sources of social identity, to call for virtue is to ask for an altruism which from the point of view of the market individual is, not just inexplicable, but irrational.

It was in the context of early eighteenth century debates about commercial society that Bernard Mandeville made the unsettling suggestion that the morality necessary to sustain society was only possible as a form of illusion. Mandeville seems to have accepted a form of psychological egoism, and much of his writing was designed to show that an overwhelming concern with self lay at the heart of the most apparently altruistic social behaviour. For Mandeville, a practice of virtue in which the individual devoted himself to the good of society was – strictly speaking – a psychological impossibility. And just as well: the point of his poem 'The Grumbling Hive' was to show that were divine intervention miraculously to inaugurate a life of universal virtue, social stagnation and poverty would be the inevitable result. Self-love was in one form or another the source of all that was valuable in social existence. Mandeville was, however, well aware that there had to be some restrictions on the cruder manifestations of self-love if social life was to be possible at all. Private vices made for public benefits, but only if kept within the bounds of a social morality:

> So Vice is beneficial found,
> When it's by Justice lopt, and bound.[20]

But how could individuals who were overwhelmingly concerned with their own selfish ends be persuaded to subordinate these to the demands of a social morality?

Mandeville's solution to this problem was disarmingly simple. Since men would only act as they ought if they were persuaded that there was something to be gained by it, the path of virtue must be provided with its own rewards. Given that there were not enough actual goods in circulation to provide the necessary rewards, it was the task of 'Law-givers and other Wise Men' to invent imaginary ones:

> Those that have undertaken to civilise Mankind . . . being unable to give so many real Rewards as would satisfy all Persons for every individual Action . . . were forc'd to contrive an imaginary one, that as a general Equivalent for the trouble of Self-denial should serve on all occasions, and without costing anything either to themselves or others, be yet a most acceptable Recompence to the Receivers.[21]

This might seem only to postpone the problem: where were the Law-givers going to discover 'a general Equivalent for the trouble of self-denial' which cost nothing, but which was sufficiently attractive to seduce men into a practice of virtue?

In the ordinary business of commercial society, it was money which functioned as the 'general Equivalent', and it had long been observed that money was a social fiction, the product of a shared imagination rather than a reality in its own right. A piece of metal was money, not because of its intrinsic qualities, but because it was believed to be such. An illusion might thus acquire the status of truth if enough people shared it. It had been a civic republican complaint about commercial society that it dealt in unrealities and fantasies, rather than the more substantial realities represented by land and its products (credit gave them even more cause for concern). It was Mandeville's genius to recognise that unreality and fantasy infected not merely the currency of market values, but also the system of moral values necessary to sustain the market. Men are, he suggested, concerned to satisfy their self-directed desires; but they are also concerned to excel their neighbours, and to be recognised as so doing. Men are, in other words, subject to the passion of pride; and they can satisfy that passion only if they can convince ourselves both that they are superior to their neighbours and also that they are known to be. It becomes a matter of relatively small importance whether they are in fact superior; it is sufficient that they are thought to be so. Though pride is the most self-directed of emotions, it leads men to become increasingly dependent on how they seem to others.[22] It is through the weakness – on some accounts, the vice – of pride, that men are led into a practice of morality. 'Skilful politicians' have succeeded in persuading those over whom they wish to rule that the most significant measure of a person's superiority is the extent to which he is able to subdue his selfish inclinations and to act on behalf of others. Men act as morality requires, not for the sake of the well-being of others nor of the society to which they belong, but to show superiority:

> It is visible then that it was not any Heathen Religion or other Idolatrous Superstition, that first put man upon crossing his Appetites and subduing his dearest Inclinations, but the skilful Management of wary Politicians; and the nearer we search into human Nature, the more we shall be convinc'd, that the Moral Virtues are the Political Offspring which Flattery begot upon Pride.[23]

So effective is this tutelage, Mandeville argued, that men are often led to risk all that is most dear to them, not just in war but in duels with the most trivial causes, just in order not to lose status in the eyes of others. But its most significant consequence is to place the restrictions on self-love which are necessary to make social life possible.

On Mandeville's view, morality is only possible as an illusion. It is based on the assumption that men are prepared to rise above their own private ends and concern themselves with their fellows. In fact, he argued, morality appeals to the most private end of all: the inner glow of being thought superior to others. Mandeville even hinted that we are secretly aware of the deception involved; when we act morally, we know in our hearts that it is not the good of others that we seek, but the conviction of our own superiority. One need not share Mandeville's psychological egoism to recognise the force of Mandeville's argument. Indeed, though Mandeville's account has never been a popular one, it is not hard to discern elements of Mandevillean cynicism in almost all versions of utilitarianism. Utilitarianism feeds on the disjunction between individual motivation and social consequence, and it finds itself with little to say when confronted with the problem of explaining why individuals might be motivated by a concern for the general happiness. Where it does not take refuge in evasion or sophistry, utilitarianism has always been apt to fall back on manipulation.[24] Utilitarianism as a moral philosophy has too often taken over the basic assumptions of Mandeville's approach, but without his wit and honesty, nor his recognition that what it provides is not morality, but a simulacrum of it.

KANTIAN MORALITY

Immanuel Kant provided a better route to market morality. Where utilitarianism takes as its starting point the beneficial consequence of market behaviour, Kant addressed more directly the conception of agency necessary to secure these results.

The market presupposes a framework of property and contract, and thus of rights and duties. Ownership involves the possession of certain rights – to use, to exclude, to sell – with respect to an object; it implies a set of correlative duties – to respect these rights – on all other individuals. To enter into a contract involves the transfer of these rights to another; where this transfer is to take place in the future, it involves a commitment to do something in the future. Now if individuals were as rationally self-concerned as market theory supposes them to be, they would only keep such commitments where these coincided with the promptings of rational self-interest. For such individuals, there could be no practice of entering into a contract with the intention of carrying it out just because it is one's commitment, especially in those cases where it turned out to conflict with self-interest. Nor could there be a practice of respecting the property of another because it is his property. There could, in other words, be no practice of doing one's duty because it is one's duty. In which case the concept of duty would have no application, nor would the correlative concept of a right.

What commercial society requires, therefore, is individuals who are able to do their duty because it is their duty, i.e. to recognise the property of others and to enter into contracts with the intention of keeping them.[25] Such individuals must be free *from* complete determination by their self-interest and thus free *to* act as morality requires. It was Kant's genius to formulate a morality in which the required notions of freedom and duty were central. Morality, Kant argued, is about duty, i.e. about what individuals ought to do whatever the promptings of self-interest; as such, it requires the existence of individuals who are free in both the above senses. Perhaps over-sensitive to the apparent paradox in identifying freedom and duty, later theorists in the Kantian tradition have focussed more on the notion of a right. But given the interdependence of rights and duties, this is little more than a matter of emphasis.

How then to derive the relevant concepts of right and duty? For Kant, the relevant notion of freedom is tied to a certain concept of rationality, not that of means to end, but of formal universality. Insofar as we are rational beings, Kant argued, we recognise ourselves as subject to principles which have universal application. To be rational in this sense, is to act on principles – which Kant called 'maxims' – which apply, not just to ourselves, but to any agent in a relevantly similar situation. The absolutely fundamental principle of morality is to: 'act only on that maxim through which you can at the same time will that it should become a universal law'.[26]

The main thrust of Kant's reasoning is that even the most self-interested individual (and Kant's view of human motivation was as egoistic as Mandeville's) must recognise that the claims that he makes for himself must also be accepted for others who are in a like position. If, for example, he claims that he is entitled to a certain object because it has been sold to him, or that he ought to be free to make his own life as he sees fit, then he is committed by a principle of consistency to recognising and accepting the like claims of others. Something of the force of Kant's argument emerges if we imagine a person attempting to provide reasons to others why his particular claims should be recognised; in these circumstances he cannot help but provide reasons of a universalistic kind. But for Kant, the commitment to principle does not arise out of the need for public justification; it is part of our nature as rational beings. As such, it provides the fundamental test of morality: it is those claims which can be willed as universal laws which define the rights and duties of rational individuals.

The key to this argument is the principle of consistency: the principle that because an individual claims something on his own behalf he is thereby committed to recognising other claims which are relevantly similar. The major move of a Kantian morality is to import this principle into the concept of reason. Rationality becomes, not just a matter of choosing the most effective means to achieve given ends, but of acting according to general and generalisable principles. This concept of reason provides a powerful argument against the free-rider, or – as Kant put it – our tendency to make an exception of ourselves to principles which we would want others to adhere to.[27]

The free-rider is concerned to maximise his own well-being. The role of instrumental reason is to seek out the most efficient means to that end. It places behaviour in a causal milieu, works out the consequences of alternative courses of action and selects that action whose consequences are such as to maximise the agent's well-being. In the crucial cases where a putative action infringes an institution on which he depends, the free-rider estimates that the consequences of his action on the behaviour of others are minimal, and that it is on the behaviour of (sufficient) others that the institution depends. So he performs the action. But if everyone so reasons and so acts, the institutions on which they all depend will collapse.

The crucial step in the free-rider's reasoning is that which treats his actions as only causally relevant to the behaviour of others. This is a step which is demanded by instrumental reason. But there is another concept of reason available: one may also treat one's actions as falling, or failing to fall, under certain concepts and principles. In which case, one treats one's actions as conceptually linked to the actions of others which are of the same kind and which fall under the same principles, even when there is no direct causal relationship. The free-rider may be taken to be committed to a certain principle of behaviour: that which is necessary if the institution on which he depends is to survive. But he also wants to make himself an exception to that principle. It is plausible to suggest that this does offend against some principle of rationality, even if it is not that of means to end. It is that of general rule to instance and it prescribes, not efficiency, but consistency. Reason in this sense requires that the individual adopts principles of action which he is prepared for others also to adopt. The relationship between his action and those of others is no longer merely causal, but conceptual as well, via general principles of which they are all instances. Only somewhat paradoxically, the causal outcome of the practice of this form of reason will be the maintenance of the institutions on which all depend.

It is often argued against moralities which rest on principles of formal consistency that they lack determinate content. This complaint may be justified if the principles are conceived as supplying the entire content of morality. However, in the way it arises here (and, perhaps, in the more plausible versions which have been argued for), it takes as its field a pre-existing conceptual content: the material world of commodity production and exchange. The role of the formal principles is not to provide a new content to morality, but rather to restrict the operation of those principles of behaviour which already exist. Self-interest is not so much overridden as constrained; what is more, it is constrained in just the ways necessary to preserve the market structures within which it operates and flourishes. The network of rights and duties defined by the principles of formal reason provides the framework of justice necessary for commercial society.

The constraints imposed by this concept of rationality will be experienced by the individual as the demands of duty as opposed to the thrust of self-interest. But on one condition: the principles of reason must be supposed to have a motivational presence in the individual. If this were not the case, reference to these principles could not constitute reasons for the individual to act in the required way, nor could they have any influence on those subject to them. Hence, the individuals subject to this form of morality must be supposed to be equipped with a form of rationality other than that of instrumental reason.

Kant himself was acutely aware of this problem. His own

solution was to posit the requisite motivation as the necessary condition for the existence of morality. Since individuals *are* subject to the demands of reason, reason *must* be present as a motivational force; that is reason must be practical.[28] But the direction of this argument may be as easily reversed. Since reason in Kant's preferred sense does not have a motivational presence, morality must be an illusion. Unless there are some grounds for positing the existence of Kantian reason, we are back with Mandeville.

Though it does not resolve the problem of motivation, a Kantian morality comes closer than utilitarianism to resolving the moral problems of a market society. But it is also important to note that despite the different accounts of the basis of morality and the nature of moral obligation, there are other quite fundamental similarities and complementarities. Both moralities are universalistic and impersonal: individuals are recognised in terms of their susceptibility to pleasure and pain, or as the subjects of rights and duties, not in terms of particular qualities or personal relationships. While Kantian morality is not directly concerned with consequences, adherence to its principles will serve to preserve the market structure and facilitate the operation of the invisible hand. Thus, adherence to these principles serves a utilitarian goal even if it is not justified by an appeal to that goal. The motivations which Kantianism assumes, with the single key exception of duty, are just those of rational self-interest which form the motivational base of utilitarianism. From this perspective, Kantianism is a necessary complement to utilitarianism, rather than something essentially opposed to it. However, for this complementarity to exist, utilitarian considerations must be subordinated to Kantian ones, and the dictates of instrumental reason contained by the demands of consistency.

COMMERCE, HISTORY AND PROGRESS

The account of market society that I have discussed in this chapter was largely constructed in the eighteenth century. However, very few eighteenth century theorists would have offered as sparse a moral scenario as the ones I have discussed so far. To some extent this is because they often appeal to considerations which are incompatible with the main thrust of their accounts of commercial society. Thus, Adam Smith and Hume both fell back on assumptions of virtue or benevolence which are inconsistent with the motivations they assumed to hold in the main business of modern life. But there is also a dimension to their thought which is central to their understanding of commercial society and which goes well beyond the utilitarianism with which so many of them have been retrospectively credited. Commercial society was justified, not just because of the happiness that it produced, but because of the way of life that it made possible. Commercial society was also 'civilised' society: it enabled the arts and sciences to flourish and provided the conditions in which humans could interact in an urbane, polished and peaceful way, respecting and even learning from the differences between them. The word 'civilisation' was coined to designate this aspect of modern social life, both as process and achievement.[29]

Commercial society, and the civilised way of life it brought with it, was the result of a historical development. While previous forms of society – hunting, pasturage and agriculture were the three prior stages identified by eighteenth century theorists of history[30] – had contained a rudimentary division of labour, and private property in some areas, these had been constrained within social structures which had impeded their full development. The immediate prehistory of commercial society was the long period in which these elements were set free. There was an enormous expansion of trade and this encouraged developments in the social division of labour; more and more property was freed from feudal encumbrance and entered the world of exchange. This process was not the result of human foresight and planning; it was the unintended consequence of what humans did with limited knowledge and quite different intentions. But there was a logic to this development which could be discerned, at least after the event. It was the task of the historians of commercial society to discern this logic and to explain the place of commercial society in world history.

The logic was progress: commercial society was civilisation, and as such it was not just the result, but the achievement of history. It was the realisation of the potential constrained within previous forms of society. This self-validation of commercial society placed it in a particular relationship, not just to past societies, but also to contemporary ones. For the prehistory of commercial society existed not just in its own past, but also in the historically present, but unformed and stagnant societies of Africa, Asia and the New World. The relationship between the commercial societies of Western Europe and the rest of the world was conceived as that between civilisation and barbarism, progress and stagnation, and the future and the past.

Though the concept of civilisation was used to legitimise oppression and exploitation, the values which it embodied were conceived of as universal and in principle available to all. The commercial societies which were developing in Western Europe were, for the time being, the privileged bearers of these values: it was this which legitimised their encroachment on those parts of the world which had not yet attained the state of civilisation. But the rationale for this encroachment was that Western Europe represented these countries' own future. In this sense, the concept of civilisation differed from that of 'culture' (another invention of the late eighteenth or early nineteenth centuries): culture refers to values which are in principle limited to a particular group or country.[31] Civilisation was, like reason, a characteristic Enlightenment value; culture, a product of romanticism, foreshadowed more accurately the nationalistic values which were to become so prominent in the nineteenth and twentieth centuries.

The values contained in the concept of civilisation go beyond anything I have discussed so far in this chapter. They are not, at least in any straightforward way, reducible to those of happiness. It is not plausible to tell the story of the historical progress towards the way of life that commercial society made possible as that of a progressive increase in human happiness. It does not require a Rousseau to point out that a way of life in which individuals relate to the world and each other on the basis of few needs and little self-awareness may be much more conducive to happiness than that characteristic of civilised societies.[32] Further, utilitarianism cannot consistently differentiate between ways of life except in terms of the happiness they provide; it has nothing to say about the possibility that some ways of life might be qualitatively superior to others. If utilitarianism has some initial appeal as an account of the value realised in a market society, it has very little to offer as an account of why such a society marks a high point in human history. It is not surprising that the move towards utilitarianism as a systematic moral philosophy was at the same time a move away from the historical self-awareness which characterised eighteenth century thought.

A more promising route towards understanding the concept of civilisation seems to be provided by the Kantian emphasis on freedom and reason. That commercial society requires a framework of formal justice means that, in principle, its members will relate on the basis of a mutual recognition of each other's freedom.

This seems to provide at least the basis for a civilised mode of existence in which individuals are both creative in their own right and ready to acknowledge and learn from the creativity of others. However, there are deep problems here. The Kantian edifice of equal right functions at best to contain the behaviour of individuals whose main concern is with themselves, and whose relations with others will range, depending on how they relate to that self-concern, from disinterest to competition. The self-seeking characteristic of the market is hardly conducive to that way of life identified with civilisation. What is more, the Kantian framework does not provide, any more than utilitarianism, a criterion for distinguishing between ways of life: these are all acceptable, even indistinguishable, just so long as their path is mapped by reference to considerations of duty.

Kant himself tried to go beyond the narrow concerns of a formal morality. These attempts are, however, among the least convincing aspects of his philosophy and are nowadays mainly of interest to specialists on Kant, rather than a living part of moral philosophy.[33] There is some reason for this: the most familiar parts of Kant's enterprise – the concept of reason as formal consistency, the notion of duty defined in terms of this, the emphasis on a certain idea of individual freedom – have continued to provide the guidelines for the most impressive attempts to construct a morality appropriate to modern society. That the morality is such a bleak one is, perhaps, more a comment on the nature of that society than on the quality of the attempts. But there is also reason to be suspicious of the failure to attend to Kant's larger project. For Kant believed that the account of morality as duty only makes eventual sense when it is placed within a larger context which embodies an overall conception of history and a cosmology which gives a point to individual existence. And this is a possibility which is not confronted by the constricted focus of most recent discussions.

Kant followed most eighteenth century theorists in the belief in a historical progress towards a commercial and civilised way of life. This belief provided a validation of the kind of society which was coming into existence in Western Europe and also a justification for its ambitions towards the rest of the world. In retrospect, these beliefs have come to seem either an embarrassment or an irrelevance. Moral philosophy and social theory have moved away from the historical teleologies and complacencies which lay behind the eighteenth century – and later – belief in progress. This is partly a matter of the narrowing of focus which has been characteristic of much recent philosophy. But it is also because history has not dealt kindly with the idea that one way of life constitutes civilisation, still less that it is uniquely exemplified by market societies. From this perspective the eighteenth century faith in Western European civilisation seems as quaint, if not as harmless, as the customs and beliefs of those less progressive societies it derided.

But there is a further question here. The belief that market societies existed in a certain intelligible relationship to an overall progressive movement of history provided the context in which the moralities considered in this chapter were initially advanced. The moralities remain with us, though the belief in the progress of history is no longer available to us. It may be, however, that some such belief is, not a historical quirk, but a necessary condition for the coherence of these moralities and the ways of life they support. Without some larger framework, it is hard to disguise the banality of the pursuit of happiness for its own sake, or the emptiness of a life lived in accordance with the demands of duty.

2

CAPITALISM: THE POWER OF REASON

Reason has always existed, but not always in reasonable form.

(Marx)[1]

In this chapter I want to draw out some of the implications of two accounts of modern society – those of Karl Marx and Max Weber. Their accounts were of course very different. For Marx, the key concept for understanding modernity was capitalism; for Weber, it was rationalisation. Weber's account was developed in explicit opposition to that of Marx. The account of the origins of capitalism that he provided in *The Protestant Ethic and the Spirit of Capitalism* was intended to refute the economic determinism he associated with Marxism, by demonstrating the independent causality of religious factors. He was always concerned to defend capitalism against its socialist critics, both by showing the inevitability of certain of its features and pointing out problems with the socialist alternative. Still, his account of modernity is a strongly nuanced one: it combines a recognition of the achievements of capitalism, with a scepticism about many of the claims made on its behalf, an awareness of its costs and a pessimism about many of its directions. It is in this duality of vision that Weber is not antithetical to Marx, despite their different political perspectives. It has often been noted that Marx was, especially in *The Communist Manifesto*, almost as much concerned to celebrate capitalism as condemn it; he asks us, as Fredric Jameson put it, 'to understand that capitalism is at one and the same time the best thing that has ever happened to the human race, and the worst'.[2] What is involved here is not the 'value neutrality' proposed – with dubious consistency – by Weber, but a recognition of the complexity and contradictoriness of the values embodied in and promised by the modern world. Any worthwhile perspective on modernity will attempt to come to terms with that complexity and contradictoriness.[3]

THE ACHIEVEMENTS OF CAPITAL

For Marx, the concept of capitalism was not an alternative to, but an extension of that of the market. Capitalism works through the exchange of commodities, and all those directly involved in capitalist economic relations are involved by virtue of their status as owners and exchangers of commodities. Even the otherwise propertyless worker owns one commodity, his capacity to work, which he exchanges with the owner of capital in return for his means of subsistence. A network of exchange relations is a necessary condition for capitalism. But not sufficient: for Marx, capitalism is not just a way in which commodities are exchanged, but a way in which they are produced – a 'mode of production'. Marx suggested however that the market – the 'sphere of exchange' – plays a disproportionate role in organising our conception of the social and economic order in which we exist. Insofar as we largely relate to each other through exchange relations – as buyers and sellers of commodities – what is merely an aspect of capitalist life is perceived as if it were the whole. This misperception is the fatal flaw – the original sin – in both common sense and theoretical understandings of capitalism. Capitalism is conceived of as the market writ large, and the specific character of capitalist production is obscured.[4]

Marx's argument here is important. Concepts derived from the market play an enormously large role in organising the consciousness and self-consciousness of modern social life. The market remains the key organising concept in all mainstream economic theory. If the argument of the preceding chapter is right, the two moralities which are most visibly at work in the modern world, and which have dominated most philosophical discussions, are structured by the concept of the market. However, I want to suggest that Marx's argument underestimates the extent to which the capitalist mode of production generates its own values – values which are not those of the market and which are even in some respects antithetical to them. In order to understand some of the most pervasive values in the modern world, we must see them as informed by – and informing – a conception of social life dominated by the capitalist mode of production. Indeed, these are the values which emerge most clearly in Marx's own account of capitalism.

The most celebrated feature of capitalism is its technological dynamism. No other social order has been responsible for as extended and as dramatic a development of the human capacity to transform nature. Thus, Marx writes:

> The bourgeoisie, during its rule of scarce one hundred years, has created more massive and more colossal productive forces than have all preceding generations together. Subjection of nature's forces to man, machinery, application of chemistry to industry and agriculture, steam-navigation, railways, electric telegraphs, clearing of whole continents for cultivation, whole populations conjured out of the ground – what earlier century had even a presentiment that such productive forces slumbered in the lap of social labour?[5]

This was written in 1847 partly in celebration of the achievements of the first industrial revolution, partly as prophecy of achievements yet to come. Unlike some of Marx's other prophecies, nothing in the past 140 years has given us reason to doubt this one.

There are a number of factors responsible for this dynamism. Any continuous increase in productivity, where this is not due to extraneous factors (e.g. climatic changes in agricultural production), presupposes an ongoing capacity to devote human ingenuity and material resources to the improvement of techniques of production. In a class society characterised by unequal control over major productive resources, that class which has the greater control will be in a position to extend the time spent on production beyond what is necessary to cater for the needs of the labouring population and to appropriate what is produced in that 'surplus' labour time. According to Marx's account, the working class in a capitalist society – the 'proletariat' – consists of those who have no productive resources of their own, and therefore have little or no choice but to work for those who do – the 'capitalists'. In return, they receive a wage which enables them to live and reproduce themselves; the capitalists appropriate the surplus labour in the form of profit from the sale of the commodities produced.[6] Marx also allowed, as a secondary case, that surplus labour might be appropriated through a mechanism of unequal exchange. An extreme, though historically important instance of this was the plunder of the New World by the European powers in the period of early modernity. A more typical case is where those who enjoy greater power within the market, perhaps by having a near monopoly of some important commodity, are able through exchange transactions to appropriate a surplus from those who enjoy less power. Despite Marx's own views, there is some reason to treat unequal exchange as the exemplary case for capitalism, and to treat the capitalists' ability to extract a surplus from the proletariat as a special instance of it, one made possible by the capitalists' greater power within the labour market.[7]

What is important in this context, however, is not the precise mechanism by which capitalists appropriate a surplus, but the fact that they have a continuing motivation to employ that surplus in improving productivity, and not, for example, to use it in the kind of unproductive consumption which was characteristic of other class societies. The basis for this is provided by the competitive structure of capital. Other things being equal, the only way in which a capitalist can continue to exist as a capitalist is to make use of whatever technological resources are available to minimise the costs of production. Hence, there is a strong motivation to return some of the surplus to the production process in order to improve the technology and ensure a more effective use of labour. Once the drive towards technological improvement is institutionalised, then it develops a momentum of its own. However, the existence of this momentum is due ultimately to the structure of capital. Within that structure, there is a dynamism, absent in other class societies, to continually revolutionise the methods of production.[8]

Capitalism presupposes a social division of labour whose workings are largely co-ordinated by the market. The improvement in techniques of production involves an ever increasing 'technical' division of labour, in which large numbers of individual workers and machines are brought together and their activities organised by their capitalist employer or his representatives ('management'). Co-operation between workers, even without the introduction of new technology, creates a productive capacity far greater than that of individual patterns of work. The simplification of particular aspects of the labour process which this made possible was one of the factors which enabled the replacement of individual workers by machines in the first industrial revolution, thus initiating a process which has led to a technology which now performs tasks of a complexity and precision beyond anything possible for humans.

One aspect of this process has been that individual workers have lost both knowledge of and control over the labour process. Another has been the creation of new forms of knowledge and control, which have become the prerogative of those who manage the production process.[9]

The power of capital is quite different from that of previous dominant classes. It is not that of simply appropriating the labour of an oppressed class, as, for example, the feudal aristocracy was able to use its political power to extract labour or rent in kind from an economically independent class of peasant serfs. Rather it consists in creating new forms of labour and appropriating that which would not have existed without it. It involves detailed planning and organising of the production process, supervision and leadership. Power is not exercised through controlling pre-existing forces, but by bringing new ones into existence. Michel Foucault has suggested that this 'new type of power . . . is one of the great inventions of bourgeois society':

> It is a mechanism of power which permits time and labour, rather than wealth and commodities, to be extracted from bodies. It is a type of power which is constantly exercised by means of surveillance rather than in a discontinuous manner by means of a system of levies or obligations distributed over time. It presupposes a tightly knit grid of material coercions rather than the physical existence of a sovereign. It is ultimately dependent upon the principle, which introduces a genuinely new economy of power, that one must be able simultaneously both to increase the subjected forces and to improve the force and efficacy of that which subjects them.[10]

The process of developing human productivity is not merely a creative one; it is also, and necessarily, destructive. Old methods of work, traditional styles and skills, sometimes entire branches of production must give way to new techniques, discoveries and forms of production, as the imperatives of profit maximisation dictate. This destruction is not limited to the very old; what was new may become out of date, and thereby old, overnight. However monumental the achievements of the bourgeoisie, they are built with the knowledge that they will not last. Unplanned obsolescence is the other side of the creative aspect of capitalism. Nor is this dialectic of construction and destruction limited to economic phenomena. The transformations which capitalism has wrought and will continue to work, involve ways of life, forms of personal and social experience, communities, institutions and the whole range of intellectual and cultural production.

> Constant revolutionising of production, uninterrupted disturbance of all social conditions, everlasting uncertainty and agitation, distinguish the bourgeois epoch from all earlier ones. All fixed, fast frozen relations, with their train of ancient and venerable prejudices and opinions, are swept away, all new formed ones become antiquated before they can ossify. All that is solid melts into air, all that is holy is profaned.[11]

Which is to say that those of us subject to the capitalist mode of production live in a world in which almost everything appears contingent, and vulnerable to change and extinction. Long established traditions do not signify stability or even continuity; they are rather especially liable to demolition by the forces of the new. Where traditional forms do exist, they do so by way of monument or nostalgia, preserved in existence by a conscious attempt to save them from the impact of change, not by their own residual strength. Even the natural world has become a human artefact. It is no longer the mysterious other to whose laws and whims the human world is subject, but is condescendingly and tenuously preserved by the operation of conservation policies. We now live in an environment dominated by the human capacity to transform it, a world without stability whose major continuity lies in perpetual transformation.

It is a contradictory world. In the words of Marshall Berman:

> To be modern is to find ourselves in an environment that promises us adventure, power, joy, growth, transformation of ourselves and the world – and, at the same time, threatens to destroy everything we have, everything we know, everything we are.[12]

This is not just the contradiction between the immense creativity unleashed by bourgeois society and its equally immense destructiveness; it is also the contradiction between the actuality of power and the equally inescapable experience of passivity. The individual in capitalist society lives within these contradictions – both created and imperilled by them.

THE VALUES OF CAPITALISM: CONSUMPTION AND POWER

> So that in the first place, I put for a general inclination of all mankind, a perpetual and restless desire of power after power, that ceaseth only in death.
>
> (Hobbes)[13]

The chaos of creation and destruction which is the glory and perhaps the tragedy of capitalism is the product of something much more banal: the mundane pursuit of profit. But even if the aim of capitalist production is profit, its end point must be consumption. The most efficient techniques of production are wasted if no one buys the product. If profit is its overriding principle, the main activity of capitalism takes place between the two poles of consumption and production.

Consumption is the satisfaction of some human want or other, and there can be little doubt that the immense productivity of the capitalist system has enormously increased the satisfaction of the wants of those who participate in the capitalist market. If want satisfaction counts as happiness, then capitalism seems to promise an increase in happiness. As with the simple market economy considered in Chapter 1, a form of utilitarianism appeals as a rationale for capitalist production. But once again, the appeal is superficial. If each individual had a fixed quantum of wants, and an ever increasing proportion of these were satisfied by capitalist production, it might be plausible to argue that capitalism delivers an increase in happiness. But human wants are as much subject to change as are the means of satisfying them. Indeed, the increasing productivity of capitalism relies as much on the creation of new wants as on the satisfaction of old ones. There is no reason to expect that there has been, or will be, an increase in the ratio of satisfied to unsatisfied wants; indeed, it is more plausible to expect the reverse. But if the satisfaction of wants counts as happiness, then the creation of unsatisfied wants must be the production of unhappiness. In which case, the utilitarian balance sheet must fall increasingly into debit.

If the satisfaction of wants is to count as an unproblematic good, the variety of human wantings must be reducible to a common measure. All other things being equal, each want will count the same, whatever its content. The utilitarian refusal to distinguish between wants seems to leave this task to the free choice of the individual, who may thus be conceived as choosing which of his wants to gratify. But it is impossible to make sense of the notion of choice here: the individual is left without any basis on which to choose between wants, except in terms of their relative intensity, duration and probability of gratification. The individual as conceived by utilitarianism becomes little more than the passive subject of his wantings, the place where various wants happen to co-exist. He is subject *to* rather than the subject *of* his wants.

A similar point was made by John Rawls when he pointed out that utilitarianism as a social morality is concerned with overall want satisfaction irrespective of whose wants they are. All wants are conflated into one system, and individual subjectivity ceases to be morally relevant.[14] But the worry here is a deeper one: the very existence of human agency becomes problematic within the utilitarian perspective. Where the individual is conceived merely as the subject of various wants, pulled this way or that depending upon their relative strength and direction, it becomes completely mysterious how such an individual might develop the capacity to step back from his current wants in order to assess the likelihood of their gratification, let alone to take account of long term and future wants in his calculation. Whatever account of individuality is compatible with utilitarianism, it is highly unlikely that individuals of this kind would be very good at performing the various calculations required by utilitarianism. Indeed, it seems even more unlikely that they would become utilitarians.[15]

Utilitarianism reduces the theoretical space for individuality to something near vanishing point. In this, it corresponds to a familiar aspect of modern life: the felt loss of self which occurs with the experience of apathy, passivity and failure of agency. Capitalism provides for the gratification of consumption needs, but denies the individual the capacity to choose what these might be. Capitalist production depends upon itself being able to call into existence wants which it can then satisfy. For the individual, the source, not just of his gratification, but of that which is to be gratified, is located elsewhere. He is subject to forces which exist outside himself, and the act of consumption is not the expression of his individuality, but the denial of it.

If consumption is one pole of capitalist life, production is the other. Production is an act or process of transformation. In its central form, it involves the transformation of objects and materials, ultimately provided by nature, into forms in which they are suitable for human use. Involved in this transformation are the various instruments of production (tools, machines, etc.) and the human activity of labour itself. Since the instruments of production are themselves the products of a previous process of production, production reduces to the two basic elements: the objects provided by nature and the human activity of its transformation. What is exercised in this process is the capacity which Marx called a '*Productivkraft*', usually translated as 'productive force' but which for present purposes may be more perspicuously rendered as 'productive power'. What is developed by capitalism is the human power to transform nature. This has involved the introduction of new machinery, new forms of co-operative labour and new kinds of knowledge; it has called into existence new skills of planning and co-ordination.[16]

These developments have taken place within the capital/labour relationship. The labour involved has been largely wage labour. On Marx's account, the wage worker is one who, lacking access to productive resources of his own, is forced to sell his capacity to work to the owner of productive resources.[17] While the situation is not usually this stark, it remains true that the wage relation is predicated on a systematic inequality in the bargaining power of the individual worker and the capitalist enterprise – an inequality which might be diminished or increased by group action on one side or the other, or by external interference. Since the wage contract means that the worker is formally under the authority of his employer for the period of his employment, the inequality between capital and labour in the labour market translates into the power of one over the other in the production process. With the development of new technology and forms of co-operation, the work of large numbers of wage labourers has tended to become merely that of executing functions conceived and co-ordinated by others. A direct corollary of this has been the development of work practices associated with knowing and co-ordinating the production process. With a sort of inevitability, the emergence of two distinct kinds of work – what Marxists refer to as the division between mental and physical labour – has been coextensive with the development of differential power relations between those involved in management and the rest of the work force. Thus, the power over nature has developed in symbiotic tandem with the power of some men over others.

As I mentioned earlier, the kinds of power which are involved here are not simply capacities to control and coerce; they are rather capacities to transform, enlarge and create. Power is not employed to constrain what already exists, but to bring the new into existence. It is power in this sense which plays a crucial role in the capitalist world, and constitutes one of its dominant values. It is a value which has not received a great deal of attention from moral philosophers. Nietzsche, for whom the concept of power was central, thought that it was antithetical to the business of morality, and, as we shall see, there is good reason for this view. But it is not hard to discern this value at work in some of the most characteristic and self-conscious products of modernity. *The Communist Manifesto* is as much a celebration of the power of bourgeois society as a critique of it. Even though Marx looked forward to a form of society free of the inequalities of power, he also thought that this society would constitute the culmination of man's power over nature. Indeed, according to one influential interpretation, Marx held that the development of power over nature is the central organising project of human history.[18]

Power is a central theme in much modern culture, especially those forms which have claimed to represent the self-awareness of the modern world. This is perhaps most explicit in the case of the Futurists' celebration of the forces released by modern society and, associated with this, their contempt for tradition and their glory in the young and the new. Thus Marinetti:

> We will sing of great crowds excited by work, by pleasure, and by riot; we will sing of the multicoloured polyphonic tides of revolution in the modern capitals; we will sing of the nightly fervour of arsenals and ship yards blazing with violent electric moons; greedy railway stations that devour smoke-plumed serpents; factories hung from clouds by the crooked lines of their smoke; bridges that stride the rivers like giant gymnasts, flashing in the sun with the glitter of knives; adventurous steamers that sniff the horizon; deep-chested locomotives whose wheels paw the tracks like the hooves of enormous steel horses bridled by tubing; and the sleek flight of planes whose propellers chatter in the wind like banners and seem to cheer like an enthusiastic crowd.[19]

(The fact that the Futurists associated the power unleashed by the modern world with nationalism, masculinity and war will be of concern to us later.) A celebration of the power of modern technology is also implicit in the way in which modernist architecture has exploited the possibilities created by modern structural engineering to create buildings which are seemingly independent of and able to dominate both their physical environments and their human inhabitants. It is not hard to trace the iconography of power, nor for that matter to respond to its appeal, in many of the most familiar and pervasive symbols of modernity: the steam train in the nineteenth century, the aeroplane in the early twentieth, the way in which the curve of an expressway completely dominates and transcends its environment, the mass political rally or demonstration, the brutal destructiveness of open-cut mining, to say nothing of the awesome machinery of war. The very fact that such symbols quickly become antiquated is itself evidence of the force of what they represent.

MODERNITY AS RATIONALISATION

For Max Weber, the development of capitalism was only an aspect – though undoubtedly a major one – of the process of rationalisation. By this he meant that certain principles of rationality have come to be incorporated in the dominant institutions and practices of the modern world – including the market and the capitalist organisation of production, but also the bureaucracies and legal apparatuses, and the establishments of science and education. Those who live within these institutions and practices cannot but make their lives within the channels socially available to them. Thus, rationalisation in an institutional or objective sense generates corresponding modes of rationality in the thought and behaviour of those subject to it.

There is no simple correlation between capitalist modernity and a specific form of reason. Rather, certain forms of reason which have always existed have become dominant in the modern world, and other forms, which historically at least have had just as good a claim to the status of reason, have been marginalised and treated as irrational. Weber did not provide a unitary account of the relevant notion of reason. In fact, there are at least three distinct forms of reason which may be discerned in Weber's account of modern Western rationalisation. These are 'instrumental' or 'means/end' reason; what I will call 'juridical reason'; and finally a concept of 'cognitive' or 'scientific' reason. In this chapter I will only be concerned with the first two of these; the notion of cognitive reason will be discussed in Chapter 4. Weber's account of rationalisation, especially in his later writings, is complex and hedged with qualification. In the following discussion, I will simplify and occasionally (with notice) go beyond the letter of Weber's account as suits my purpose.[20]

Easily the dominant form of rationality in the modern world is instrumental rationality. It is most clearly present in the market place, the production process and, subsuming both, capitalist accounting procedures. In many discussions, this form of reason is simply identified with rationality *per se*.[21] Many of its elements have already emerged in the preceding chapter. Individuals are rational in this sense if they select from the range of possible actions which are open to them that action which is, on the best evidence available, most likely to achieve a given goal. Where an individual's goals conflict, reason will select those goals which are most likely to be achieved, taking into account the intensity and duration of the wants involved. Instrumental reason treats all wants as having a right to gratification; its function is to point towards the ways in which they might be gratified and, by taking into account their relative strength and the contingencies of the world, to introduce a ranking amongst them.[22]

Two conditions must be satisfied prior to the application of instrumental reason. It presupposes the existence of ends to which alternative routes are available; it also presupposes the existence of agents who consider themselves free to choose between these alternative routes. These conditions are by no means universal. If, for example, a certain kind of activity is essentially connected to a goal, as perhaps I may only achieve excellence in a craft if I work in accordance with certain pre-existing standards and traditions, then that activity does not fall completely within the logic of instrumental reason. Or if I conceive certain kinds of activity as necessary for my being the kind of person I am – if, for example, I am destined to be a soldier by a family tradition that I could not dream of breaking – then that activity ceases to be subject to instrumental choice. The instrumental rationalisation of the modern world has, however, militated against these two conditions. It has encouraged a conception of the world in which objects, events, agents and activities exist in external and contingent relationships with each other.

The overriding concern of instrumental reason is efficiency. Since its only measure of efficiency is quantitative, it is most effective when its materials – ends, potential means – are conceived in quantitative terms. Instrumental reason's preferred form of existence is as a calculation of quantitative input and quantitative output. However, definite material conditions had to exist before so much of social life could be conceived under the aspects of profit and loss, and expressed in the language of capital accounting which Weber took to be the formal paradigm of instrumental rationality. These included the competitive 'battle of man with man' in the market place,[23] the existence of money as a means of measuring value and – perhaps most significant of all – the separation of the working population from the means of production. Only a legally free, but economically dependent labour force would, Weber argued, have the incentive and the docility necessary to become disciplined participants in the capitalist labour process.[24]

Much of the time, Weber wrote as if instrumental reason was neutral between different ends. Still, it is implicit in his own account of capitalist rationalisation, that there are certain preferred ends towards which it is directed. After all, 'capitalism is identical with profit and forever *renewed* profit, by means of continuous, rational capitalistic enterprise'.[25] The aim of capitalist enterprise is and must be profit. What this means is that the capitalist and his agents must act in such a way as to maximise their returns, not so that they might consume the proceeds, but in order that these returns might be used to maximise their returns in the next round of activity. And they must continue to act with this end, indefinitely. This is a form of rational activity which is directed towards an end, but where the end is always a means towards a further end of exactly the same kind. Insofar as individuals have ends of this kind, they must have desires which are never satisfied and which are, in a certain sense, unsatisfiable.

Weber's analysis of the Protestant ethic was intended to show how this kind of insatiable desire, rationally pursued, came into existence. Anxiety about whether he was destined for salvation led the Calvinist entrepreneur towards a life of relentless activity combined with austere self-denial – of production without corresponding consumption. It thus provided the psychological impetus necessary for capitalist development to begin. However, once capitalist institutions and practices were well established, and society was objectively rationalised in this sense, the individual capitalist had little alternative but to conform to it. Whether or not the capitalist entrepreneur is concerned with his salvation, he must still be prepared to match his competitors in reinvesting his profit in improved and expanded production, or he will not be able to compete effectively with them and he will soon be replaced by someone who is. For capitalists, as against feudal lords, consumption wants must be subsumed under the rational pursuit of profit, i.e. subordinated to the pursuit of an end which is primarily conceived, not as an end, but as a means towards further ends.

It has long been noted, especially by theorists of the Frankfurt School,[26] that instrumental reason seeks power in the sense of control. To conceive of things or persons as means towards the achievement of one's goals is, other things being equal, to seek to control them. However, the operation of that form of instrumental reason which is especially characteristic of capitalist modernity seeks power in an even more direct sense. To pursue ends which are means to further ends, is to pursue, not ends as such, but the capacity to pursue ends; it is thus identical with the pursuit of power for its own sake. The rationalisation of the institutions characteristic of capitalist modernity – the market, the organisation of production – means that the individuals who live their lives within these institutions will direct their activities towards power. Those who are rational in this socially dominant sense must subordinate their other goals to the efficient pursuit of power. It is ironic that the apotheosis of instrumental reason is a form of reason which has lost its concern with goals, and focusses its attention on the 'instrument' itself.

The emergence of Western modernity involved a second principle of rationality which is quite distinct from, and is often opposed to, instrumental reason. This principle is not explicitly distinguished by Weber, and has not received a great deal of attention from his commentators.[27] However, it is implicit in his discussion of the 'formal rationality' associated with the law.[28] This form of rationality – juridical rationality (my term, not Weber's) – has an objective social existence in the law and judicial institutions, and in certain parts of the state bureaucracy; like the instrumental rationalisation of the capitalist market, it generates corresponding modes of rational behaviour on the part of those who are subject to these institutions. This form of reason requires the consistent and impartial application of general legal principles to particular cases.[29] Individuals are formally rational in this juridical sense when they conceive of their actions as an instance of principles which also apply to other actions which are relevantly similar. Thus, the judge or bureaucrat is concerned to establish the appropriate description of some action and then to apply to it the relevant principle. If instrumental reason is concerned with efficiency, this form of reason is concerned with consistency.

Juridical rationality will rarely exist in a pure form, even in the legal and quasi-legal apparatuses of the state. It will typically be enmeshed with practices informed by other concepts of rationality, e.g. instrumental reason, even that obsolescent form of reason (which Weber called 'substantive reason') which is directed towards the achievement of particular ethical ideals. There will be conflicts between these forms of reason; in such cases, Weber suggests, each party to the conflict will think the others irrational.[30] Juridical reason will also exist in the motivations and behaviour of the individuals subject to these institutional structures. This will generate conflicts – internal to the individual – between the dictates of instrumental reason and the demands of juridical rationality.

Juridical reason is, of course, Kant's moral law in another guise. But where the moral law was supposed to exist first and foremost in the motivation of the individual moral agent, juridical reason's primary form of existence is institutional. As such, it provides the legal structure necessary to define and protect the rights of owners of property and makers of contracts. As a derivative of this it encourages individuals to think of themselves and others as bearers of rights and duties. If the arguments of Chapter 1 are correct, then this concept of reason provides the most plausible way of explaining and justifying the rights and duties appropriate to the market. These arguments are strengthened when we move from the market to an explicit consideration of capitalism. Capitalism works through the market: it requires a market in which the means of production may be purchased, a labour market in which it may recruit its work force, a money market through which it can raise funds and a commodity market so that it may sell its products. If a framework of rights and duties is necessary to sustain the market, it is also necessary to sustain capitalism. However, the forces which capitalism generates are much more potentially destructive than those at work in the market. What is at work is not merely a rational concern to further one's self-interest, but an insatiable drive towards power.

REASON, REPETITION AND FRUSTRATION

> 'Yours is the bread that satisfieth never.' (Faust to Mephistopheles)
>
> (Goethe)[31]

Instrumental rationality is embodied primarily in the institutions of production and exchange, but it informs a large range of other areas of human activity as well. To be rational, in the dominant capitalist sense of this term, is to pursue power as an end in itself. Power is a value in capitalist modernity in the strongest sense: it is an intrinsic good, which is pursued for its own sake. While it may – usually does – serve other ends, these do not provide its justification. Power does not stand in need of a legitimising principle outside itself.

Power is not the only value engendered by capitalism, though it is undoubtedly the dominant one. Consumption is another, and this too is pursued for its own sake. In the form which is most characteristic of capitalism, the desire to consume has the same repetitive and insatiable character as the desire for power. Both may be rationally pursued, but neither defines an object which can ever be achieved. While capitalism has massively increased our ability to achieve our goals and to satisfy our needs and wants, it has done this at the cost of severing any intelligible connection between the exercise of these capacities and the gaining of satisfaction and happiness.

If power is the dominant value in capitalist society, then the demands of juridical reason constitute the social morality required to limit its operation. Juridical reason is embodied in the judicial institutions and the government bureaucracy, and it encourages corresponding modes of rational behaviour in those subject to these institutions. The socially induced disposition to act in this way – or, at least, to think that one *ought* to act in this way – provides at least a substitute for that more ethereal motivation posited by Kant as necessary for the existence of morality: a readiness to do one's duty just because it is one's duty. But juridical reason can only have a tenuous existence in the modern world. Both within the legal and bureaucratic structures, and within the individual, it will constantly be confronted with the demands for efficiency; and there seems little reason to suppose that it will often, or ever, win out against those demands. (Within the bureaucracy, of course, it may become the vehicle of a will to power working through those institutions;

but that is another story.) The kind of power which capitalism creates as a value is the drive to transform, to create, to control and organise, and to transcend limits. Power will always strive to push beyond the constraints imposed by the formal requirements of impartiality and consistency. If one's life is devoted to the pursuit of power, then one will not accept the limits imposed by the demands of morality. Except, of course, if they are the means towards power, or – the opposite case – they are imposed by a greater power. Nor is there a reason why one should. Juridical rationality will always appear to the instrumentally rational individual as a frustration and an encumbrance, a source of needless inefficiency.

The social morality defined by juridical reason is essentially the Kantian framework of individual rights and duties: the freedom to own property and to enter into contracts of exchange, together with the restrictions necessary to allow for the corresponding freedoms of others. Formal justice consists in the mutual recognition of these rights and duties. Capitalism operates through precisely the same framework of justice as that necessary to sustain the market: it recognises the rights of the wage worker when it offers him a wage in return for his capacity to work, and when it offers to sell him its products in return for his wage. The worker is under no formal compulsion to accept either offer. But just to the extent that capitalism generates power as a value, it reveals the framework of right to be a façade. For the power of capital in the labour market is predicated on the lesser power of those whose ability to work it purchases; its capacity to find a market for its products presupposes the lesser power of consumers. The formal rights of the worker do not correspond to real capacities. And intervening between the purchase of labour and the sale of the commodities produced is the process of production. This is, paradigmatically, the expression of the power of capital over both the material world and labour.

Within the market, freedom is appropriately conceived as a matter of right: it is the right to own, to exchange and to enter contracts, and it is the right not to be interfered with in the enjoyment of these rights. But within capitalism, freedom is more appropriately conceived as a matter of power: it is the power to act on and to change the world, and perhaps the power to express and change oneself in so acting. Capitalism works through the market and must in principle recognise the freedoms of the market. But capitalism also generates a concept of freedom as power, and this must undermine the concept of freedom as right. But – paradoxically – power is a value which capitalism can promise, but never deliver.

Instrumental reason promises, if nothing else, the efficient realisation of an individual's goals. However, in its characteristically capitalist form, it takes as its goals ends which are essentially unrealisable. Where it is directed towards consumption, its aim is not the satisfaction of one's pre-existing needs and wants, but the act of consumption itself. The gratification achieved with the attainment of a particular object must immediately give way to the quest for further objects. What is achieved in consumption is not satisfaction, but repetition. The goal of power is equally unattainable. In part, this is because the power sought is essentially comparative: it involves power over others, so that having must mean having more than others. Since one's achievements are always liable to be undermined by the achievements of others and one can never be sure what those achievements will be, one must constantly strive to increase what one has.[32] But it is also because the power which is sought is not the capacity to carry out a particular task or range of tasks, it is rather the means to acquire further means to further means, and so on indefinitely. Whatever ends are achieved are valued only insofar as they are means towards further ends which are themselves means. Whether or not this programme of endless deferral of ends is coherent,[33] it is certainly unsatisfying. What is achieved is not the efficient realisation of goals, but endless and compulsive repetition.

There are of course modalities in the experience of power. The industrial workers described by Marx exist in a subordinate position to capital because of their lesser power within the labour market. Within the production process, the power of their collective work is brought into existence by, controlled by and experienced as belonging to capital.[34] But however large the holdings of any individual capitalist, he too is subject to forces which he may influence but cannot control. He is, together with his fellow capitalists, not to mention his employees, subject to market forces which are generated by their various activities but which are only dimly comprehended and not controllable as such.

More fundamental than the laws of the market, and more threatening, is the historical dynamic of capitalism. If the forces of the market have some semblance of comprehensibility (to the extent that it makes sense to speak of 'laws'), this is certainly not true of the temporal movement of capitalist society. This is only partly a matter of the unpredictability of the cycles of expansion and contraction to which the capitalist economy is subject. More significantly, it is because the process of creation and destruction which is the very dynamic of capitalist development is the creation of what is as yet unknown and unpredictable, and the destruction of what is known and predictable. Where the invention of the new is part of the dynamic of social change, the future must always remain a matter of guesswork.[35] If there were those in the eighteenth and nineteenth centuries who felt able to place the dynamic of modern society in a comprehensible historical framework, there are few who would share this confidence now. Insofar as we can have an overall perspective on capitalist development, it is of power out of control. The values generated by capitalism – consumption, power – do not provide criteria in terms of which the historical dynamism of modern society can be conceived as the progressive realisation of some ideal. If there is a direction to modern history, it is one which is not available to us. But without a concept of progress or direction, there is only change and chaos. It is as if the power that other ages had ascribed to nature and which has long been tamed by capitalism has reasserted itself at the level of history.

If power is a value engendered by capitalism, it is a value which is denied to just those individuals who value it. It is massively present in capitalist society, but paradoxically it is always absent. This is because the powers that modernity call into existence – the forces of production and destruction, of capital, of bureaucracy, of the market and even of history – are collective powers. In one way or another they result from the joint action of many individuals. But where there is no mechanism for the collective control of these powers, and where the dominant mode of experience is individual possession, it can only be experienced as anonymous and alien: as belonging elsewhere. Where actual power is always other, it may be enjoyed only in simulacrum, as fantasy or representation.

3

THE PRIVATE SPHERE: VIRTUE REGAINED?

> 'Cause when love is gone, there's always justice.
> And when justice is gone, there's always force.
> And when force is gone, there's always Mom. Hi Mom!
> (Laurie Anderson, 'O Superman')[1]

Probably some form of the distinction between public and private spheres of social life has been drawn in every society. However, there is a good deal of divergence in the way in which the distinction has been drawn, partly with respect to which activities are marked public and private (e.g. kin relations are part of the public world in many societies; in modernity, they are aspects of private life), but also with regard to the significance of the distinction. My concern in this chapter will be with the specific form of the distinction in the modern world,[2] and in particular with its significance with respect to conceptions of morality. I will suggest that there are two conceptions of morality at large in the modern world, one appropriate to public life, the other to private. The two moralities are often at odds with each other; however, in a deeper sense they are complementary.

The distinction between public and private is also a key component in conceptions of masculinity and femininity. Men are characteristically ascribed those attributes necessary to operate in the public world, women the attributes appropriate to private life. These social identities enter crucially into the way in which men and women are aware of each other and themselves; they also mean that men and women are subject to quite different conceptions of morality.

PUBLIC AND PRIVATE – MASCULINE AND FEMININE

The arena of public life is already before us: it consists of the rationalised institutions of capitalist production, market exchange and bureaucratic administration discussed in Chapters 1 and 2. One way to approach the realm of private life is to bring out the way in which these institutions presuppose a further dimension of social existence which has not so far been characterised. A market society as described in Chapter 1 would not reproduce itself. To suppose that it would assumes that purely self-interested individuals will enter into relationships with each other in order to produce, nurture and care for other self-interested individuals just like themselves. But if we are to make sense of the apparent sacrifice of self-interest involved here, we would need, at the very least, to posit the existence of goods of a different kind to those involved in ordinary market transactions, and we would also need to suppose that there are human relationships – certainly those between parent and child, probably those between parents – which are different in kind to the contractual and voluntary engagements for mutual benefit typical of the market. Nor is the position very different when we broaden the account to include capitalism and rationalisation. We might imagine that one way of rationally maximising one's power is to bring children into the world and to look after them in return for future favours, but this story wears thin very quickly unless we assume, what it needs to explain, that there are commitments of kin which are different in kind to other relations between individuals in the capitalist world.

What these considerations show is that the accounts of social life discussed in the first two chapters are incomplete with respect to that aspect of human existence concerned with the bearing and caring for children. In fact, their major proponents have all, more or less explicitly, assumed the existence of a realm of social existence which has this responsibility and which is qualitatively different from that sphere of society which was the main object of their concern. The eighteenth century theorists of commercial society took for granted a realm of domestic life in which individuals, especially women, were moved, not by rational self-interest, but by emotion and a concern for others.[3] Though Marx worried that the dynamic of capitalism was destroying the sphere of family life, he also took this sphere for granted as the place in which the capitalist labour force was reproduced.[4] Weber went further: he argued that a necessary condition for the rationalisation of the processes of production, distribution and social organisation was their institutional separation from the family and, more generally, from the erotic and the emotional. Thus,

> The modern rational organisation of the capitalistic enterprise would not have been possible without two important factors in its development: the separation of business from the household, which completely dominates modern economic life, and closely connected with it, rational book-keeping.[5]

Both the market and the bureaucracy operate 'without regard for persons' and on 'calculable rules'. The principle of calculable rules is of particular importance to the modern bureaucracy:

> Its specific nature, which is welcomed by capitalism. develops the more perfectly the more the bureaucracy is 'dehumanised', the more completely it succeeds in eliminating from official business love, hatred, and all purely personal, irrational, and emotional elements which escape calculation. This is the specific nature of bureaucracy and is appraised as its special virtue.[6]

It is the exclusion of the personal, the emotional and the domestic which allows for the impersonal calculation which is essential for modern rationality. This does not and could not mean the elimination of these elements from social existence; but it does involve their being confined so that they do not infect the domain of the rational.

Weber's account brings out the two-sided nature of the distinction between public and private. The dominant conceptions of market activity, capitalist production and bureaucratic administration exclude the feelings, relationships and commitments which are characteristic of familial, sexual and emotional life. Society can, therefore, only be rationalised, in the senses appropriate to these conceptions, if these relationships lead a marginalised existence elsewhere. This creates a conception of domestic life as a distinct social space which is the appropriate place for emotion, attachment and sexuality. These are now conceived of as non-rational – according to Weber, irrational – aspects of human life, and properly separate from and subordinate to the larger questions of production, distribution and social organisation. It is this particular structure of exclusion and subordination which marks the modern form of the distinction between public and private spheres of social existence.

This distinction maps on to another: that between male and female. The sphere of domesticity represents the feminine principle in social existence. This is not just because women have, as a matter of fact, largely inhabited the private world and have been impeded from entry into public life. It is rather that the characteristics which are associated with the modern family are conceived of as feminine, even when they are possessed by men, and a concept of femininity has been constructed in terms of these characteristics. It is the woman who is supposed to embody in her existence as wife and mother the principles of family life and the practices of love, nurturance and support that it requires. This conceptual association between the feminine and the domestic exposes a parallel connection: that between masculinity and the public sphere. This does not just reside in the fact that it has been largely men who have dominated the world of production, distribution and administration. It is rather that the capacities which are required by public life are conceived of as male, even or especially when they are possessed by women, and the form of identity constructed by public life as a form of male identity. Masculinity has been an implicit presence in my account of the market, capitalism and rationalisation; hence, the pervasive use of the male pronoun in the first two chapters. This presence only becomes explicit, however, when the account is located in a larger context. The maleness of the public sphere only emerges when it is placed in relationship to the private – and explicitly – feminine domain.

Men are called upon to play a dual role. On the one hand, they participate in the public world as representatives of the household unit. Domesticity has its place in the wider world through this representation. On the other hand, men represent the public world of production, exchange and administration within the family. Thus, the duality between public and private also informs the private sphere. Indeed, that this must be so is clear from the perspective of reproduction. If the domestic realm is to reproduce, not just the physical individuals, but also the structure of individuality required by public life, then it must contain within itself a representation of that public individuality. In this way, the private realm provides the principles of its own transcendence. This duality also provides its constitutive authority structure: public reason against private emotion, the opportunity to seek power in the public world against the weakness of being contained in the private.

While the family is the most significant institution within the private sphere, there are other human relationships which, excluded by the dominant conceptions of public life, are deemed to find their proper place in the realm of the private. The rational behaviour required by the market, capitalist production and bureaucratic administration is characteristically impersonal in form: individuals are treated as exchangeable means to independent ends or as instances of general principles. Where there are relations in which individuals figure as the objects of non-transferable emotions, these relations are located in the realm of private life. The private is thus the realm of the personal, as against the impersonal public world. As such it includes family relationships, but also includes relationships of personal friendship and, for that matter, enmity.

The private realm has those characteristics which are denied representation within the public world, but which are necessary for social life. The relationship between the two spheres is one of presupposition, in that each requires the existence of the other, but also one of opposition, in that the characteristics of each sphere are just those which are excluded from the other. This kind of opposition is especially characteristic of modern societies, and perhaps specific to them. Aristotle, for example, took friendship (*philia*) to be properly constitutive of public relationships between citizens, not a phenomenon of private existence.[7] According to the patriarchal theories of political sovereignty criticised by Locke, the authority of the monarch over his subjects is directly analogous to that of the father over his family. It was one of the achievements of early liberalism to displace a traditional form of patriarchal authority in the public realm while retaining it in the private.[8] In this way it began the task of grounding a qualitative distinction between the two realms of social existence.

This form of the distinction between public and private, male and female, is the product of modern history. With the emergence of capitalism, distribution of the social product came to be largely determined by the workings of an impersonal market, not by tradition, status or obligations to kin. The main activity of production moved outside the household and into the factory, and the concept of work – though certainly not the reality – became nearly synonymous with wage labour. Larger questions of social administration and law came to be the province of specialised bureaucracies. These developments provided the background to and the impetus for the accounts of modern society I considered in the first two chapters. In tandem with them was the construction, mainly through philosophy and literature, of a sentimentalised conception of private life, in which the family, divorced from other social functions became primarily concerned with love, the domestication of sexuality and nurture.[9] Part of this process was the construction of corresponding images of masculinity and femininity, with women equipped with those capacities necessary for the sphere of private life, and with men having the capacity both to function in public life and also to mediate between the two spheres. This division of labour between the sexes was also a division of authority: in virtue of his role in the public sphere the man had authority – as father, husband, head of household – over the members of his family, including his wife. The sentimental family was also the patriarchal family. If formal equality of right is characteristic of the public sphere, neither equality nor, as we shall see, right exist in the realm of domestic relations.

If the modern world is responsible for these representations, it has never created a closely corresponding reality. Women have never just existed within the private realm; they have often been, and are increasingly, wage workers. Capitalist enterprise, in its continual search for markets and its more fluctuating need for labour, has relentlessly colonised the realm of private life. However, even where these distinctions are undermined, they are recreated. The kind of work which is considered most appropriate for women in the public sphere is, in terms of its content and its status, an extension of their domestic roles. Thus the ubiquitous image of women as secretaries, nurses and child care workers. Where women do have full-time work, it is still supposed that this is merely supplementary to their primary domestic activities. The wages women receive are almost always less than those of men, even where the jobs are comparable. Where capitalism has appropriated for itself responsibilities which have been associated with the private sphere, and has taken on itself the task of providing meals and leisure activities, it has done so under the sign of the very family whose functions it usurps.

ARE THERE TWO MORALITIES?

> But it is obvious that the values of women differ very often from the values which have been made by the other sex; naturally this is so. Yet it is the masculine values that prevail.
>
> (Virginia Woolf)[10]

> Over the past ten years, I have been listening to people talking about morality and about themselves. Halfway through that time, I began to hear a distinction in these voices, two ways of speaking about moral problems, two modes of describing the relationship between self and other.
>
> (Carol Gilligan)[11]

The values and morality which are appropriate for the world of the market, capitalist production and bureaucratic administration form part of the public face of modernity; as such, they contrast with those values and moralities appropriate to the private realm.

Within the market, the identity of each individual is given independently of specific activities or relationships. The value which moves the individual to act is an instrumentally rational concern for his own long term well-being. To conceive the market as a capitalist one broadens our conception of this individual. His motivation now appears as the – still rational – concern both to maximise his power (i.e. his capacity to act on the world, to control and organise others) and also his consumption activities. Relationships between such individuals will be impersonal, in that individuals will figure in such relationships only through the medium of the property they own or (almost but not quite the same thing) the power they represent. They will thus be interchangeable with any other individuals with equivalent property or power. The scope of relations between individuals will only be limited by the extent of the market.

A morality which will be appropriate to these relations will be equally impersonal and universalistic. It will concern transactions between individuals whose personal qualities are unknown to each other and are, in any case, only relevant through the medium of property or power. It will specify the rights and duties which hold between owners of property and makers of contracts. Its major component will be a principle of formal justice which will require the reciprocal recognition of these rights and duties. It will abstract from the personal relationships within which individuals may exist and from the emotions which they may feel towards each other. Against the values (power, consumption) which actually move these individuals, the dictates of morality will take the form of a set of constraints on their doing what they would otherwise (and may still) want to do. Their own rights they will take to be the minimal conditions of agency; the rights of others as impediments to that agency. Morality – the requirement of justice – will appear as the voice of duty demanding that those impediments be accepted. Its force will be that of rational consistency: my claim to a right must, in consistency, be conceded to others. However, the claims of morality exist in opposition to the values which motivate the individual in his day-to-day public life.

Within the private sphere, matters are very different. Here, relationships are personal, in that individuals are the objects of non-transferable emotions, and particularly, in that they are the repositories of special value and commitment. The particularity here is not necessarily that of specifiable characteristic: it is picked out through the personal possessive pronoun: the commitments are to '*my* child', '*my* wife' or '*my* friend'. Paradoxically, the impersonal and universal sphere is also that of rampant egoism; the sphere of private life, thus egocentrically demarcated, is one in which egoism is, in principle, transcended.

Certain relationships, for example that of friendship, are not possible within the public sphere, and must therefore find their place in the private realm. Within the public sphere, other individuals are valued only insofar as they are means towards certain distinct ends. But to be a friend of someone involves, *inter alia*, that one be prepared to act in respect to that person for his or her own sake. So to act is, at least normally, a means towards ends which one does have: it usually gives one pleasure, for example, to help a friend. But to help a friend in order to experience the resultant pleasure is not the same thing as helping the friend for his or her own sake, and this is the motivation necessary for friendship. Only somewhat paradoxically, certain ends may be achieved only if they are not pursued as such.[12]

If friendship is not a matter of instrumental reason, nor is it a matter of public morality. It involves commitments, but these are not matters of duty, at least insofar as this concept is defined in the public sphere. Friendship involves a readiness to do things for one's friend, but this readiness must spring from desire, not duty. One helps one's friends because one wants to, not because one thinks one ought to – though one may think that too. Of course, things may not always be so clear cut. The demands of friendship may on occasion conflict with one's desires; in such cases, they may well appear as duties, and be carried out as such. But these cases cannot be the central ones. Where duty comes to play more than a peripheral role in a relationship, then that relationship has ceased to be one of friendship. Further, what one is ready to do for a friend one is not, at least in the same way and for the same reason, ready to do for others. If there is justice in friendship, it is not a matter of formal consistency: one's friends get, or should get, more than is due to others. These commitments may be displayed as instances of general principles – e.g. 'People ought to give more attention to the needs of their friends than to the needs of those who are not their friends' – and it may be that such principles can be justified in the name of an impersonal and universalistic morality. But this is irrelevant. Reference to such general principles does not provide the motivations required by friendship. Where one acts towards another because of a principle of this kind, friendship is absent.[13]

In modern society, friendship is a relatively marginal phenomenon. It is excluded by the values and morality of mainstream public life; and within the private sphere, personal life is largely dominated by the demands of more intimate relationships, and especially those constituted by the family. Within the family, relationships are particular: other individuals are valued because they stand in specific and uniquely identifying relationships (husband, child). They are also personal in that individuals are conceived to be the non-replaceable objects of certain emotions. If individuals in the public sphere seek ends which essentially pertain to self (and, perhaps, to those represented by the self), within the sphere of family relations individuals are assumed to take the well-being of others as a sufficient basis for action. Not, of course, of all others: only those within the same private sphere. This may be construed as altruism, as against the self-interest which is characteristic of much public existence. But to do so would be to blur an important distinction, and risk misconceiving the structure of motivation and – more fundamentally – of identity which is involved.

Where goods are conceived individualistically, we may envisage an individual choosing between seeking his own good or that of another. In this case, the altruistic individual is one who sacrifices his own good in order to achieve the good of the other. Were we to discover that an apparently altruistic person is actually seeking a good of his own, perhaps the secret pleasure of being considered morally worthy, we would cease to think of his actions as altruistic. Though genuinely altruistic behaviour differs in its object from self-interested behaviour, it is subject to the same instrumental logic. If it is to achieve its goal, it should be informed by the same means/end rationality as its self-directed counterpart.

The behaviour associated with the private sphere belongs to a different genre. The goods which the mother seeks, for example, are the goods of those specific others for whom she has responsibility; but in addition to these, she achieves her own good. Motherhood is a form of identity which defines the well-being of the individual in terms of her contribution to the well-being of others. Where an individual conceives herself primarily as a mother, then achieving the good of those specific others does not involve a sacrifice, but is a way of achieving her own good. The good of others is not merely a means to the mother's own good: it is a component of it. Maternal behaviour is not, like the behaviour of the altruist, governed by the norms of instrumental reason. The mother's own good may be achieved by helping others, but is not sought as such. Helping others is not simply one way of achieving that good; it is the only way. What is more, it is often the case that the children (or husband) whom she cares for can only be cared for in certain respects by someone who *is* their mother (or wife). It is, for example, only when the child recognises that it is his mother who is comforting him that he is comforted. This may be in part because it is only the mother who knows how to do it (i.e. has the requisite knowledge), but it is also because the child needs attention from that particular person. What is more, that she give such attention is expressive of the identity of the mother, and essential if she is to maintain that identity. What is involved here is not a contingently effective means of securing certain results, but behaviour which is essentially linked both to the identity of the agent and the effects it is intended to secure. The concept of 'care', which has been central to many recent discussions of the idea of a female ethic, is probably best thought of as involving this kind of intimate relationship between the identity of the agent and the effects which are achieved.[14]

If maternal behaviour is not instrumentally rational, nor is it governed by the demands of formal consistency. As with friendship, there may be general norms involved here (e.g. 'Every mother ought to love and care for her children'), but what is required of the mother, as of the friend, is not action which is determined by the norm, but action which springs from what the mother wants to do. What is involved here is a notion of commitment and responsibility, not duty as this is defined in and required by the public sphere.

That form of identity which is constructed within the family expresses itself in behaviour which is emotional, in a sense which is contrasted with those forms of reason which are dominant in the public sphere, and is directed towards particular others. What moves men to action in the public sphere are emotions which have been transformed by the requirements of reason into channels of efficiency and consistency; feminine emotions, devoid of reason, are infected by excess and particularity. Hence, the lack of a sense of justice which such moral theorists as Rousseau, Hegel and Freud have – notoriously – supposed to be characteristic of women.[15] This lack, if such it is, should not be confused with a lack of morality as such. Femininity is defined within a different arena of moral discourse to the one in which the public discourse of justice, that is, of universal and impersonal right, is constructed. The two arenas are not independent; indeed, each presupposes the other. But the two conceptions of morality exist in a state of tension; they relate in different ways to the motivations of those subject to them and, at least sometimes, make incompatible demands on them. Hence, their essential complementarity is only ensured where the private sphere is properly subordinate to the public conceptions of reason and justice which are, in principle, embodied in the male head of household.

There are other ways in which the two moralities may be contrasted. Public morality takes the form of duty and, as such, imposes itself on the non-moral inclinations of those subject to it. Transgression of duty is an ever present and conceptually available possibility. The individual is aware that the path mapped out by the rational pursuit of self-interest (power, consumption) passes through the boundary defined by morality. To cross that boundary may involve punishment or even guilt, but that is all. The self of the transgressor remains intact. The corresponding conception of female identity is, on the other hand, defined much more tightly in terms of existing within certain relationships and carrying out certain associated activities. Withdrawal from these relationships or failure to carry out the associated activities is always possible, but these will take a different form and have different consequences to a transgression of public morality. They will involve, not just punishment or guilt, but a real threat to individual identity. To conceive of such failures in systematic terms is to envisage, not a mere infringement of the moral law, but a loss of self. In this sense, the morality of the private realm is part of the identity of those subject to it in a way that the morality of the public world is not.

The realm of the private also infects masculinity. While male identity is abstract with respect to specific public activities and relationships, it also represents the domestic world in that sphere. Insofar as they are breadwinners, men have responsibilities to their families. Male identity within the family is that of representing the public order of reason (efficiency, consistency) and power, and this partially depends upon their carrying out these responsibilities. A failure here (e.g. unemployment) may also occasion, not just guilt at transgression, but a threat to male self-identity.

DUTY AND VIRTUE

The contrast between public and private morality instantiates a more general contrast: that between a morality of duty and one of virtue. Public morality is a set of universal precepts: it places certain limits on the actions of those subject to it. Private morality informs the identity of its subjects: acting in certain morally required ways is necessary to express that identity. Hence, to be moral is to be a certain kind of person and to know how one should act given that one is that kind of person. Morality is a form of character.

I do not wish to put too much store on the word 'virtue'. It is protean in its uses, and has a role within most conceptions of morality.[16] However, there is a fairly specific moral tradition in which a concept of the virtues has a special place – a tradition which may be called, after its most significant protagonist, 'Aristotelian'.[17] According to this tradition, a virtue is a character trait of a certain kind, a disposition to act in certain ways. Thus the virtue of courage (or of charity) is the disposition to act courageously (or charitably) when the occasion arises. It is an important part of the tradition that the exercise of these dispositions requires judgement, and that acquiring the disposition is at least partly a result of education and practice.

A character trait counts as a virtue only if its characteristic behaviour is thought of as contributing towards some ideal of the good life, both for the virtuous individual and also the society to which he or she belongs. The contribution is of two kinds. The first is that of means to ends: virtuous behaviour will be conducive to the good life both for the individual and the society to which he or she belongs. For example, courageous activity will, by and large, lead to a better life both for the courageous individuals and their society. The second is that virtuous behaviour will be partially constitutive of the good life both for the individual and the society. To act courageously is part of living well, and a society whose members characteristically act courageously will be, at least in that regard, a flourishing society. The second sense is important: the virtuous activity is not just a contingently available means towards some desirable end state; it is itself part of that desirable state of affairs. There is also a certain openness about the nature of the ideal to which the virtuous activity contributes. Even those who participate in it would be hard put to provide a complete account of just what it consists in, particularly if they were to take account of the possibility of change and development. While virtuous behaviour is goal directed, its goal does not have the conceptual determinacy which would allow the formulation of Weber's 'calculable rules' by which it might be achieved. Virtue requires, as Aristotle recognised, the exercise of a kind of judgement which is not merely that of applying a pre-existing principle.[18] Indeed, the exercise of such judgement is in itself one of the important virtues.

An ethic of virtue presupposes that there is a systematic convergence between that behaviour which is conducive to the good of the individual and that required to sustain the society to which he or she belongs. This is secured by an assumption about the identity of the individuals who are subject to the ethic. The Aristotelian ethic, for example, is addressed to the (adult, male, free) citizens of a – presumably idealised – Greek city state. It is assumed that the identity of the individual, his conception of what he most essentially is, is given by his membership of that political community. For such an individual to live well is, *inter alia*, to perform those activities – military, political, cultural – associated with being a citizen, and these activities are just those which are required to sustain that form of social life. Conflicts of responsibilities may arise (though Aristotle seems to have thought that these could only arise through misunderstanding), but in general the identity of the individual moral agent ensures that there is a harmony between the individual and the social good. Thus Aristotle's ethics largely takes the form of advice: this is the way to live well. If a citizen takes this advice and uses it with judgement, then he will achieve the well-being (*eudaimonia*) which is the goal of individual existence (unless he is dogged by misfortune); that is, he will participate responsibly and fully in those activities which constitute a full human existence. In this way, he will also contribute to sustaining the community which makes that life possible.

The situation is quite different in the modern public world. Here the good of the individual is conceptually distinct from the good of the society in which he exists, except insofar as it is a very tiny part of it. The individual in pursuing his own good may contribute to the overall social good, but only through indirection. That he so contributes forms no part of his own well-being. We have no conceptual difficulty in thinking of successful tax evaders or corporate criminals as people who may live well, though at the expense of the society which provides them with the conditions of their activity. In public life, individual identity is not constituted by a specific social role nor by the carrying out of certain activities. Hence, there is a need for curbs on how individuals might pursue their own well-being, and morality must take the form, not of advice on how to live well, but of duty.

This is partly a matter of the self-directed aims of individuals in the public sphere. As I suggested in Chapter 1, an ethic of virtue presupposes a continuity between individual motivation and overall social consequence. But this assumption has become difficult if not impossible to sustain in the modern world. But it is also a matter of the dominant instrumental form of reason. Suppose that a particular individual does, mysteriously, take the overall social good as his aim. Such an individual will not be nearly as ready as his self-directed neighbour to opt out of his social responsibilities. However, there will be very many social goods for which his contribution will play a vanishingly small part. The institution of property will not collapse just because he steals something from a corporation which will not feel the loss, and perhaps where stealing will enable him to contribute substantially to some other social good. Insofar as his behaviour is governed by means/end rationality, the altruist will always contribute to those social goods to which his contribution will make a substantial difference rather than to those where his contribution will make very little difference. Hence, the more distant social goods will be as unsustained by the altruistic as by the self-interested individual.

This is, of course, the kind of problem to which Kantianism

purports to provide a solution. The point here is not to rehearse that solution, but to register the difference between this situation and that which is assumed by Aristotle and the virtue tradition: that individuals will perform the required activities, not just because they think that they will contribute eventually to some end they believe in (though they will think that too), but because performing them is a way of expressing their identity, and is thus a component of their own well-being as individuals. This kind of identity is not available in the modern public sphere, and for that reason an ethic of virtue is not available either.

The contrasting private realm does, however, provide identities of this kind. Being a mother is, for example, assumed to involve a set of responsibilities to others which are both necessary to sustain the family and also a mode of individual fulfilment. Not to carry out these responsibilities is conceived to be a failure on the part of the woman to understand what her nature is. There are various character traits, e.g. the capacity to care, empathy, constancy, etc., which manifest themselves in the appropriate behaviour, and which are the characteristically feminine virtues. Women are from babyhood destined to assume this identity: to be the mother of their future children and the wife/mother of their future husbands.[19] There is also a complementary male identity: that of head of household/breadwinner. This too involves responsibilities which are also conceived to be forms of the good life for the individual. But masculinity is also constituted within the public morality of duty, so it is in the figure of the woman/mother/wife that there is an unambiguous representation of modern virtue.

The English word 'virtue' is derived from the Latin *virtus* which comes in turn from *vir*, meaning man. For the stoics, to have *virtus* was to have the manly qualities necessary to cope with a life constantly threatened by the unpredictable interventions of the goddess Fortuna.[20] This etymological connection with maleness is born out in the history of the concept. Aristotelian virtue (*arete*) was only possible for those qualified to be citizens, and this excluded women. The virtues associated with the civic republican tradition in early modern England were also associated with citizenship, land ownership and maleness.[21] So it is at least somewhat paradoxical that the modern bearers of virtue are, paradigmatically, women. However, there is a common thread. The appearance of virtue as a primary moral concept is only possible on the assumption of a social identity which is also a moral identity.

To be a citizen of an ideal Athenian state as conceived by Aristotle, or a citizen of a basically agricultural republic as conceived by the civic humanists, or to be a mother as this identity is constructed in the modern private realm, are all, in the relevant senses, moral identities.

THE TEMPTATIONS OF VIRTUE

The morality of duty is a bleak one. It ignores, or considers only indirectly, many aspects of human life and personal relationship, and in its very universality, it seems to have no place for the particularities of human existence. The image of morality that it presents is that of the law court and the bureaucracy: it represents order and restraint against desire and pleasure. It is easy, therefore, to be attracted towards an ethic of virtue, which finds a place for much that is ignored or marginalised by the morality of duty and which links the moral life, not with constraint but with personal fulfilment.

There are, however, reasons not to succumb too readily to the temptations of virtue. Those communities which have been invoked to support an ethic of virtue have often been highly restrictive, and the identities they have provided have been exclusive ones. The Athenian *polis* idealised by Aristotle excluded slaves and women from citizenship, the virtues recommended by Aristotle were those necessary to sustain a privileged and parasitic way of life and the responsibilities of the citizen did not extend far beyond the boundaries of this restricted community. Often the communities have been hierarchical in structure, and the different identities and their associated virtues have been defined in terms of that hierarchy. For example, late medieval Christendom, at least as portrayed by MacIntyre, provided a social context for a practice of the virtues, if not quite the same virtues as those recommended by Aristotle.[22] This community was a universal one, at least in principle, and it also provided an identity, that of being subject to the one God and the one salvation, common to all its members. But that identity was articulated within a complex hierarchical structure, both religious and secular, and to live the virtues appropriate to one's station was to reproduce that hierarchy.

The development of a market economy was incompatible with this kind of hierarchical structure, not least because it required a concept of identity such that individuals were not tied to particular places within society, but were able to move from occupation to occupation in response to market forces. As I have argued in Chapter 1, the identity required by the market is that of an individual who is not tied to particular activities and responsibilities. This identity is, ultimately, that of the individual bearer of rights, and defines a basic, if formal, equality between all those engaged in market transactions. The concept of right is that of an entitlement to certain kinds of freedom, e.g. to own property, to buy and sell, to enter into contracts, and so on. Even the freedom to sell one's capacity to work in the capitalist labour market is a genuine freedom compared with the serf's feudal ties to a particular master. These concepts of freedom and equality have significant limitations, and are compatible with substantive inequalities and unfreedoms. We have already encountered a sense of freedom – as the power to act on the world, to create and control the conditions of one's existence – which is provided only meagrely and unequally by the capitalist market. But the point here is that even the limited concepts of freedom and equality which are satisfied (or satisfiable) in the modern public world go beyond what was available in the preceding culture.

A framework of virtue need not be, as the medieval one was, one of inequality. Aristotle's conception of the *polis* was of a limited and exclusive community, but its citizens were equal members of it. But a certain concept of freedom does not seem to be available within a virtue ethic. For that ethic presupposes that the individual has an identity which is sufficiently substantial to provide an answer to the more significant moral questions which arise for the individual. But a question which that identity cannot answer is whether or why the individual should assume that identity. If my identity as an Athenian citizen, when this is properly understood by me, provides a way of deciding the most important choices that arise for me, this is because being an Athenian citizen is not in the same way a matter of choice. But in the modern public world, most identities are conceived of as matters of choice; or, to put this slightly differently, identities are conceived of as roles which are only contingently related to their bearer. Even where they are not strictly chosen (I may have no choice but to be unemployed) they are conceived as if they are, at least potentially, objects of choice. And this is sufficient to destroy the unproblematic assumption of identity which constitutes the basis for an ethic of virtue.

There are two consequences of this. First, it allows for a new concept of freedom. A virtue ethic presupposes an identity which, from the perspective of modernity, is a potential restriction on one's freedom. For Aristotle, for example, to be free was to be a citizen and free activity was fulfilling the privileges and responsibilities of citizenship. But for the abstract individual of the capitalist market, citizenship is in principle a matter of choice; it is an object of freedom, not its subject. Second, certain ways of answering questions and making decisions about how one should live become unavailable. Those identities which, in an ethic of virtue, provide the criteria for answering these questions and making these decisions are now themselves subject to question and decision. But how then to go about answering these questions and making these decisions? If no other criteria suggest themselves, then these will become matters, not of reason, but of arbitrary choice.

I shall return to these questions in the next chapter. It is sufficient here to note that the attractions of a virtue ethic are closely tied to its limitations. While it provides for a conception of the moral life which is apparently less restrictive than that provided by a morality of duty, this is because the assumptions it makes about the identity of the individual mean that there is less to restrict. It is just because the modern world generates a more absolute conception of individual freedom that it requires a more restrictive conception of morality. But on the other hand, if the morality of duty allows for a more encompassing notion of freedom, it does so at the risk of placing the whole of morality within the scope of individual choice, and removing it from the domain of reason. This is no small matter: the rational morality of duty stands in peril of itself becoming a matter of non-rational decision.

Within the modern world, a virtue ethic exists in the private domain in a subordinate relationship to the public morality of duty. It can only exist to the extent that it denies to its subjects the kind of identity constructed in the public world. To be a woman/wife/mother must be conceived, not as a choice which some women (and perhaps some men) might make, but as an inescapable destiny. To be a head of household/breadwinner must be a necessary part of man's fate. What is social and contingent must appear as natural and necessary.

While these identities and their associated virtues are very different to those constructed in the premodern world of medieval Christendom, they are just as surely incompatible with capitalist market relations. Hence, their existence depends on their isolation: a quarantine such that these identities do not become contingent roles which may or may not be chosen. Once they become subject to choice, the individual chooser has defined him- or herself independently of them. The self who chooses no longer has the moral identity which is necessary for the virtue ethic. Self-fulfilment becomes a matter of free choice, not working through a given destiny.

The borders of the quarantine are drawn by the public/private distinction. I have already noted that even where these are undermined by the operation of the capitalist market they are reinscribed: the marketing of leisure packages and pre-cooked food is conducted in terms of those family virtues that it erodes; the roles ascribed to women in the public sphere of work replicate the caring and subordinate tasks they are allotted in the domestic realm. Perhaps this process is reaching its limits. If the model of family life drawn in the previous pages ever approximated to the norm, it has long since ceased to do so. The contemporary reality is as much single-parent families, working mothers and unemployed fathers as it is the breadwinner/homemaker couple described above. If the model of the patriarchal but caring family still constitutes a norm, this is because it corresponds to many of the aspirations and needs which are denied recognition in the impersonality of modern public life, not because it is a statistical average. The force of this concept is not to be measured by its empirical adequacy, but by the strength of the emotions attached to it, the effectiveness of the rhetoric that employs it and the stridency with which it is defended.

It is not the point here to chart the historical processes by which the identities described in this chapter have been undermined and reaffirmed. What is more significant in this context is the fact that any process of evaluating these identities is liable to undermine them. For an individual to subject her or his identity (as wife/mother or breadwinner/head of household) to such a scrutiny is to render that identity vulnerable, insofar as it brings into play a concept of rational agency beyond that of the identity in question. It involves the application of criteria in terms of which the identity may be assessed and, perhaps, found wanting. To ponder the identity in question is to render contingent what must be assumed as necessary and inescapable if it is to found an ethic of virtue.

In fact, the only criteria of assessment which have so far emerged are those provided by the public world of instrumental and juridical reason (it will be important later that there are others) and the form of identity which is most readily available from which to pass judgement on the private world is that form of abstract individuality constructed through the capitalist market. Thus, the place which is almost inevitably occupied by the individual who is led to subject her or his identity to rational scrutiny is already predefined. In which case, the activities involved in family life and other private relationships appear, not as ways of expressing one's identity, but as more or less rational means of achieving independent ends, and the responsibilities involved in personal relations take on the guise of duties. This kind of rational assessment changes the nature of that which is assessed, and the private realm can only survive such assessment by ceasing to be itself.

4

LIBERALISM AND NIHILISM

SCIENTIFIC REASON AND THE STATUS OF VALUE

> The fate of our times is characterised by rationalisation and intellectualisation and, above all, by the 'disenchantment of the world'.
>
> (Weber)[1]

In Chapter 2, I suggested that there were two distinct forms of reason implicit in Weber's account of the rationalisation of the modern world. The dominant and most pervasive form is instrumental reason: it is embodied in the market place, the capitalist organisation of production and it affects almost all other human activities and relationships. Instrumental reason is concerned with efficiency: it takes the ends of human activity as given and is concerned to calculate the most effective way of achieving those ends. In its characteristically capitalist form it is concerned with production for the sake of further production, consumption for the sake of further consumption, and above all, profit for the sake of further profit. In other words, it is concerned not with ends in themselves, but with ends insofar as they may be used to pursue further ends. To be rational in this sense is identical with the pursuit of power, not as a means but as an end in itself. The second form of reason, juridical rationality, is not so clearly distinguished by Weber. It is that form of reason which is concerned, not with efficiency, but with consistency – the relationship of general rule to instance. This form of reason is embodied in the law and in many organs of the state bureaucracy.

There is a third and prima facie distinct form of reason involved in Weber's notion of rationalisation: 'scientific' or 'cognitive' reason (my terms, not Weber's). It is 'the kind of rationalisation [which] the systematic thinker performs on the image of the world: an increasingly theoretical mastery of reality by means of increasingly abstract concepts'.[2] The aim of this form of reason is knowledge: it is concerned with questions of truth in some realist sense of that term, as well as with related questions of probability, explanation and coherence. Individuals are rational in this sense if their beliefs and judgements are arrived at or tested by methods which are more likely than available alternatives to yield true beliefs and judgements. Its favoured techniques are those of controlled observation, repetition, abstraction and quantification, and the inductive formation and testing of theories. Individuals who are cognitively rational are, if not in possession of the truth, at least oriented towards it. They are on the path towards understanding the world as it is, and not as they want it to be. Rationality in this sense is embodied in the modern institutions of scientific education and research.

Modern scientific reason is responsible for a concept of truth as corresponding to a world whose lineaments are revealed by the methods of science. Weber argued that as a consequence of this, we can no longer look to that world to discover the larger significance of our individual doings and strivings, nor to discern the values that our doings and strivings might instantiate.

> Who – aside from certain big children who are indeed found in the natural sciences – still believes that the findings of astronomy, biology, physics, or chemistry could teach us anything about the *meaning* of the world? If there is any such 'meaning', along what road could one come upon its tracks? If these natural sciences lead to anything in this way, they are apt to make the belief that there is such a thing as the 'meaning' of the universe die out at its very roots.[3]

The aspirations of modern science to describe and explain the world imply that nothing in it corresponds to the claims of religion and morality. These are expelled from the domain of truth, and must find some other status. If people found meanings and values in the premodern world, it was because they had invested it with their own hopes and desires and then failed to recognise them as such.

This is the burden of the claim that we now live in a 'disenchanted world' – a world devoid of intrinsic meaning. J. L. Mackie has spelled out the 'queerness' of supposing that such a world might contain values. How could objective values relate to or co-exist with those characteristics revealed by science? If they do exist, by what means could we come to know of them? And what possible relevance could they have to our existence?[4] Mackie's argument lays down a challenge. Once we have accepted that modern science has a primary role in saying what the world is like, how can we give a clear sense to the supposition that anything which exists in the world could be a standard by which we should guide our lives? As far as I can tell, this challenge has not been met.[5]

It is important to retain however, as Mackie did not, Weber's recognition of the historical limitations of this argument. It is not difficult to envisage a different conception of the world in terms of which it exemplifies a moral order of a certain kind. To have knowledge of such a world would involve knowing one's place in it and how to act with respect to it. In this world, there would be no difficulty in supposing that values had an objective existence. But no such conception is available now. We may regret the disenchantment which has destroyed this conception, but we cannot pretend that it has not taken place. To live in the modern world is to recognise that values and meanings only exist insofar as they are created by us. If science defines the realm of cognitive rationality, then questions of value fall outside that realm. Instrumental reason serves values; it does not say what they should be. Values are not therefore matters of objective existence or rational belief, but of subjective and non-rational choice.

Weber himself was uncomfortably aware of a problem this created for the status of science. If it was science which revealed a world in which values are matters of non-rational choice, then the commitment to science is itself a matter of non-rational choice. The procedures and results of science cannot validate themselves, and the choice of science as a way of life – as a 'vocation' – is no more cognitively rational than the choice of religion.

If scientific reason cannot provide its own justification, it must seek it elsewhere. Weber argued, somewhat guardedly, that it may be justified in part by its usefulness in pursuing the aims of instrumental reason,[6] and this claim has been made in a much less guarded fashion in more recent years.[7] But Weber had good reasons for his hesitation. As he well knew, there are many cases where misconception or ignorance increases one's chances of success. A soldier will often fight more effectively if he is unaware of the high probability of defeat; a capitalist will pursue a profit with more vigour if he is convinced that he deserves it. If we define truth in realist terms, e.g. as correspondence to the world, it emerges that there is only a contingent and defeasible connection between beliefs which are true in this sense and the effective pursuit of one's aims. If on the other hand, we define truth in terms of pragmatic efficacy, then we must give up the claim that any particular set of 'truths', e.g. those of science, has a privileged status. Science serves certain interests, religion serves others. If from the perspective of modern science, a religious view of the world objectifies the desires and hopes of those who hold to that view, the same may now be said of science itself. The scientific world is an objectification of those desires which work through the institutions and practices of science. This world is disenchanted not because the objective procedures of science have revealed it in its bleak actuality, but because the values it serves lie outside it. The meaningless world revealed by science has no more claim to be the real world than the meaningful world displayed by religion.

It may be that there are those who take the understanding of the world as it is in itself as their aim in life; indeed, it was probably this lonely commitment – to 'knowledge ... for its own sake', to 'science as a vocation' – which Weber was, against all his principles, advocating.[8] Such 'objective men' who desire to reflect the world like mirrors, are, Nietzsche suggested, 'precious instruments' who need to be taken good care of; their role however is to be used by those who are mightier. In the modern world, it is the will to power which dominates that ineffectual form of reason directed towards truth.[9]

Weber's position is an attempt to come to terms with the subjective and arbitrary nature of value as revealed by scientific reason, and in particular, to insulate science itself from this subjectivism and arbitrariness. The attempt is unsuccessful: if values are non-rational, then so too are the values embodied in the enterprise of science, and it must give up its pretensions to a special status. Nietzsche's position is the more consistent one: science, along with morality and religion, is to be understood, not in terms of objective truth and falsity, but in terms of the aspirations, projects, hopes and fears of its proponents. The scientific picture of the world is an expression of a particular kind of will to power, and to seek objective guarantees of its veracity is a timid evasion.

According to Nietzsche, nihilism arises when 'the highest values devaluate themselves'.[10] Nihilism 'stands at the door' of modern civilisation, not merely because it is no longer possible to believe in certain ultimate meanings and values, but because the most important sources of meaning and the most important values have turned against themselves, and revealed their own meaninglessness and lack of value. Where science provides the standard of objective knowledge, morality can only be a self-deluding subjectivity. But from there it has had its revenge: the pretensions of science to secure objective truth are themselves exposed to reveal the same subjectivity as had been revealed in morality and religion.

The administered self-destruction which was Nietzsche's favoured technique for dealing with the claims of morality and truth was not intended to clear the way for new truths and a new morality. Its purpose was to rid the world of both. It is important to recognise what is at stake here. It may be that the practices of science can survive all the better without the pretensions of providing a privileged account of the world as it really is. However, if science is merely a vehicle for various interests and desires, what ought these to be? If values are merely matters of non-rational choice, this question is unanswerable. The failure of science to make good its claim for objectivity makes it all the more necessary to rescue morality from the swamp of subjectivity. Conversely, if morality is more than an artefact of human desire, it may be that moral values will support an enterprise of understanding the world as it is.

There are other reasons to be concerned with morality. It is not just a method of social control and co-ordination; it also provides coherence to individual existence. Moral values provide a significance and direction to our lives beyond that which is provided by our individual desires and goals. We often seek reasons which are not simply the epiphenomena of our desires or decisions, nor of the desires and decisions of others. We desire standards to assess which of our desires to cultivate and which of our goals to pursue. Morality even promises a satisfaction – that of living as one ought – beyond those provided by doing what one wants.

Morality can only play this role if it is something more than an artefact of human desire. The paradox of morality in the modern world is that it lays claim to an objective status which is no longer available to it. Whatever is objective is *for that reason* not a value. It may be that we have no option but to accept this position and reject the enterprise of morality, much as an earlier generation rejected religion. This was more or less Nietzsche's position. Morality makes a claim to truth which it can no longer sustain. Insofar as morality itself posits truth as a value, it requires us to reject morality for its own mendacity – and with it, of course, we must reject the moral value of truthfulness.[11]

The failure of morality to live up to its own claims for itself throws us dangerously back on our own resources: the only significance and direction in our lives is that provided by us. It may be that nihilism – the 'repudiation of value, meaning, and desirability' – is, as Nietzsche thought, the fate of modernity. But Nietzsche himself thought that it required exceptional heroism even to contemplate this result, let alone to live with it. It may be that there is more than a hint of delusion in the widespread contemporary belief that we can take it in our stride.

THE PROJECT OF LIBERALISM

> That we have one conception of the good rather than another is not relevant from a moral standpoint.
>
> (John Rawls)[12]

Contemporary liberalism accepts the Weberian thesis that values are not part of the objective world and are – *for the most part* – matters of individual choice. Its project is defined by the qualifying phrase 'for the most part'; it is to locate and defend a sphere of value which, while not part of the objective world, is not a matter of choice either.

For the liberal, the idea that the world does not contain objective values is often allied with a thesis about freedom: individuals are – or should be – free to choose their own values. The term '*good*' is appropriated to designate those values which fall within the area of human freedom. Since there is no reason to suppose that all individuals will choose the same values, and less to suppose that they should, the liberal envisages a pluralist society – one characterised by a variety of ways in which individuals pursue their own chosen conceptions of the good life. Within certain limits, there are no objective standards on which to assess such acts of value creation and hence no reason to suppose that one way of life is superior to another. This is the area of human freedom. However, individuals may pursue their conceptions of the good in such a way as to conflict with the ways of life of others, so there must be limits to the ways in which individuals pursue their chosen ways of life. This is the area of restriction, or of '*right*' as this term has come to be used; its main component is a concept of justice.

By and large, the liberal does not think it possible – or even desirable – to say very much about the good. There are certain basic necessities of human existence, and there are other things which are necessary or useful for doing almost anything a person might choose to do, so it is possible to identify some relatively uncontroversial goods.[13] But above this limit, and perhaps even below it, there will be a wide variety of different ways in which individuals will choose to live, and there are no rationally compelling grounds on which any one of these can be picked out as exemplifying *the* good life. However, the greater the variety in individual conceptions of the good, the more it is necessary to place limits on what each individual does in order to allow for other individuals to pursue their chosen ways of life. Somewhat paradoxically, the greater the freedom which is envisaged, the more extensive the restrictions which are required. If liberals see no good reason for providing a theory of the good, it is essential for them to provide an account of justice. Since this is the part of morality which constrains the desires and choices of those subject to it, it cannot be left to those desires and choices to determine.

The project of liberalism is to construct an account of justice which resists the subjectivity which it allows to the good. It has been Kant who has provided the main inspiration for the recent liberal theorists who have taken up this challenge. The principle of justice is sought, not in the fabric of the external world, nor in the content of individual desire or choice, but in a structure of human thought and action. This is, in a sense, a structure of subjectivity; but if it is widely shared, or universal, it will have the requisite impersonal and objective status. A key role in determining the content and the force of the principle is played by the concept of reason. We understand and are subject to the demands of justice insofar as we are rational beings. In which case, these demands will not be external constraints, but will in principle be accepted – and perhaps even worked out for themselves – by the very people who are subject to them. The principles of right are in this sense self-imposed and their restrictions, self-restrictions; they are, therefore, the products of freedom.

For Kant, the principles of morality are presupposed by our everyday moral practice. That one has the capacity to know and to act on the basis of these principles is 'transcendentally necessary' for the validity of these demands. There is a certain ponderous emptiness here: the transcendental turn is made just in order to keep morality a going concern. Most contemporary liberals have rejected Kant's transcendental turn and its accompanying metaphysics. For them, the principles of morality cannot be established by *fiat*; they must be discovered or created in the real world as it is revealed by ordinary experience and modern social science. As we shall see, this is no easy matter.

Gewirth

Of recent attempts to construct a theory of right, Alan Gewirth's attempt to elicit a principle of right from the structure of action is closest to Kant in one important respect: the deployment of a concept of reason as formal consistency or universality. Gewirth summarises his argument as follows:

> First, every agent implicitly makes evaluative judgements about the goodness of his purposes and hence about the necessary goodness of the freedom and well-being that are necessary conditions of his acting to achieve his purposes. Second, because of this necessary goodness, every agent implicitly makes a deontic judgement in which he claims he has rights to freedom and well-being. Third, every agent must claim these rights for the sufficient reason that he is a prospective agent who has purposes he wants to fulfil, so that he logically must accept the generalisation that all prospective agents have rights to freedom and well-being.[14]

Gewirth provides a wealth of detail in support of this argument. For my purposes, however, it is sufficient to concentrate on one step in it: the move from the agent's own claim to have rights to freedom and well-being, to Gewirth's conclusion that the agent 'logically must accept' that all who are relevantly similar, i.e. all who are prospective agents, have precisely the same rights. This step depends on a 'general logical principle of universalisability: if some predicate P belongs to some subject S because S has the property Q . . . then P must also belong to all other subjects S_1, S_2, . . . S_n that have Q'.[15]

This principle does have some claim to be a principle of reason: indeed, it is precisely the principle of formal consistency which is at the heart of Kant's doctrine of practical reason. It is also the principle of juridical reason which plays an important though subsidiary role in Weber's concept of rationalisation. But what is this for individual agents who, according to Gewirth, must 'on pain of contradiction' accept that others have the same rights as they claim for themselves, and are 'logically committed' to respecting these rights?[16] But can a logical commitment have such binding practical consequences? If I say or write something, I may be 'logically committed' not to contradict it; but I may easily choose to do so, perhaps through wilfulness, but perhaps also because of the demands of rhyme or wit, paradox or irony, or in general because of the pursuit of what I take at the time to be a greater good. If on a particular occasion I can most effectively pursue my chosen conception of the good by ignoring the demands of logic, why should I not do so? Probably I will usually make use of a principle of formal consistency the better to achieve my goals; indeed, in many cases, I will be foolish not to. But in the particular cases which Gewirth is inviting us to consider, the application of this principle will not aid, but interfere with the effective pursuit of my goals. What reason is there for me to adopt the principle in these cases?

This point may be put differently. Gewirth argues that reason involves consistency. This may be so of one concept of reason; but there is *another* concept of reason – that of choosing the most efficient means to secure given ends. In many cases the demands of the two concepts of reason coincide. But in the cases which are crucial for morality, they do not. It may be, as Gewirth has argued, that as a logical reasoner, I ought to allow others the same freedom and well-being that I claim for myself and regulate my behaviour accordingly; but it may equally be the case that as a rational pursuer of my chosen conception of the good life, I ought to override the freedom of others. Gewirth provides no reason why the first – logical – 'ought' should take precedence over the second – pragmatic – one in determining what *I* ought to do.

It was precisely this kind of consideration which led Kant to posit the primacy of practical reason; only thus could he secure the overriding commitment which he thought crucial to morality. Gewirth accepts that the commitment to right must override others, and attempts to found it on the existence of 'rational and conatively normal' individuals who accept 'the reasons of deductive and inductive logic' and have 'the self-interested motivations common to most persons'.[17] But he fails to show why rationality in his logical sense defines a commitment which must in principle take precedence over other considerations. This leaves us where we started: if formal rationality is a matter of choice, so too are the principles of right which it is used to construct. Gewirth has not shown that these impose obligations upon individuals whatever they desire or choose.

Rawls

The most influential recent attempt to construct a liberal theory of justice is that of John Rawls.[18] Rawls makes use of one of the most recurrent and powerful myths in the repertoire of modern political thought: the story of an originating contract in which the free and rational individuals who are subject to the institutions of civil society come together to decide what these should be. The attraction of this story is that it bases legitimate authority on the free choice of those subject to it. Rawls' use of the myth is avowedly hypothetical (in this, as in much else, he follows Kant). The commitment is not that of an actual contract, but it is such as to invite the assent of reflective and reasonable moral agents.

Rawls asks us to imagine an 'original position' in which those who are subject to the claims of justice consider what principles they would accept to determine the basic structure of society. Their deliberations take place behind a 'veil of ignorance': they do not know what specific position they will occupy in society, what particular characteristics and capabilities they will have (even their sex is not known to them), or what conception of the good life they will espouse. They are, however, equipped with a general knowledge of society and its workings, and also with a concept of rationality in the familiar – instrumental – sense.[19] They can also work out a list of 'primary goods' such as freedom, self-respect, power and wealth, which 'every rational agent is presumed to want', and which 'have a use whatever a person's rational plan of life'.[20]

Individuals in the original position will all reason in precisely the same way and, assuming that there is an optimal solution to the problems they are faced with, they will all agree to it. Rawls argues that since they cannot tell how they personally will be affected by the outcome of their deliberations, they will choose arrangements which will maximise the well-being of the worst off. They will arrive at two basic principles:

> First: each person is to have an equal right to the most extensive basic liberty compatible with a similar liberty to others.
> Second: social and economic inequalities are to be arranged so that they are both (a) reasonably expected to be to everyone's advantage, and (b) attached to positions and offices open to all.[21]

The point of the first principle – the 'Equal Liberty' Principle – is to give all individuals the rights to speech and assembly, political activity, conscience, personal property and the rule of law. The point of the second – the 'Difference Principle' – is to ensure that inequalities in the possession of the primary goods not covered by the first principle, e.g. wealth, income, authority, are only justified if everyone, even the worst off, benefits from them. Rawls also argues that individuals in the original position will agree that the Equal Liberty Principle should take priority over the Difference Principle: all citizens must be guaranteed their basic liberties *before* there can be any question of trade off in the distribution of other social goods.

The device of the original position eliminates the need to appeal to a concept of rationality other than that of instrumental reason. Ignorance imposes impartiality. If other assumptions are held constant, instrumental reason will in this context deliver much the same conclusions as a more Kantian conception in a less exiguously described situation.

It is a moot point whether individuals in the original position would arrive at Rawls' two principles (why not gamble?). But there is a more fundamental question. Why should we *care* what they would decide? After all, it is not immediately clear why we, who have a fair knowledge of our situation, capacities and interests, should feel any commitment to principles arrived at by hypothetical individuals who are somewhat like us, but lack most of our more interesting characteristics and almost all the knowledge relevant to our lives. As Gewirth complains, it is not usually considered rational to base our commitments on wilful ignorance.[22]

There are various passages in *A Theory of Justice* where Rawls seems to suggest that our 'representatives' in the original position are in some sense our 'real selves'. By acting on the principles which would be arrived at in the original position,

> persons express their nature as free and rational beings subject to the general conditions of life. For to express one's nature as

> a being of a particular kind is to act on the principles that would be chosen if this nature were the decisive determining element.[23]

But elsewhere in the book, and more explicitly in his later writings, Rawls distances himself from the idea of grounding morality on metaphysical necessity. He argues instead that in our everyday social existence we recognise ourselves as subject to considerations of justice, and that the device of the original position articulates this pre-reflective moral consciousness. At this point, Rawls is closer in spirit to Hegel than to Kant.[24] He assumes that we possess a certain moral understanding as a matter of cultural fact, and that it is in virtue of this that we can be inducted into a theory of morality.

Certain ideas about justice are, he claims, already involved in modern, Western, democratic life, and these ideas are embodied in the account of the original position.[25] We know, for example, that it is not fair for individuals to be able to tailor rules in order to suit themselves, and we can recognise that this condition of fairness is secured by the veil of ignorance. Similarly, we can be persuaded that the original position represents the other circumstances – freedom, equality, rationality – which, on reflection, we can see to be necessary to arrive at just principles. This procedure need not simply reproduce our antecedent moral convictions; these may be modified, transformed or even rejected through the process of philosophical argument and reflection. The aim of the procedure is to reach an ideal 'reflective equilibrium' in which our actual moral convictions and the principles delivered by moral theory will have come to coincide.[26]

While there is a danger that the mutual interaction of moral theory and pre-reflective moral judgement will only reproduce our parochial moral certainties, there is a corresponding promise: that of explaining why we in the real world should be committed by the deliberations of those who are not. Rawls' claim is that we recognise the procedure as expressing not our metaphysical identity, but our already existing, if socially formed, nature as moral beings. The story of the original position delivers *reasons* for us to act in the ways prescribed, because it articulates an already existing moral consciousness. This assumes the existence of a widespread and effective sense of justice:

> the parties as agents of reconstruction are assumed to have an effective sense of justice . . . [which means] that they have the

> capacity to understand and apply the various principles of justice that are under discussion, as well as a sufficiently strong desire to act upon whatever principles are eventually adopted.[27]

No doubt an 'effective sense of justice' does play a large role in the rhetoric characteristic of the liberal, democratic tradition. Presumably too the agents to whom Rawls' arguments are addressed do have the capacity to 'understand and apply' the principles of justice. But whether this corresponds to a 'sufficiently strong capacity' to act on these principles is a good deal more dubious. The rationalisation of the dominant institutions of modern public life means that most of us must be, most of the time, instrumentally rational in pursuing our goals. If we were not ready to assess available activities and social relationships in terms of their contribution to these goals, then we and those dependent upon us would suffer. Rawls' assumption that individuals have a sense of justice implies that we are *not* just like this; that we are ready to restrain the pursuit of our goals by considerations which are instrumentally non-rational. Curiously, however, in his account of the original position, he assumes that its inhabitants *are* just like this: they are instrumentally rational, and while they are not necessarily self-interested, they are disinterested in others.

There is a paradox here. If we assume, as Rawls does, that we are equipped with a lively sense of justice, then we will not recognise those who lack that sense as our 'representatives'. To do so would be treat our commitment to justice as being on a par with all our other inclinations. But on Rawls' own view, a sense of justice is a much stronger commitment, one which is even prior to our sense of the good. If we have a sense of justice, we will – properly – be reluctant to divest ourselves of it, or be moved by the reasoning of those without it. If on the other hand we do recognise those in the original position as representing our own motivations, it will be because we lack a sense of justice. In which case, we will find that the deliberations of our 'representatives' have no purchase on our own.

The device of the original position – like that of the social contract – is a way of abstracting individuals from the social relations in which they exist. Its point is to generate principles by which actual social relations may be assessed. The problem with Rawls' use of this device is not that it is unrealistic; indeed, in certain respects it is too realistic in its representation of the isolated individual of modern social existence. The description of the original position precisely mirrors the abstract individuality and instrumental rationality characteristic of modern public existence. But if real life individuals are like this, they will *not* acknowledge the force of the principles arrived at in the original position, certainly not to the extent of overriding their own informed judgements.

Rawls' assumption that a sense of justice already has a cultural existence occupies the place that should be filled by an argument why people should be moved by, and give priority to, considerations of justice. In order to mount such an argument it would be necessary to claim that it is *good* that individuals be just, and this would be to subsume the theory of justice under a theory of the good. There is more than terminology at stake here. To argue directly that individuals should include an ideal of justice within their conception of the good would be to claim that living in certain kinds of relationship with others constitutes part of the good life itself, not a means through which people may pursue their own versions of it. This would require a conception of the social nature of human existence. The device of the original position is an attempt to arrive at a concept of justice by means of the ruminations of individuals considered in abstraction from their relationship with each other. It thus simulates the isolation which is both the pre-condition and the effect of the dominant institutions of modern public life, and it promotes conceptions of the good in which relations with others count as means, not as part of the good life itself. But the existence of individuals of this kind is compatible neither with a theory nor a practice of justice. They do not have, and are probably not capable of, a sense of justice.

Habermas

> The goal of coming to an understanding is to bring about an agreement that terminates in the intersubjective mutuality of reciprocal understanding, shared knowledge, mutual trust, and accord with each other.
>
> (Habermas)[28]

> If, by some misunderstanding, people understood each other, they would never be able to reach agreement.
>
> (Baudelaire)[29]

There is some awkwardness in treating Habermas as a liberal given that his intellectual origins lie in a tradition of Marxist critical theory which has been hostile to liberalism. But in the respects which are important here, he must be counted as such. As Habermas himself says: 'my Marxist friends are not entirely unjustified in accusing me of being a radical liberal.'[30] He has characterised his work as 'an attempt to reconstruct Kantian ethics'[31] and accepts the characteristically liberal view that the aim of moral theory is to provide, not an account of the good, but a theory of justice:

> Deontic, cognitive and universal moral theories in the Kantian tradition are theories of justice, which must leave the question of the good life unanswered. . . . One should not place excessive demands on moral theory, but leave something over for social theory, and the major part for the participants themselves.[32]

Like Gewirth and Rawls, Habermas attempts to construct a theory of justice without appeal to *a priori* arguments. But he takes the implications of this position much more seriously than they do: if the presuppositions of a morality of justice are to be discovered in the real world of modernity, then that world must be analysed by the best available social theory. Thus much of his work consists of a critical encounter with the major attempts to comprehend the modern social world, especially those of Marx and Weber.[33]

Habermas takes over from Marx the idea that the productive forces are one of the primary dynamic elements in human history, and that capitalism has been responsible for an unprecedented development. He interprets this development along Weberian lines in terms of rationalisation: the achievement of capitalist modernity is the liberation of instrumental reason from the constraints within which it operates in other forms of society. Unlike earlier critical theorists (e.g. Adorno, Horkheimer, Marcuse), Habermas limits his critique of instrumental reason: while he disputes its imperialist pretensions to constitute the whole of human rationality, he does not reject it altogether.[34] However, Habermas criticises Marx for overemphasising production and ignoring – what is crucial for Habermas – communicative interaction. Habermas locates the genesis of this idea in the early writings of Hegel, but criticises Hegel and, following him, Marx for turning away from it in favour of a concept of human action based on the paradigm of production

– in Marx's case, of material production.[35] Habermas argues that the Marxian idea of the social relations of production should be expanded so as to include this intersubjective dimension of human existence. In a related vein, he criticises Weber for having too narrow a concept of rationalisation. There are, Habermas argues, two distinct dimensions in which the modern world has been rationalised. The first, which was recognised by Weber, involves the primacy of instrumental reason; the second, which was largely unnoticed by Weber, is that involved in communication. If instrumental reason is directed towards success, communicative reason is oriented towards mutual understanding, and is paradigmatically exemplified in those discursive activities, 'speech acts', which take this as their goal.[36]

Much of Habermas' energy is devoted to expounding the concept of communicative reason. He argues that communication – of which speech is the exemplary form – presupposes a concept of agreement based on reason, and that whenever we involve ourselves in communicative action, we make a commitment to the principles which are necessary to make a rational agreement possible. According to Habermas' general theory of speech acts ('universal pragmatics'), when we make a speech act we commit ourselves to the meaningfulness of what we say, we implicitly claim that it is true, that we are sincere and that we have a right so to speak. Any of these claims may, in principle, be contested; in which case the speaker is committed to providing an intersubjectively acceptable justification for it.[37]

In practice, most speech acts fail to satisfy the principles of communicative reason. But it is Habermas' claim that they at least raise these claims to validity.

> In action oriented towards reaching understanding, validity claims are 'always already' implicitly raised. . . . In these validity claims communication theory can locate a gentle but obstinate, a never silent though seldom redeemed claim to reason, a claim that must be recognised de facto whenever and wherever there is to be consensual action.[38]

However defective a particular speech act may be, it yet invokes an 'ideal speech situation' in which the promises it makes will be redeemed. Such a situation exists where the consensus is achieved without the use of force or deception, and where all involved have the opportunity and the means to participate in the communicative process of obtaining agreement. The rationalisation of society in this communicative sense would mean:

> extirpating those relations of force that are inconspicuously set in the very structures of communication and that prevent conscious settlement of conflicts, and consensual regulation of conflicts, by means of intrapsychic as well as interpersonal communicative barriers.[39]

Habermas' thesis is that the modern world has been rationalised, not only in the directions recognised by Weber, but also in the sense of communicative reason. While capitalist production embodies instrumental reason at work, it has also massively increased the nature and scope of communicative interaction. But there is a tension between the two forms of reason. The operation of instrumental reason in the social world – what Habermas refers to as 'strategic action' – is often incompatible with the demands of communicative reason. It may require deception, generate unequal access to the means of communication and knowledge, and produce what, in the light of the ideal speech situation, must be counted as 'systematically distorted communication'. Habermas sees it as characteristic of capitalist modernity that it tends both to expand and also to erode the sphere of communicative rationality. But even distorted communication pays its dues to the ideal of undistorted communication: it pretends to be, what it is not, meaningful, true, sincere and morally appropriate. However distorted an act of communication, it still contains a transcendent moment: an implicit reference to a radically egalitarian and free society.

Habermas' strategy has several attractions. Language exists both as fact and as value: it is an empirically given human practice and a normative structure. As a practice it is nearly inescapable: it is hard to conceive of any human society which does not involve the use of language. But it is also a rule-governed human activity: a network of linguistic rules defines the possibility of communication, and we cannot participate in linguistic activity without accepting these rules. If, as Habermas argues, these rules are not only narrowly linguistic (like the rules of grammar) but include principles with a broader and more substantive content, then it is plausible to argue that modern individuals are, *qua* language users, committed to them. They may not follow them in practice, but the principles have a normative force which they cannot evade.

However, it is highly doubtful whether communicative action has the unified structure which Habermas assumes. Habermas constructs his concept of communicative rationality only by treating a range of speech acts (e.g. story telling, jokes, role playing, the use of words to arouse or comfort, etc.) as secondary to the serious business of truth, truthfulness and the rest. Even this putatively central case is only arrived at through a process of idealisation. It is hard not to suspect circularity here; that the principles of communicative reason play a large role in picking out the central cases of communicative action which are then used to derive the principles.[40] Prima facie, it is just as plausible to argue that, once we get beyond purely formal considerations, the uses of language are as heterogeneous as the human activities they imbricate. The views of the later Wittgenstein are instructive here. Habermas applauds Wittgenstein's analysis of various 'language games', but regrets that 'in Wittgenstein and his disciples, the logical analysis of the use of language always remained particularistic: they failed to develop it into a *theory of language games*'.[41] Habermas does not recognise the principled nature of this refusal. Wittgenstein's use of the term 'game' was intended to suggest that the various language games lacked anything very significant in common. Wittgenstein's reluctance to develop a theory of language was precisely due to the fact that he did not wish to impose a false unity on the heterogeneity of the various linguistic practices.

In practice, language is used as much to conceal as to reveal, and as much to generate misunderstanding as understanding. This is not just because it is a vehicle for the ideological dominance of a ruling class. It is an important part of the language of the oppressed, the deviant and even those who merely wish to emphasise their difference, that communication with those who are other is coded, masked and elusive. Creating a distinction between those who understand and those who do not is part of the process of negotiating difference and plurality. Perhaps this is distorted communication; but these practices provide a space for divergence which is precluded by Habermas' ideal of consensual transparency. Even where mutual understanding is aspired to, there is no guarantee that it is achievable, even in principle. Incommensurability between two discourses – and the ways of life they express – may be such that mutual understanding is only possible at the cost of suppressing difference.[42] A conflict of interests might be so intense and deep-seated that there is no possibility – at least no *rational* possibility – of uncoerced agreement. Communication may clear the air and show what is at issue; but in this case, mutual understanding will preclude agreement. At that point, the force of arms must replace the force of argument.[43]

Even if we assume that communication does involve a commitment to principles as substantive as those posited by Habermas, it is not clear that these have a normative force which must override all other commitments. On Habermas' own account, modern individuals exist within two symbiotic but opposed forms of rational structure. Many of their activities must be governed by the norms of instrumental reason: they must earn their living, maximise their capacity to cope with future contingencies, secure as far as possible the futures of those dependent upon them – all in the ways which are made available by the market, the capitalist organisation of production and so on. Of course, they must also involve themselves in communicative activities, and if Habermas is right, they are thereby committed to the principles of communicative reason. But, as Agnes Heller has asked,[44] why should *this* commitment override those defined by the norms of instrumental reason? This is not just a matter of which commitment will in practice win out, but of which *should* win out. No such principle of adjudication is provided by communicative reason, which is after all one of the parties in the dispute. But in the absence of such a principle, we are back with an arbitrary choice ('decisionism' in Habermas' terms). At this point, Habermas' problems are parallel to those of Gewirth: he is unable to show why the principles of communicative reason should take precedence over the other principles which inform the behaviour of the individual.

Habermas touches on this point when, in response to Heller's criticism, he suggests that the choice between instrumental and communicative rationality is only available to the individual in the most abstract sense. Withdrawal from 'communicatively structured spheres of life, means retreating into the monadic isolation of strategic action: in the long run this is self-destructive'.[45] But someone who opts for instrumental over communicative rationality does not have to withdraw from communication. He/she will communicate strategically and be a free-rider on the communicative rationality of other participants. It may be that communicative rationality is not just a commitment that we must make and perhaps not keep, but that it is a component in individual well-being, i.e. part of the good. In this case, there is a reason for the individual to choose communicative reason over its competitors. But this would require a different kind of argument; not a theory of universal pragmatics but an account of the good. It would also move the debate outside the terrain of liberalism.

Heller has also pointed out that in providing a purely instrumental account of production, Habermas ignores the 'anthropological meaning of work'.[46] For Marx, as for Hegel, labour is not simply the activity of satisfying pre-existing ends. It is also a way in which humans express and transform their nature; in acting to satisfy old needs, they generate new ones and new kinds of human activity. It is both a creative and a self-creative activity. When production is conceived in this way, it cannot be subsumed under the norms of instrumental reason. Its goals do not have a clearcut conceptual existence prior to the activity, and the desires which give rise to the activity are transformed by it. Labour is not merely an available means to a desired end. It is a necessary form of human self-expression and of human self-making. From the perspective of the anthropological meaning of work, the fact that capitalism has turned labour into an instrumental activity is not a sign of progress but of alienation.

My point here is not to resurrect a conception of morality in which labour is fundamental, and everything else derivative. Indeed, changes in the nature of work in the contemporary world render Marx's conception of labour as a 'metabolism' between humans and the natural world increasingly problematic.[47] But just as it is possible to elicit a deep structure of communicative rationality beneath the distortions of contemporary communicative practices, it is also possible to posit a normative dimension of human creativity within the instrumentally rationalised world of capitalist production. The concept of work also has a claim to be considered in the derivation of our fundamental moral values. But there are many other human activities which are not reducible either to communication or to production. These include playing, singing, dancing, making love, raising children, writing (if not publishing) books and so on. Why should all these significant human activities be subject to norms derived from the concept of communication? What is the reason for singling out one human activity, however pervasive and inescapable, as the sole basis for morality? By attempting to give communication a privileged significance, Habermas neglects the normative aspects of other human activities.

Habermas has accepted too uncritically the instrumental rationalisation through which human activities and relationships in the modern world have been drained of normative significance as they come to serve values which are extrinsic to them. Since Habermas has explicitly conceded work to the logic of instrumental reason, and implicitly other human activities as well, these are not available to enter into the construction of basic moral values. Even if communication were the only bulwark from which instrumental rationalisation could be resisted, this would still leave the individual – and the wider society – torn between two conflicting forms of rationality. Habermas' account of modernity provides no basis to think that communicative reason will win out against instrumental reason, nor does he supply the individual with a good reason to prefer it.

Even as an object of potential choice, the principles embodied in an ethic of communication are unattractively abstract and formalistic when compared with the various intensities and pleasures of those human activities and relationships which have not completely succumbed to the logic of rationalisation. If there are principles to be discovered with which the encroachments of instrumental reason and the vagaries of subjectivism are to be combated, then we must seek them in a wider and richer range of human activities than merely communication. This requires recognising that these activities have a dimension which is not captured by instrumental reason, or by communicative reason for that matter. It also involves moving beyond the terrain of justice, and attempting to provide an account of the good.

LIBERALISM, NIHILISM AND THE FAILURE OF COMMUNITY

> Nihilism stands at the door: whence comes this uncanniest of all guests?
>
> (Nietzsche)[48]

Liberalism has given up trying to discover what constitutes the good life; it leaves this in the domain of individual choice. It has limited itself to providing a theory of justice. This self-abnegation has left it without anything worthwhile to say on the vast range of moral issues which concern, not restriction and obligation, but guidance and advice. It is also self-defeating. The arbitrariness which liberalism concedes to the good cannot but return to infect the domain of justice. If we are to do better than liberalism we must provide *reasons* why people ought to be just. We must go beyond liberalism and locate a concept of justice within an account of the good – not just for a particular individual, but for all individuals subject to the demands of justice. Justice must be conceived, not as a constraint upon individual's pursuing their good, but a component of it.

To many liberals, the idea of a unitary good has seemed incompatible with a commitment to pluralism. The extent of this incompatibility will, however, depend upon how narrowly the good is specified. Anyway, the failure of liberalism to deliver a theory of justice shows the need for *some* limits to the pluralism it espouses. The idea that it may fall within the province of moral theory to say something substantive about the good life has seemed to some to be inconsistent with individual freedom of choice. But this is a confusion. To argue that there is an objective good does not provide a justification for compelling people to choose it. It is plausible to suggest that freedom of choice is necessary both to know and to pursue the good life. There is no incompatibility between a theory of the good and a commitment to freedom.

There are, however, certain conditions which must be satisfied if a theory of justice as a good is to be more than an idle wish. Justice involves a recognition of the rights and perhaps the well-being of others. For justice to become a part of our good, the claims and concerns of others must enter into the structure of our desires, not merely as contingently available means to their satisfaction, but as their objects. They must enter into the conception of our own well-being. While desires of this 'intersubjective' sort are familiar enough, they are usually limited in scope, concerned with specific others connected by ties of intimacy, emotion or family commitment. Justice in the public sphere concerns relations with people who are far beyond our ordinary emotional reach; it requires, therefore, a bond of a more impersonal kind. Communication, as Habermas conceives it, has something like the requisite impersonality and scope. But the appeal of communicative activity in this context is precisely due to the extent to which other human activities have been structured by the logic of instrumental reason and drained of their intersubjective dimension. The use of language will only have the moral authority to resist the further encroachments of instrumental reason, if it is itself embedded in a more comprehensive theory of the human good.

If intersubjectivity is to serve as the foundation for a theory of justice as a good, it must be established at the level of individual identity. We must be able to provide an account of the self which makes essential reference to its relationship with other selves. Individual identity must be constituted by the existence of the individual within a network of relations with others, so that self-awareness involves an awareness of those relations, and the concerns of the self include a reference to the concerns of others. Only with this more inclusive concept of individual identity will concern for oneself be, not only compatible with, but necessary for a theory and a practice of justice.[49] For such individuals, relations with others are not merely means for the satisfaction of their ends, nor is action directed towards the satisfaction of the interests of others only contingently related to their own satisfaction. To act for another is also to act for oneself; the satisfaction and happiness of that other is part of one's own satisfaction and happiness.

This concept of individual identity presupposes a certain form of social life – a 'community' (in the somewhat specialised sense in which this term translates *Gemeinschaft* as against *Gesellschaft*) in which individuals recognise that certain social relationships are constitutive of their own self-awareness. To act justly, i.e. with due regard to the claims and concerns of others in the community, will not be to restrain the pursuit of one's own good in order to secure the good of those others. It will be a way of pursuing one's own good. Even where the relationship between the just act and the good of others is highly tenuous, e.g. where the action contributes only marginally to some distant good, people will conceive of the action as part of the good life, and justified for this reason. They will not be free-riders.

Many liberals have rejected concepts of this kind as irredeemably unclear. Rawls, for example, mentions the concept of community in order to dismiss it:

> For reasons of clarity among others, we do not want to rely on an undefined concept of community, or to suppose that society is an organic whole with a life of its own distinct from and superior to that of all its members in their relations with one another.[50]

The trouble with the concept (apart from Rawls' tendentious characterisation of it) is not that it is unclear or confused. Recent 'communitarian' critics of liberalism such as Michael Sandel have gone a long way towards characterising a notion of community in terms acceptable to the analytic tradition. Indeed, Sandel has argued persuasively that some such conception is presupposed by some of Rawls' most characteristic positions.[51] The problem with the notion of community is not its obscurity, but its unavailability. The dominant forms of modern public life – the market, the capitalist organisation of production, the bureaucracy – are incompatible with community in this sense. Those who have invoked the concept against liberalism have simply evaded the central problem which liberalism is attempting to confront: the place of values in a value-free social world.

For Weber, the world of modernity is disenchanted through the application of scientific reason: it is as if the cold clear gaze of objective knowledge has revealed a world without value. However, insofar as scientific reason is itself informed by instrumental reason, there is no ground to suppose that its findings have a privileged claim to reveal the world as it essentially is. The disenchantment of the world follows, not from knowing it in its unadorned truth, but from conceiving it as a means to ends which are independent of it.

This suggests a further dimension of disenchantment: the expulsion of value from the social world. The capitalist market and organisation of production have located the individual within a network of interdependencies more extensive than in any other form of society. Paradoxically, however, they also function to sever the individual from constitutive links with other individuals – at least in the public world. Individuals conceive of themselves as the self-contained centre of their needs and desires, and others exist as the means through which these needs and desires may be satisfied. The instrumental rationalisation characteristic of modernity requires that one's own activities, as well as one's relationships with other individuals, be conceived of as means for the achievement of distinct goals. The capitalist organisation of production, and the way of life associated with it, focuses these goals on consumption and – above all – power.

In this context, people can no longer look to the wider social world for the source of their identity nor – what amounts to the same thing – find in it the values and meanings to guide their lives. The only place left to look for these are within the individual; but the process through which the constitutive links between the individual and society have been severed is also the process by which people have been drained of the resources to provide their own values. Underlying the liberal emphasis on the freedom of people to choose their own conception of the good is the failure of liberalism to confront the arbitrariness of this freedom where people are devoid of standards to inform their choosing. The reality to which this freedom is subject is the process of rationalisation and the socially imposed goals of consumption and power. The order of the modern world

> is now bound to the technical and economic conditions of machine production which today determine the lives of all the individuals who are born into this mechanism, not only those directly concerned with economic acquisition, with irresistible force. Perhaps it will so determine them until the last ton of fossilised coal is burnt.[52]

As Weber saw, the rationalisation of society has delivered not freedom, but its opposite.

Nihilism arises in part through the collapse of objective values and the incapacity of individuals to provide their own. It is the emptiness of absolute freedom: freedom as arbitrariness. But it is also the opposite: the subject *of* this empty freedom is also subject *to* the 'iron cage' of modern capitalist rationalisation. Certain socially imposed goals work through this apparent arbitrariness. Nihilism here derives from the unsatisfying and essentially unsatisfiable nature of these goals.

Liberalism is a diluted nihilism. It implicitly recognises the nihilism at the centre of modern social existence, and attempts a holding operation: to contain nihilism within the limits necessary for social life to continue. But it is of the nature of nihilism – as of the drives towards power and consumption which are the masks of nihilism in the modern world – to destroy or subvert limits, especially those of morality. So the attempt fails.

5

THE ILLUSORY COMMUNITY: THE NATION

> No more arresting emblems of the modern culture of nationalism exist than cenotaphs and tombs of Unknown Soldiers. The public ceremonial reverence accorded these monuments precisely *because* they are either deliberately empty or no one knows who lies inside them, has no true precedents in earlier times. . . . Yet void as these tombs are of identifiable mortal remains or immortal souls, they are nonetheless saturated with ghostly *national* imaginings.
>
> The cultural significance of such monuments becomes even clearer if one tries to imagine, say, a Tomb of the Unknown Marxist or a cenotaph for fallen Liberals. Is a sense of absurdity avoidable? The reason is that neither Marxism nor Liberalism are much concerned with death and immortality.
>
> (Benedict Anderson)[1]

NATIONALISM, LIBERALISM AND PHILOSOPHY

The form of liberalism discussed in the preceding chapter is very much a philosopher's construction. Nevertheless, its principles were part of a political movement which, though it received its name only in the early nineteenth century, is able to trace its intellectual and political origins well into the eighteenth and seventeenth centuries. It has been the task of philosophy to use its preferred techniques of asepsis and abstraction in order to articulate and to defend or criticise principles which have had – and continue to have – a much untidier form of existence.

In the nineteenth century, liberalism was often allied with another discourse: that of nationalism. The characteristic liberal principles of individual right and formal justice were combined with claims to national sovereignty and self-determination. Most nineteenth century theorists did not find any tension between the two discourses: they were assumed to support each other.[2] Twentieth century history has shaken, if not destroyed, this assumption. Nationalism itself has developed in ways incompatible with liberalism; and it has often allied itself with ideologies (socialism, fascism, conservatism, religious fundamentalism) which have been hostile to liberalism. When it has come to the test, nationalism has shown itself to be a more potent political force than liberalism. Where there has been a conflict between the two, it has almost always been nationalism which has been victorious, and successful nationalist movements have been able to treat the principles most central to liberalism with contempt.

Despite this, nationalism has largely been ignored by modern philosophers. There are a number of reasons for this. There have been no theorists of nationalism to rival Locke, Kant, J. S. Mill, Tocqueville and the rest of the liberal pantheon, so there is no 'great tradition' of nationalism for contemporary philosophers to continue. Liberalism as a political practice has been congenial to the practice of philosophy, while the power of nationalism has often been demonstrated against those principles and forms of life with which philosophy has been associated. The practice of modern philosophy has been cosmopolitan in its affiliations, with only shallow roots in local cultures. Too easily, nationalism has been assumed to be a form of unreason, a pathology which is not worthy of and is perhaps unavailable to the techniques of philosophy.

Yet nationalism has shown itself markedly superior to liberalism in attracting allegiance in the modern world. Despite its concern with the individual, liberalism has never been very good at supplying the individual with a reason or a motive for accepting its principles. In assuming the existence of a social world which is devoid of values, liberalism has assigned the task of creating them to the vagaries of individual choice. It then discovers that it has no strong argument against the individual who chooses values which are antithetical to those of liberalism. The nation on the other hand, presents itself as a social world which does provide values by which an individual might live. It is a community – a *Gemeinschaft* – and to belong to it is to identify oneself through that belonging. Our national identity – being Australian, or German, or French, or whatever – enters into our conception of what we are. It is not a property which we might have or lack; and though it might on occasion be chosen, it is a choice of a particularly significant kind. Our national identity is a form of self-awareness; it is also a form of other-awareness. It identifies those who share that identity, and whom we have a special responsibility to help. It also identifies those who are other, and whom on occasion we have a special responsibility to harm. Our national identity will often lead us to do things which would not be recommended on the basis of a more narrowly conceived self-interest. The moral values associated with nationalism are often incompatible with the more universalistic values espoused by liberalism. Nevertheless, nationalism provides the individual with a reason – or at least a motivation – for accepting its values; liberalism does not. The greater affectivity of nationalism is due in large part to its superiority in this respect.

Nationalism is a paradoxical phenomenon. The major theorists of modernity conceived of it as an atavism, destined to dissipate when subjected to the rationalising and cosmopolitan tendencies of the modern world. It is easy now to see that they were wrong, at least in the short term. Nationalism has not withered away: it remains one of the most potent forces at work in modern – and modernising – societies. Still, those who underestimated the staying power of nationalism had powerful arguments on their side. Modern social life is atomistic and cuts the individual off from broader constitutive relations; it is also universalistic and places the individual in a network of dependencies which traverse national boundaries.

> In place of the old local and national seclusion and self-sufficiency, we have intercourse in every direction, universal interdependence of nations. And as in material, so in intellectual production. The intellectual creations of individual nations become common property. National one-sidedness and narrow mindedness become more and more impossible.[3]

It is not surprising, therefore, that Marx and others treated nationalism as a residue from a premodern past with little survival value. However, in its most essential features, nationalism is a creature of the modern world. It is historically almost coextensive with the emergence of capitalist market societies – though it is not, of course, unique to them. While nationalism often appeals to premodern cultural traditions, and usually claims a premodern – sometimes primeval – genealogy, it is a quintessentially modern phenomenon. Indeed, its birth can be dated with some precision: it emerged as a significant historical force around the end of the eighteenth and the beginning of the nineteenth centuries.[4] Along with its near enough contemporary liberalism, nationalism is an artefact of the modern world. It is in the modern world, therefore, that we should pursue its aetiology.

MARKET SOCIETY AND THE STATE

The rationalised modern world of capitalist production and exchange requires a framework of property and exchange. This in turn presupposes the existence of a law making and law enforcing body, i.e. the state. In a certain limited sense, the capitalist market is a sphere of freedom: obligations are incurred as a consequence of decisions which the individual is not – at least legally or politically – compelled to make. But this freedom is only possible if it is contained within a realm of necessity. There are certain overriding obligations – to respect the property of others and to keep one's commitments – which are incumbent upon all individuals, and are not the result of choices which they are free to make or not to make. The existence of freely chosen obligations is only possible on the basis of obligations which are not freely chosen. As Durkheim recognised, the sphere of the contractual rests on the foundation of the non-contractual.[5]

The identity of the market individual is abstract in the sense that it is not defined by specific activities and relationships, nor by particular obligations. Abstract individuality is that form of identity which is free of obligations except those which are specifically entered into. So where certain obligations are *not* matters of choice, but are necessarily incumbent on the individual, they must be supposed to be part of the identity of those subject to them. Thus, the abstract individuality of the market presupposes a more determinate form of identity.

The differences between these forms of identity emerge in a stark form when we consider the content of the obligations embodied in the state. The sphere of production and exchange requires a coercive force able to protect society from internal recalcitrance and external threat. The state must claim the right both to punish its citizens, and also to require that they sacrifice themselves – their property, even their lives – on its behalf. The obligations incumbent on the citizen go beyond anything which would voluntarily be assumed by the individuals involved in market activity – except, perhaps, as the result of deception or miscalculation. The state embodies the power of death; and for the market individual death is the ultimate sacrifice of self-interest and the final irrationality.[6]

Sacrifice of self-interest at the behest of the state is not just a residual power to be exercised *in extremis*. A society made up of individuals whose relationships were based solely on the calculations of instrumental reason would lack the social cohesion necessary to maintain itself in existence. Social behaviour must be informed by a propensity to restrain the operation of rational self-interest, i.e. to keep one's contractual agreements and respect the property of others even when one would profit by fraud or theft.[7] The residual power of the state over life and death is an extreme form of the more muted and less dramatic sacrifice of self-interest required by day-to-day social existence. Still, the extreme form is important: it symbolises in a stark and exemplary way what state power is about. Prisons and wars may not constitute the major business of the state; but that the state has the capacity to punish its citizens and call upon them to die on its behalf is essential to its existence.

In order to make sense of the obligations involved here, we must conceive of the state as embodying a more fundamental community than that of the market, a *Gemeinschaft* underlying and making possible the *Gesellschaft* of economic life. It must define a form of identity which subsumes the abstract individuality characteristic of the market. This identity may appear as part of the pre-social order of things, as 'natural' as one's sex, or it may be recognised as socially and politically structured. It may on occasion be an object of choice, but not on all occasions: its characteristic role is to structure and limit the choices that the individual makes. It must be inescapable. Insofar as it defines goals for which we might sacrifice our particular interests (e.g. property, profit, even life itself), it must provide a kind of self-fulfilment which overrides those interests. It must involve a sense of self which transcends other identities, a self which has its being as part of a more encompassing and wider set of relationships. The self is thus defined as a member of a community with others who share that deeper identity.

The preceding arguments have largely been drawn from Hegel's *Philosophy of Right*. However, Hegel supposed that the requisite community could be defined in terms of its institutions. In this he followed a strong eighteenth century theme. Patriotism was the sentiment owed by citizens, not to their nation, but to the rationally structured political community to which they belonged. Such a state might provide the conditions of existence of a specific and unique language and culture, but its political legitimacy did not rest on a claim to embody that particular culture. The Hegelian state represented a universal and rational principle which transcended such particularity. Indeed, the culture and language themselves only had value insofar as they pointed towards something more absolute and universal. The moral authority of the state resided, not in the emotions it engendered and depended upon, but on its universality and rationality. For citizens of the state, patriotism was not a mere sentiment, but a form of self-knowledge.

Hegel was aware of the emergence of nationalism, especially in the writings of such compatriots as Fichte, Herder, Schleiermacher and Fries, but he was contemptuous of it. It substituted feeling for knowledge, and particularity for universality; and it appealed to a romantic intuition of nature against the demand of reason.[8] Nevertheless, Hegel's own 'court of judgement', history, has – so far at least – come down decisively in favour of particularity: the community that has provided the sense of identity required by modern social and political life has been the nation. What has legitimised the state has not been its instantiation of universal principles, but its claim to embody a particular national spirit. Hegel who, probably more than anyone else in the eighteenth and nineteenth centuries, recognised the problems confronting modern society, and who was very clear about the conditions a solution must meet, was totally wrong about what the solution would be.

NATIONAL IDENTITY

> A nation is a soul, a spiritual principle. Only two things, actually, constitute this soul, this spiritual principle. One is in the past, the other is in the present. One is the possession in common of a rich legacy of remembrances; the other is the actual consent, the desire to live together, the will to continue to value the heritage that all hold in common.
>
> (Ernest Renan)[9]

What is a nation? A nation is a principle of identity, or – better – it is a number of principles of identity. It collects together a diverse range of people and groups, traditions and ways of life, into one.

Just what the principles are and how they relate to each other vary from nation to nation. The way in which each nation cherishes its uniqueness is not just illusion: each nation does have its own story to tell. Still, there is a common pattern to these stories.

Every nation claims to stand in a specific and privileged relation to a homeland – the 'ground' in a near literal sense of its national identity. The nation provides its members with an inalienable collective property: the land in which they have the right to lead their lives. It thus recovers a relationship to the land – a spatial location and identity – which the modern world has destroyed for most people. The land is the source and often the object of those cultural productions which have a place in the national heritage: it has a special place in the nation's literature, popular culture and the various rituals of national celebration and commemoration. The national landscape is something more than a physical space; it is endowed with spirit and personality (think of the American West, or England's 'green and pleasant land'). At the same time, those characters and ways of life which are assigned a role within the national culture take on something of the substantiality of the land which has formed them.

If the national homeland provides its members with a spatial location and identity, the nation's history provides them with a location and an identity in time. Nationalism is the discovery or creation of a common past – it is the story of the victories and triumphs, defeats and betrayals which have formed the nation. This narrative defines the nation as an entity which endures through time;[10] and it provides a link between those who live now and those who have lived in the past. The narrative does not, however, merely connect the past and the present; it extends into the future. The nation is a principle of identity which unifies what was with what is; it also defines a perspective on what will be. National identity is the recognition that members of the nation – past, present and future – have a common destiny.[11]

In some cases, national identity has seemed to depend upon blood or race; even today, it is not hard to find such notions lurking behind the most civilised façades, ready to be mobilised in the face of real or apparent threat. Where the sense of identity is congealed in this way, the foreigner is irredeemably alien. However, though closure of this kind is always a possibility, the more normal case is to allow entry to those foreigners who are prepared to participate in the nation's culture and assume its identity. 'Naturalisation' is a choice which most nations – more or less uneasily – allow some aliens to make.[12] As the word suggests, naturalisation is conceived as a commitment of an unusual kind. In some respects it is like a religious conversion: it is the commitment to a new identity, even a new 'nature'. One may assume the identity for all sorts of narrowly selfish reasons; but once it is assumed, it transcends self-interest. The assumption of a new national identity may have the appearance of a contract; if so, it is – as Hegel remarked of marriage[13] – a contract which transcends the viewpoint of contract.

To many theorists of nationalism, the existence of a common language has seemed to be the key to a sense of national identity. Clearly there is something in this, though the existence of multilingual nations should make us wary of pushing this theory too far. Much energy has been devoted by the proponents of various nationalisms to preserving, discovering and occasionally even creating national languages.[14] A national language allows for the constitution of a single mass audience, and for the dissemination and sharing of experiences through that audience. The development of universal literacy, and the associated growth of the print and other media, were of crucial importance in the historical development of nationalism.[15] A common language, especially as this is embodied in newspapers, songs, novels and other cultural products, provides the foundation for a widely shared intersubjectivity: the recognition that others have the same kinds of capacities and goals as oneself. This feature of language is at the heart of Habermas' attempt to construct a 'discourse ethics' on the basis of a universal speech community. However, for the users of a national language, difference is as important as identity; and actual particularity is more significant than potential universality. The national language provides a medium through which a community becomes aware of itself as a community; but it also provides a way of identifying those who are not members. What is significant about a nation's language is not the features it shares with the languages of other nations, still less its formal universality, but the features which make it unique: the national idiosyncrasies of accent, pronunciation, idiom, sentence order and the like.

The nation is not just a form of community, it is also a principle of political right: a government is legitimate if and only if it is a form of national self-government.[16] Nationalism is not the only principle of legitimacy which has been important in the modern world, but it has certainly been the most important. Whatever the political form of a modern state, whether it be dynastic, authoritarian, democratic or liberal, the major source of its capacity to exercise power over its subjects is its claim that it is the nation state, i.e. the political expression of a pre-existing community. Democratically elected leaders have authority, not because they have been chosen on the basis of rational principles of political right, but because these particular procedures are inscribed within the political culture of the nation. Those monarchs who continue to receive deference and obedience do so, not as members of a dynasty who have the God given right to rule, but because that dynasty has been able to establish itself as a symbol of the nation.

The discourse of nationalism has a certain affinity with that of liberal democracy. Perhaps it was for this reason that they were for so long assumed to be complementary. The nation does not recognise hierarchies of authority: each individual is equally subject to its authority. If in most premodern forms, political authority was a complex and indirect affair, where individuals owed authority to the state through a network of more localised bonds, in the modern world, each individual is directly subject to the state. Liberal doctrines of individual right, and democratic principles of suffrage and representation have played a role in legitimising this relationship; but these are often transcribed into the language of national identity. The rights are the rights of the 'true born Englishman' (or American, or . . .); the electoral procedures are those through which the voice of the nation speaks; all too often they are dispensed with when another way of establishing that voice is discovered. In the final analysis, the spirit of nationalism is incompatible with more than a conditional allegiance to liberal right and democratic rule. It is the nation which claims an absolute and direct authority over its subjects. This relationship is not unlike the relationship between God and the individual which, always latent in Christianity, was made explicit by the Protestant Reformation. And like God, the nation has the final say on the validity of other forms of authority, and the right to override them when necessary.

The characteristic experience of nationalism is of the emergence for consciousness of a pre-existing unity – a principle which underlies the nation's culture and history, and which provides the ideal to which these should aspire. This experience misconceives the nature of nationalism, and diminishes its achievement. The nation is not the formative reality behind history and culture; it is their artefact. The prehistory of modern nationalism involved the decline of a cosmopolitan high culture on the one hand, and the destruction of a multitude of non-literate local cultures on the other.[17] There were no pre-existing national cultures to be hidden from history and later unearthed by national historians and archivists. It was the emergence of nationalist movements in the nineteenth century which created the project of a national history, and it was this project which has created a corresponding historical past. The past culture was not so much discovered by nationalist historians and archivists as invented by them. Of course, the invention took account of existing traditions and customs, of real and not fictitious similarities and divergences. But it involved a process of selection, such that other traditions, similarities and differences were ignored. This process of selection was – and is – itself a matter of dispute and struggle. Different political programmes invoked different conceptions of the nation, and different conceptions of the nation required different accounts of its traditions, culture and history. But political struggle has almost always been carried on under the sign of the nation. What is in dispute are different conceptions of the nation, not a conception of the nation against another form of community.

The creation of a national culture and history is not just a matter of selection; it also involves the creation of an identity out of similarities, and a difference out of diversity. The nation is something more than a collection of similarities; it is an entity in its own right. Those traditions which are assigned a place in the national heritage become properties of the national substance; those events which play a role in the nation's history become episodes in the development of that substance. The nation exists through the network of similarities and dissimilarities; it is the reality which underlies and ultimately explains them. The history of the nation is not merely the emergence of certain institutions, practices and forms of rhetoric; it is the coming to self-consciousness of a historical subject. The nation is a substance, and those who belong to the nation and who recognise each other as so belonging, participate in that substance. It is a community of identity, not merely of similarity. The identity is compatible with vast distances in space and time, and massive inequalities in power, wealth and status. On the other hand, other divergences of language or culture become differences, signifiers of an otherness of substance which overrides similarities.

The nation is a creature of modernity. In principle, it should be possible to explain its origins and its continued existence in terms of other features of the modern world. My project here, however, is a much more modest and preliminary one: it is to see how far it is possible to understand the phenomenon of nationalism in terms of the concepts discussed so far. These will certainly not provide an explanation of nationalism; they do, however, enable us locate it.

In the first place, the market imposes a certain social homogeneity on the sphere of public life. While market relations create massive inequalities, and in their capitalist form presuppose them, they also create a form of identity, that of the abstract individual, which is common to all participants. This identity finds political expression in the legal framework of free and equal juridical subjects (property owners, contract makers).[18] Despite isolation and competition, there is a sense in which market individuals can recognise each other as sharing a common identity. The market also imposes mobility: horizontal, as participants move from one sphere of activity to another in response to market demands; and vertical, as fortunes are made and lost. It requires a common conceptual currency in terms of which exchanges are made, and it assumes a common instrumental rationality.[19]

The capitalist market militates against the existence of the culturally isolated and heterogeneous communities which have been characteristic of most premodern societies. Though the capitalist market has been international from its very beginnings, the existence of various domestic markets – larger than the village or town, but smaller than the world – has always been of importance to capital. This has been partly a matter of securing a market big enough to be worthwhile and small enough to dominate, with respect both to the sale of commodities and, especially, to controlling the supply of labour. The existence of these privileged spheres of economic activity do not, as some Marxists have argued,[20] explain the emergence of nationalism; however, they have created the social space necessary for the emergence of a common national culture.

The second major resource required for the construction of a concept of national identity is provided by the sphere of domesticity. The nation is constructed through a relocation of the relations and identities constituted within the private realm. The nation is – something like – the family inscribed in the social space created by the market.

It is a familiar feature of the rhetoric of nationalism that it invokes the language of family and kin relationships. One's country is 'home'; it is androgynously one's 'fatherland' or 'motherland'; the national language is the 'mother tongue'; and the ties of nation are often presented in terms of 'blood', 'inheritance' and the like.[21] In part, this is a matter of relocating the considerable psychic investment one has in one's family in a wider and more encompassing web of relationships. The emotions and needs which are extruded from the sphere of commodity exchange by the operations of impersonal and rational self-interest, are not merely contained within the private realm, but are focussed on and suffused through the nation. What has made this possible is the construction of a new form of identity on a model to that constructed in and through the family.

The main feature of national identity, as of that form of identity constructed in the private sphere, is that it is constructed, not through separation (the 'isolation effect' of the market), but in terms of relationships with others. Thus, the aspirations of a specific individual come to be inextricably bound up with others. An action which from the point of the self-directed market individual would be a pointless piece of altruism, becomes a mode of individual self-fulfilment. To have the identity in question (that of family or nation) is to be subject to certain emotions, e.g. those of shame or pride, which are provoked by actions which are not necessarily one's own, but rather are the actions of those who share that identity. Certain kinds of activity, e.g. the nurturing or supportive activity required to support members of one's family, or the patriotic deed required by one's country, are conceived of, not merely as instrumentally effective in achieving certain ends, and certainly not of one's self-directed ends, but as expressive of one's identity and necessary to sustain it.

National identity is a way of conceiving oneself – though, of course, not the only way. It is a form of self-awareness which provides a source of pleasures and pains, desires and frustrations, powers and weaknesses, which are not available to other forms of self-awareness. To assume or discover this form of identity is to recognise, not just one's kin with others, but also that the nation is the basis of this kinship. Here the parallel with the family is something more than metaphor. The family is the source of one's physical existence; but it is equally the source of a certain kind of social identity. So too is one's country. Just to the extent that this mode of social existence enters into one's conception of what one is, then to that extent the nation is one's parent – one's father *and* mother – and one's fellow nationals constitute one's kin.

There are several significant agencies through which this form of identity is constructed. The first is the state itself. It is a familiar point that the capitalist market requires effective administrative and coercive institutions, but also that it tends to undermine the customs, beliefs and relationships which traditionally legitimise the authority of those institutions.[22] Hence, the modern state has had the task of constructing its own form of legitimacy. The exigencies of the market economy have provided it with the means to do this: a centralised education system and a large measure of control over language and culture. Nationalism is brought into play to provide the content. A variety of specific cultural artefacts have been employed in this task, but the necessary conceptual and psychic resources are provided through the relocation and enlargement of that form of identity associated with the family. A complementary role is played by the media, related cultural bodies and those whose way of life associates them with the media and culture ('intellectuals' in a broad sense). For those involved in cultural activities, the national language and traditions are the *sine qua non* of their activities. Hence, the media and the institutions of culture have been concerned to protect their domestic cultural heritage; they have shared with the state a concern to enunciate, develop and protect the local and particular against the universal and the cosmopolitan. Intellectuals have always been amongst the most enthusiastic proponents of national identity.[23]

A final agency in the formation of a national identity arises through the structures of individuality constructed through the capitalist market and the family. Take the market individual first. For such an individual, other persons and relations will only have significance to the extent that they mediate between the individual and his ends. The locus of meaning is essentially self-referential. But the task of providing one's own meaning is a daunting one; and is constantly threatened by the demands of ordinary living, by the very limited power that individuals have over the conditions of their existence and by the instability and change which are characteristic of capitalist modernity. Perhaps above all, the individual is faced with the actuality of mortality: death can only be experienced by the individual as a rude invalidation of what life is about. It is not just the end of meaning; it also renders what was meaningful, meaningless. To a limited extent, the sphere of domesticity provides a stability lacking in other areas of life, and a framework of purposes which go beyond the individual. However, it too is limited in scope and vulnerable to larger and more impersonal forces. A more universal and satisfying transcendence is provided if the individual can find an identity within a more global framework of relations. Within that framework, particular strivings have a significance that they cannot have within the market or even the family. The nation provides a glimpse of strength and power, and of a stability and continuity able to contain the transience of everyday life. It provides a spatial anchor in a world which has destroyed any other stable relations to a privileged space; and it provides a temporal identity by imposing a historical teleology on an otherwise chaotic and meaningless flux. More significantly, it defines – indeed, gives birth to – a kind of identity which promises an existence beyond that allowed by human biology. The nation may not be immortal, but it presents itself as such, and immortality is the promise it makes to its members.

To the extent that femininity is constructed through the family, it is already relational, and exists in a framework of meaning beyond that of the individual. It may be that the attractions of national identity will be weaker for this reason. Nevertheless, the domestic sphere is a limited and parochial one, existing within a wider sphere of relations, but excluded from them. If the nation can provide the relational and feminine within a more universal context, it will provide compensations and gratifications for this form of identity too. However, there are significant differences in the ways in which femininity and masculinity are incorporated within the nation.

War is only one of the many activities undertaken by the modern state. Nevertheless, it is essential to its functioning that the state have the moral capacity to wage war, so the business of war takes on a unique significance. Modern nationalisms have largely been forged through wars; but even – perhaps especially – where this has not been the case, the commemoration of war has a central place amongst the rituals of nationalism. Patriotism may be demonstrated in any number of ways; nevertheless, it is service in war which constitutes its exemplary form.

Waging war involves using violence in order to kill the citizens of an enemy state, to destroy its resources and in any way possible to eliminate its capacity to resist.[24] One respect in which war is significant is that it demonstrates that the moral force of nationalism overrides that of conventional morality. However, the rituals of nationalism do not especially emphasise the inflicting of violence, destruction and killing. What they do emphasise is the aspect of suffering and death. The main significance of war for the nation is that it shows that men – and sometimes women – have been prepared to suffer and die on its behalf. These acts of sacrifice define the nation – and the state which is the embodiment of the nation – as having a value beyond the other goods of individual life. In this way, and perhaps only in this way, the nation is able to show itself worthy of existing.

For the man, self-sacrifice in war demonstrates the achievement of a more encompassing form of identity. It shows that the aspirations which have moved him to act (to suffer, to die) are not those of the particular individual who represents his household in the world of production and exchange, but are those of an individual who has identified his existence with that of the nation. These aspirations are, at least symbolically, common to all those who share this deeper identity. In nationalism, as in religion, the voluntary act of self-sacrifice establishes an identity which transcends that of the individual who dies. Death is the paradoxical proof of immortality. It is the achievement of a locus of meaning sought by, but denied to individuals in their ordinary material existence.

The ways in which masculine and feminine identities are constituted within the nation are significantly different. Up to a point, the relationship between men and their nation replicates that between the worker and his family. The male identity as defender of the nation is as inescapable as that of breadwinner. The nation is the family – the mother – to be fought for and protected in the wider world by its male representatives. But the symbolic value of these activities is very different to those of the market and the capitalist work place. Not only does it require acts of destruction and self-sacrifice, it also involves a commitment to one's fellows beyond anything conceivable in the world of economic activity. In the national rituals of commemoration, what is celebrated are not the acts of murder and destruction, but the comradeship, mutual caring and readiness for self-sacrifice amongst those who fought. What is forged in the ritual commemorations of war is a kind of identity – exemplary for nationalism – which transcends the isolation and separation characteristic of the market. War is not so much the construction of a new and virulent form of masculinity, as the recovery for men of that relational form of identity constructed within the family. It is, curiously enough, the return of the feminine.

Insofar as the nation, on whose behalf men fight and die, is the family, its members – those 'at home' – are wives, mothers and children. Those who fight and die do so, not merely as citizens, but as fathers, husbands and sons. The iconography brought into play involves a universalisation of the moral and gender framework of the domestic realm. Each man/soldier is father/husband/son to every woman; each woman is mother/wife/daughter to every soldier. It is as thus constituted that women carry out their allotted tasks of child care and nurture, or take on new responsibilities in the hitherto male public world; it is thus that they enjoy the fruits of victory, suffer the agonies of defeat and experience the anxieties and pains of loss and bereavement. Women do have a place in national identity, though a different one from men.[25] The form of identity they are assigned does transcend the limits of the domestic and the particular. However, it does so, not by transforming but by universalising their domestic identity.[26]

It is in times of war that the always latent conflict between the demands of the nation state and the claims of liberal morality are most likely to become explicit. The state will restrict the movement of individuals, require that they undertake certain kinds of work, perhaps even military service, and restrict the right of emigration. In practice, the liberal can only conduct a holding operation against this *raison d'état*, attempting to curb its worst excesses. The political weakness of liberalism in times of crisis is a reflection of its moral emptiness. Liberalism does not provide an ethic by which people might live, nor a principle of social cohesion. For these, it is parasitic on other forms of morality. Nationalism provides a principle of unity for the various elements in modern society (the family, the capitalist market, the state); however, it may on occasions of national crisis override the values embodied in these subordinate spheres of social life. Nationalism is the guardian discourse of modern society; however, like other guardians, it is always liable to turn on those it protects.

IMAGINATION, ILLUSION AND COMMUNITY

> In the state . . . [man] is the imaginary member of an illusory sovereignty, is deprived of his real individual life and endowed with an unreal universality.
>
> (Marx)[27]

Nationalism works by constructing a form of identity which provides guidance to those subject to it. To know what my national identity is, is to know how I should act, and who has the right to tell me how I should act. These guidelines do not take the form of duties which impose themselves on what I actually want to do – even though they may be enforced by the state. Rather, they inform me as to what I – really – want to do. They are often incompatible with the dictates of a more narrowly conceived self-identity. One's national identity may require helping or harming others, even risking harm to oneself; very often, it will require action which is instrumentally irrational. Yet national identity has its rewards. It offers the individuals pleasures and powers, possibilities and meanings which are not otherwise available. It is effective as a moral identity just because it offers something to the individual who assumes it.

There is a lot to be said against an ideology which has been responsible for the insularity, xenophobia, destruction and death which can be attributed to nationalism. But perhaps there is as much to be said in favour of a commitment which has encouraged so much selflessness, heroism and creativity. It is probably too soon to draw up the balance sheet. We do not yet understand it well enough, nor is there a clear moral position from which to do the accounting. Whatever the final evaluation, it will need to do justice to the strengths of nationalism: its capacity to inspire individuals to go beyond the limits of their own narrowly conceived aspirations and sympathies. However. it will also need to bring out the inescapable element of illusion in the way that nationalism works. Nationalism has inspired heroism, devotion, effort and creativity, but only by pretending to be what it is not.

The claim that nationalism involves illusion is, of course, a familiar one. For many liberals, the ultimate reality is the self-contained individual, and the assertion of any form of collective identity is incoherent. For some Marxists on the other hand, the only genuine collective identity is that of class, so the notion of a national identity can only function to obscure this more basic reality. For both the liberal individualist and the Marxist there is a more fundamental reality against which the claims of nationalism can be measured and found wanting. But the notion of a 'fundamental reality' appealed to here is highly dubious. Every social entity – even the individual – exists in and through institutional structures and social consciousness. National identity exists largely because people think of themselves and are encouraged to think of themselves in this way. But on its own, this gives us no reason to think of national identity as an illusion, any more than any other form of identity is an illusion.

Benedict Anderson has recently argued against 'false consciousness' views of nationalism in a similar vein:

> It [the nation] is *imagined* because the members of even the smallest nation will never know most of their fellow members, meet them, or even hear of them, yet in the minds of each lives the image of their communion. . . . Gellner makes a comparable point when he rules that 'Nationalism is not the awakening of nations to self-consciousness; it *invents* nations where they do not exist.' The drawback of this formulation, however, is that Gellner is so anxious to show that nationalism masquerades under false pretences that he assimilates 'invention' to 'fabrication' and 'falsity', rather than to 'imagining' and 'creation'. In this way he implies that 'true' communities exist which can be advantageously juxtaposed to nations. In fact, all communities larger than primordial villages of face-to-face contact (and perhaps even these) are imagined. Communities are to be distinguished, not by their falsity/genuineness, but by the style in which they are imagined.[28]

On this account, to regard the imagining that goes into constituting the nation (or some other group) as false or illusory is as out of place as it would be to regard a novel or a piece of music as false or illusory. (It is one of the many strengths of Anderson's book that it provides an illuminating account of the role of cultural artefacts, such as novels and music, in the formation of a sense of national identity.)

Anderson's conception of the nation as an 'imagined community' is an illuminating one. It does not, however, rule out a distinction between communities which are in some sense 'true' and those which are 'false'. Indeed, this distinction is implicit in Anderson's own account of the development of nationalism. Nationalism is, as Anderson convincingly shows, an artefact; but it is characteristically experienced as if it were part of the natural order of things. It is a contingency created by historical circumstance and creative imagination; but it is conceived to be a necessity which expresses itself through history and the imagination. Nations are the products of relatively recent times; but they present themselves as eternal. The analogy with religion which Anderson himself draws is a telling one. Nationalism and religion are both human products; however, their effectivity depends on their not being experienced as such. Neither can survive self-knowledge. The nation is, as Anderson and others have convincingly argued, the product of human imaginings; but it works by suppressing that knowledge.[29] To give due weight to the significance of creativity – of imagination in Anderson's sense – in constituting certain kinds of human community, does not necessarily eliminate a role for concepts of truth and falsity. The nation is an illusory community, and not just an imagined one, because of the necessary role of unrecognised falsity – of illusion – in its constitution.

In his more general and programmatic statements, Anderson often writes as if any aggregate of persons could imagine themselves (or 'be imagined into') a community; as if suitably creative 'imagining' is not merely necessary, but also sufficient to constitute a community. This pushes the role of consciousness too far. Not every kind of society can be said to constitute a community. It is at least a further condition that the various members of the community exist in certain relations of interdependence on each other and independence from others, that they are conscious of this, and that this consciousness enters into their dealings with each other in some fundamental and constitutive way. No doubt these conditions are hard to render precise, but they cannot be ignored, especially as the 'imagining' of the nation will take as its material the network of relationships which exist – or are imagined to exist – between members of the nation. This introduces another dimension in which an imagined community may be an illusory one: where the relations which are held to constitute the community are significantly misconceived. A community of 'Aryans' held together by a mythological line of descent and a racially distorted genetic theory would surely be an illusory, and not just an imagined community, though the illusion will have real effects. A modern nation state which is built on the nostalgia for a past which has never existed, on a community of enterprise which can only exist in extreme situations or in symbolic form (such as war and its commemoration, national achievements in sport), and which requires the withholding from consciousness of dissonant elements, is also an illusory and not just an imagined community.

There is no doubt that imagining the nation does answer certain needs – for identity, stability, meaning – which are denied in the more mundane aspects of modern life. This explains something of the strength of nationalism; indeed, its strength is in almost inverse proportion to its validity. It is just because modern society does not provide for community, that it exists in merely imagined form. The phenomenon of nationalism shows something of the human capacity for community and transcendence of particularity. However, the nation imagines the community, not as an aspiration towards something which ought to exist, but as something which already does. To explain what nationalism is and how it works is to destroy the illusion which is essential to it; it dissolves necessity into contingency, the natural into the social and identity into similarity. Nationalism cannot survive this process.

6

MODERNITY AND MADNESS: NIETZSCHE'S APOTHEOSIS

> Rather than the death of God – or, rather, in the wake of that death and in profound correlation with it – what Nietzsche's thought heralds is the end of his murderer.
>
> (Foucault)[1]

NIETZSCHE, PHILOSOPHY AND MADNESS

Some years ago, Al Alvarez suggested that there is a kind of modernist writing which attempts to combine self-conscious lucidity and precision with an exploration of themes – such as death, madness and destruction – which occupy the extreme limits of human experience. On Alvarez's view, such writing carried with it grave risks for its author; in extreme cases, insanity or suicide. Sylvia Plath, whom Alvarez had especially in mind, had taken love, rejection, anger, destructiveness and, above all, her own death as her chosen subject matter. Her suicide could be regarded as a kind of occupational hazard of the work she had undertaken; it was 'simply a risk she took in handling such volatile material'.[2] In a similar vein, I want to suggest that madness was an occupational hazard of Nietzsche's writing. That he went mad was not merely an external contingency which – rudely, tragically – brought Nietzsche's career as a writer to a close, any more than Sylvia Plath's suicide is merely accidentally related to the themes of her poetry. By choosing the themes that he did, Nietzsche exposed himself to the threat of madness.

Of course, Nietzsche did not – could not – foresee his own collapse into silence, passivity and pitiful dependence. Still, he was aware of the risks of his enterprise.

> Few are made for independence – it is a privilege of the strong. And he who attempts it, having the complete right to it but without being *compelled* to, thereby proves that he is not only strong but daring to the point of recklessness. He ventures into a labyrinth, he multiplies by a thousand the dangers which life already brings with it, not the smallest of which is that no one can behold how and where he goes astray, is cut off from others, and is torn to pieces limb from limb by some cave-minotaur of conscience. If such a one is destroyed, it takes place so far from the understanding of men that they can neither feel it nor sympathise – and he can no longer go back! He can no longer go back even to the pity of men![3]

Nietzsche's collapse less than three years after writing this passage is a strong argument against dismissing it as mere rhetoric. His madness is glimpsed and prefigured in almost all that he wrote in the last desperate years of his creative life. If we factor out the megalomania, obsession and hyperbole from Nietzsche's writing we are not left with anything recognisable as a Nietzschean contribution to philosophy. If there is such a contribution – if Nietzsche is worth studying as a philosopher – then his madness is an issue within philosophy.

Of course, Nietzsche's madness is not *just* a philosophical problem. It was a personal tragedy and a humiliation – deepened, not diminished, by Nietzsche's apparent unawareness of what had happened to him. No doubt there are medical, psychoanalytic, even sociological explanations of his deterioration and eventual collapse. But there is also a philosophical story to be told. After all, it was Nietzsche himself who held that 'every great philosophy has . . . been . . . a confession on the part its author'.[4] The last major work he completed before his final collapse was the autobiography *Ecco Homo*. Its subtitle, 'How One Becomes What One is', refers to the philosophical project that Nietzsche was engaged in over those last years – that of remaking the self. The mental disintegration of its author signalled in the most dramatic way possible the failure of that project.

Madness was a risk, or a threat, implicit in Nietzsche's conception of philosophy. It was not, however, inevitable. I am not tempted by the romantic notion that Nietzsche's madness was the necessary consequence of his pushing beyond the limits of Western philosophy and reason. Indeed, I see little evidence – except for his characteristic hyperbole and self-aggrandisement – that he pushed beyond those limits. The threat of madness which pervades his philosophy, perhaps the madness which was his, was a much more local and contingent phenomenon. Nietzsche's madness was not the excluded other of Western reason; it was part of the logic of modern Western society. Despite his protestations of 'untimeliness', Nietzsche was a creature of his – and our – times.[5] His achievement lay in his insight into the nihilistic tendencies at large in the modern world. He was pitiless in his contempt for the evasions and sophistries of those who would continue as if nothing was amiss. Intellectual rigour, a respect for truth if nothing else, demanded that nihilism be confronted and worked through. The remedy, if there was one, did not lie in evasion, but in attack: nihilism must be pushed to its limits in order that it go beyond itself. The project of 'becoming what one is' – at one with his call for 'new philosophers', 'free spirits', even an '*Übermensch*' – was the project of moving beyond nihilism.

Nietzsche's tragic flaw was that he remained within the field of force of the nihilism that he so acutely diagnosed. Madness was the outcome, not so much of his confrontation with nihilism, as of the inadequacy of the intellectual and moral weapons he had at his disposal. His final position in philosophy was a dead end: a desperate, but futile act of defiance. Nietzsche's enterprise of creating a new self was a symptom of the ills of modernity, rather than a solution to them. There is a threat of madness close to the centre of modern life, and it was Nietzsche's achievement to show that one can ignore this threat only at the cost of evasion and sophistry. It says something of Nietzsche's commitment to reason and truth, and the courage which must always underlie such a commitment, that he refused this evasion. To recognise the courage and the commitment does not, however, require us to accept the conclusions. Nietzsche too must be pushed beyond himself.

THE GENEALOGY OF THE MORAL SUBJECT

> It is to be *inferred* that there exist countless dark bodies close to the sun – such as we shall never see. This is, between ourselves, a parable; and a moral psychologist reads the whole starry script only as a parable and sign-language by means of which many things can be kept secret.[6]

Parables are for concealing meaning, as well as displaying it. Morality is a network of signs, hieroglyphs and secrets; like a dream, or a neurotic symptom, it always says both more and less than it claims. To recognise this is to call attention to the need, not just for a psychology of morals, but also for a semiology and a natural history; in a phrase, it calls for a 'genealogy' of morals.

What are the secrets kept by the 'starry script' of morality? One of Nietzsche's best known claims is that '[t]here are no moral phenomena at all, only a moral interpretation of phenomena.'[7] But this is hardly news to us, nor, I suspect, to Nietzsche's contemporaries. Despite his boast that he was the first to formulate the 'insight' that 'there are no moral facts whatever',[8] this was over a century after Hume. Anyway, the impact of this claim is immediately overshadowed by that of the much larger thesis that in precisely the sense in which there are no moral facts, there are no facts of any kind: '[F]acts is precisely what there is not, only interpretations'.[9] Morality may only be an interpretation of the world, but so too is everything else, even science, as well as the claim that science and morality are only interpretations.[10]

Nietzsche's view is not a relativist one: he certainly does not think that all interpretations are equally valid. Much of his energies were spent trying to demonstrate the unacceptability of certain interpretations, and in particular, to show that the moral interpretation of the world is not a tenable one and should be left behind: 'Morality is merely an interpretation of certain phenomena, more precisely a *mis*interpretation.'[11] The slogan 'Beyond good and evil' means beyond morality: the moral interpretation of the world is one which should be rejected. But why precisely should it be rejected? Is it on grounds of truth or of morality? If so, as critics have always been keen to point out, there is more than a hint of self-refutation here. If there are no facts, how can we appeal to the concept of truth? And what moral reasons can we have for rejecting morality?

In order to answer these questions, we need to get clear about Nietzsche's 'perspectivism'.[12] All views of the world are the creations of a particular set of interests and a particular location with respect to the world: these determine which questions are asked, which insights are gained and which aspects are overlooked. There is no one perspective which can make good a claim to provide a privileged account of what the world is like. Some accounts may be more adequate than others – because they are more comprehensive, contain fewer internal inconsistencies, are more exciting and stimulating, are more aesthetically pleasing or are more 'life enhancing'. However, this greater adequacy is achieved by developing a particular perspective, not by denying it. The insights of a particular perspective are the result of concentration; the price of these insights lies in what is overlooked. A perspective is a particular structure of knowledge; but it is also – and necessarily – a structure of ignorance. What is characteristic of most accounts is that they deny their perspectival character: they present themselves as the product, not of a particular point of view, but of how the world is – of the 'facts'. They claim knowledge, but deny a corresponding ignorance. They characteristically deny their own origins.

This provides some of the critical edge to the strategy Nietzsche calls 'genealogy'. In part, genealogy involves unpacking the desires and needs, hopes and fears which have found expression in a particular account of the world. Philosophy is a confession;[13] morality a sign-language of the emotions.[14] The genealogist must learn to read philosophy as a confession; discern the emotions represented in morality. Even the most impersonal discourse is the expression of a specific kind of psychic structure, and it is Nietzsche's task to uncover that structure. It is for this reason that he often refers to himself as a 'psychologist'.[15] But his enterprise is not – or not only – that of discerning the particular motives which might lead an individual to invent or subscribe to a particular view of the world. Nietzsche's enterprise is also an historical one: moralities, and metaphysical and religious doctrines are located with respect to specific historical contexts and political struggles. Yet the point of Nietzsche's stories is clearly not historical explanation in a conventional sense. It is rather to identify the cultural residues which continue to dominate individual and social life so that they be understood and their power resisted. We may never overcome the past, but we may combat it, and genealogy is part of that struggle.[16]

The stories which Nietzsche tells are more like fables than actual histories. He is not worried about consistency and is impatient with detail. This is partly because he is not concerned with the past as such, but the past as it is located in the cultural present. Here, there is no significant distinction between myth and history. Nor does – or could – Nietzsche claim any epistemological privilege for his genealogies: they are *his* stories, *his* truths and they are informed by *his* values. They say 'This is how I see things' rather than 'This is how things were'. Their critical dimension lies in the challenge they present to the reader to find and defend an alternative account. Often enough, even to attempt to meet this challenge is to risk defeat, as the existence of *any* genealogy will undercut the pretensions to universality and objectivity required to sustain the position being defended.

Perspectivism is a general epistemological position, and genealogy applies as much to science as to morality. However, while Nietzsche is often critical of the self-image of science, he does not – at least after his early writings – attack it with anything like the ferocity he directed at morality. Part of the difference was that Nietzsche thought that science could survive the discovery of its own limitations; indeed, that it is likely that the achievements of science will be better appreciated when it is recognised to be a human creation, rather than a register of pre-existing facts. On the other hand, morality will not survive the discovery. Without its claim to a non-perspectival status, morality crumbles. Nietzsche's position here is the reverse of what has become orthodoxy. For him, science can do without the claim to objectivity; morality cannot.[17]

Some of the deeper reasons why morality must claim a non-perspectival objectivity will emerge later. For the moment, it is sufficient to note that moral judgements present themselves as unconditional, i.e. as something which must be accepted by everyone, whatever their interests or desires. In the Kantian language that Nietzsche despised, the dictates of morality are categorical, not hypothetical. According to Nietzsche, the human need which finds expression in morality is 'the worst of all tastes, the taste for the unconditional'.[18] The good which is posited by morality is supposed to be a good for everyone; but this claim to universality is fraudulent. Goods belong to their owners: they are private possessions:

> 'Good' is no longer good when your neighbour takes it into his mouth. And how could there exist a 'common good'! The expression is a self-contradiction: what can be common has ever but little value.[19]

This bogus universality is associated with another feature of moral evaluation, that it is characteristically dichotomous. Moralists, like metaphysicians, believe in 'antithetical values';[20] they must falsify the complex and multi-valued nature of reality. Whatever characteristics are selected as exemplifying the good, these will be found always to exist together with and to depend upon what is evil.

> Examine the lives of the best and most fruitful people and ask yourself whether a tree that is supposed to grow to a proud height can dispense with bad weather and storms; whether misfortune and external resistance, some kinds of hatred, jealousy, stubbornness, mistrust, hardness, avarice, and violence do not belong among the *favourable* conditions without which any great growth even of virtue is scarcely possible.[21]

The alleged good of altruism is parasitic, Nietzsche argues, on egoism;[22] sickness is necessary for self-knowledge;[23] '"higher culture" is based on the spiritualisation and intensification of cruelty';[24] the 'profoundest and sublimest form of love' grew from 'the trunk of that tree of vengefulness and hatred, Jewish hatred'.[25] Everything of value will be found to depend at some stage of its history upon an opposed value; no system of morality has achieved dominance without the use of methods which are, by its own criteria, immoral: 'Everything praised as moral is identical in essence with everything immoral and was made possible, as in every development of morality, with immoral means and for immoral ends.'[26] The creation of new values always involves the destruction of other values: 'If a temple is to be erected, a temple must first be destroyed'.[27] The great moralists in history have had to be capable of equally great immorality as a necessary condition for their achievements. To advocate the good and deplore the evil ignores their interdependence; it is also a recipe for mediocrity and stagnation. Belief in the antithetical values of morality is only possible on the basis of a wilful – indeed hypocritical – blindness.

The moral interpretation of the world presupposes the existence of agents who may be held accountable for their actions. It posits subjects who are distinct from, but nevertheless causally responsible for what they do. Nietzsche argues that the freely willing moral subject is a fiction, though a deep seated one. It is in part generated by the subject/predicate structure of language. In too literal minded a fashion we transpose grammar onto the world, and suppose that there must be a subject underlying every attribute and every action, as if – to use Nietzsche's own example – there must be lightning apart from the flash.[28] Descartes' inference from the existence of a thought to a self whose business it is to think is based on just this assumption that the structure of language must mirror that of the world.

> 'There is thinking: therefore there is something that thinks': this is the upshot of all Descartes' argumentation. But that means positing as 'true *a priori*' our belief in the concept of substance – that when there is a thought there has to be something 'that thinks' is simply a formulation of our grammatical custom that adds a doer to every deed.[29]

There is no subject underlying our various beliefs, thoughts and actions; *a fortiori* there is no subject which is causally responsible for them.

But how does this misinterpretation arise? Grammar may suggest it, but it is not the whole story. What are the desires and fears – what kind of will – finds expression in this fiction? What is the genealogy of the moral subject? Ultimately, the fiction of the moral subject is created and maintained by the practice of morality itself. Nietzsche provides two overlapping, though not altogether consistent stories about the genesis of morality.

The first is the story of what he called 'slave' or 'herd' morality. Once upon a time, there were two kinds of people, the masters and those over whom they ruled. The dominant morality – or better, the dominant mode of evaluation – was that of the master. It was an expression of his respect and esteem for himself: he judged himself to be 'good', and – consequently – what he did to be 'good'. There were others like himself – other masters – whom he also respected: they were worthy of a fight or friendship. Then there were those over whom he ruled: they were unlike him in the respects that counted, and he marked this difference by designating them 'bad' (or 'base': '*schlecht*'). But the badness of his slaves was largely a matter of indifference to the master: he was concerned with pursuing his own life and creating his own values. The master did not claim universality for these values: they did not prescribe how others (and certainly not the slaves) *ought* to act; they simply described how he *did* act.

The slave, on the other hand, did not act; or, at least, his actions were subject to the command of his master. To act on his own behalf would be to deny his status as a slave, and this he was afraid to do. If the master's sentiment towards the slave was the 'pathos of difference', that of the slave towards the master was '*ressentiment*', the hatred nourished in those who were afraid to act.

> The slave revolt in morality begins when *ressentiment* itself becomes creative and gives birth to values: the *ressentiment* of natures that are denied their true reaction, that of deeds, and compensate themselves with an imaginary revenge.[30]

Slave morality is essentially reactive. It focusses on the object of its fear – the master – and designates what he does as 'evil' ('*böse*'); the slave is, by contrast, 'good'. It thus reverses the values of the master. What is good to the master is evil for the slave: the master himself, his superiority and the characteristics which exemplify that superiority – worldly success, wealth, fame, pride, brutality and the like. What is bad to the master is good for the slave: submissiveness, self-denial, equality. This is not a simple reversal of the content of values; their polarity is reversed also. For the master, the primary value is good, and what is not good is bad; for the slave, the primary value is evil, and what is not evil is good.

The 'revaluation of values' was commenced by the Jews and carried through by Christianity. Paradoxically, the slave revolt in morality which was brought about by the fear of action has come to dominate European moral sensibility. Morality in the modern world *is* slave morality. If success is measured in worldly terms, it is the slave morality which has been successful. Not only has it captured morality, it has also subjugated man himself. For better or worse, modern man – the 'last man' – is the moral subject.

The development of the moral subject is a complex one. Nor is the story one of simple decline: here as elsewhere Nietzsche eschews antitheses. Because the man of *ressentiment* lacks the 'trust and openness with himself' which is characteristic of the noble, because he is 'neither upright nor naive nor honest and straightforward with himself', he acquires subtlety and complexity.[31] It was owing to the 'priestly form of existence'

> that man first became an *interesting animal*, that only here did the human soul in a higher sense acquire *depth* and become *evil* – and these are the two basic respects in which man has hitherto been superior to other beasts.[32]

The man of *ressentiment* hates; but he also fears, and therefore does not act. He internalises his hatred, which comes to pervade all that he thinks and does. The noble man, however, acts on his emotions and forgets the wrongs that have been done to him. It is not simply that the action dissipates the emotion; it is rather that forgetting is a sign of strength: it clears the way to live one's own life.[33] The slave does not act, and does not have the strength to forget; so he remembers. (Nietzsche remarks somewhere that the Christian knows how to forgive, but not how to forget.[34]) The I is in part constituted by continuing hatred and the memory of past injuries. This I, the subject of morality, has a continuity and an intensity of focus not available to the noble. The power of *ressentiment*, turned inwards, has created a subject for the emotions which are denied expression: an I which is born of frustrated desire, a desire all the more intense because it is denied recognition.

The master does not distinguish what is from what ought to be. His judgement that the slave is bad (or base) does not imply that the slave ought to be different. He would probably not make much sense of the idea: for him, the slave simply *is* weak. The slave, on the other hand, thinks that the master freely chooses to do what he *ought not* do. Nietzsche's critique of this reasoning is worth quoting at length:

> To demand of strength that it should *not* express itself as strength, that it should *not* be a desire to overcome, a desire to throw down, a desire to become master, a thirst for enemies and resistances and triumphs, is just as absurd as to demand of weakness that it should express itself as strength. A quantum of force is equivalent to a quantum of drive, will, effect – more, it is nothing other than precisely this very driving, willing, effecting, and only owing to the seduction of language (and of the fundamental errors of reason that are petrified in it) which conceives and misconceives all effects as conditioned by something that causes effects, by a 'subject', can it appear otherwise. For just as the popular mind separates the lightning from its flash and takes the latter for an *action*, for the operation of a subject called lightning, so popular morality also separates strength from expressions of strength, as if there were a neutral substratum behind the strong man, which was *free* to express strength or not to do so. But there is no such substratum: there is no 'being' behind doing, effecting, becoming; 'the doer' is merely a fiction added to the deed – the deed is everything.[35]

We might say that *ressentiment* creates a new kind of subject: the subject of morality:[36] the conception of an agency which is separable from what it does. However, we should keep in mind

Nietzsche's insistence that the subject of morality is a fiction, a misinterpretation of the complex phenomena of subjectivity. It is a misinterpretation engendered by weakness. The failure of the man of *ressentiment* to act on his hatred expresses his weakness just as the actions of the noble express his strength; but both are interpreted by morality, not as expressions of character, but as acts of choice.

Nietzsche provided a second – perhaps complementary, perhaps inconsistent – account of the genesis of an essential component of morality: the 'bad conscience' or 'soul' – the consciousness of guilt, the awareness that one is not as one ought to be. This kind of self-awareness internalises the gap between 'is' and 'ought' which the man of *ressentiment* has projected onto the world. It is, Nietzsche suggests, a necessary consequence of the trauma suffered by the human animal as a consequence of the entry into social life.

> I regard the bad conscience as the serious illness that man was bound to contract under the stress of the most fundamental change he ever experienced – that change which occurred when he found himself enclosed within the walls of society and peace. The situation that faced sea-animals when they were compelled to become land-animals or perish was the same as that which faced these semi-animals, well adapted to the wilderness, to war, to prowling, to adventure: suddenly, all their instincts were disvalued and 'suspended'.[37]

On this account, it is social life itself, not the fear of the master, which turns the desires of the individual back on themselves: the bad conscience – or soul – is the product of this reaction.

For social life to be possible, man must acquire 'the right to make promises';[38] that is, he must learn to undertake obligations and to carry them out. (Nietzsche probably had Kant in mind here.) Men must remember what they have undertaken to do, and this memory must impose itself on what they would otherwise do. They must acquire a sense of right and wrong, and – above all – of guilt. There is pain involved here: 'only that which never ceases to *hurt* stays in the memory'.[39] Punishment for breaches of morality is not by itself sufficient to produce guilt: unless the experience of pain is already associated with guilt, i.e. it is felt to be deserved, punishment will only induce prudence, not the consciousness that one has done wrong. What is required, and what is provided by social life, is a mechanism of self-punishment: the human will must be turned on itself. The human capacity for violence and destruction plays a dual role here. It is the occasion for guilt – for the awareness that one is not what one ought to be. It is also responsible for the pain of guilt: turned on itself, it administers the violence necessary for the wound to remain active in our consciousness. Nietzsche suggests that it is the enactment of this self-inflicted violence which creates the stage on which it takes place: the whole theatre of our inner life:

> All instincts that do not discharge themselves outwardly *turn inward* – this is what I call the *internalisation* of man: thus it was that man first developed what was later called his 'soul'. The entire inner world, originally as thin as if it were stretched between two membranes, expanded and extended itself, acquired depth, breadth and height, in the same measure as outward discharge was *inhibited*. . . . Hostility, cruelty, joy in persecuting, in attacking, in change, in destruction – all this turned against the possessors of such instincts: *that* is the origin of the 'bad conscience'.[40]

Social man is a sick animal, and his soul, his conscience, are the symptoms of his illness. It is in virtue of that illness that each of us is now subject to morality: we have the right to make promises on which social life depends. Each individual is now a moral subject.

The story of the bad conscience exemplifies Nietzsche's tendency to construe all social life as a form of servitude. Elsewhere, in *The Gay Science*, he provided a brilliant account of the emergence of consciousness out of the need to communicate. With the development of language and consciousness, man has gained in subtlety and complexity, but he has also lost access to what is specific to himself. What is captured in language, and thus in consciousness, is what is average and common; what escapes capture is our unique individuality. Here, Nietzsche explicitly identifies the social with the herd: 'My idea is . . . that consciousness does not really belong to man's individual existence but rather to his *social or herd nature*.'[41]

There is a tension between the parable of the masters and slaves, and the stories of the origins of the bad conscience and of consciousness. If the former threatens to construe all social relations as either mastery or slavery, the latter threatens to reduce them all to slavery. If the former allows for the possibility of a form of life which is beyond morality, the latter does not. This is not to say that Nietzsche ever recommended a return to the life of mastery – his project was to go forward, not backward. Still, mastery does provide a glimpse of life without morality. In the story of the sick animal, on the other hand, morality is the price we pay for social existence. Here the alternative to the moral life is something pre-human ('animal' in the pejorative sense beloved by philosophers). Again, it is important not to impose too strict an antithesis on Nietzsche's thought. The emergence of bad conscience had meant a loss of a certain rude vitality; but it was a pre-condition for much else. It was 'an illness as pregnancy is an illness'.[42] It has indeed given birth to everything that is recognisably human in history. Yet it is also clear that its time is coming to an end. What then is the alternative? How can one live beyond guilt and beyond morality?

BEYOND MORAL SUBJECTIVITY: THE ETERNAL RECURRENCE

The subject of morality is a fiction, created by fear and trauma and sustained by the practice of morality. The struggle against morality is the struggle against the 'unselfing' of man.[43] Moving beyond morality means discovering or creating a new self. But what is the self? How do we 'become what we are'?

Up to a point, Nietzsche's position is similar to Hume's: the self is nothing but a collection of sensations, passions, thoughts and the like.[44] But far more than Hume, Nietzsche emphasises the existence of the body as the ground of these sensations, passions and thoughts. The I is not a mental I, but a bodily I: '"I", you say, and are proud of the word. But greater is that in which you do not wish to have faith – your body and its great reason: that does not say "I", but does "I".'[45] If anything, it is the body which feels, wills and thinks. But ultimately, the body too stands in need of unification. It could not on its own constitute the unity of a self. Nor could consciousness, that late developing and superficial phenomenon, do the job.[46] The self is unified through power. The various bodily passions, desires, needs and thoughts exist in diverse relations of compatibility, complementarity, tension and contradiction. This diversity gives way to unity when an order of hierarchy and dominance is established amongst them. Certain desires establish their priority, and others fall into place beneath them.

The impression of freedom of the will arises because the self is constituted by the commanding will and takes pleasure in the obedience of the now subordinated aspects of the self.[47] It expresses itself in action, and there too it experiences the feeling of freedom.

But this is not freedom of the will as the moralist understands it. It is the freedom of artists to create as they must,[48] the freedom of the bird of prey to express its nature by carrying off the lamb[49] and, perhaps, of the philosopher to pursue his 'campaign against morality'[50] into madness. It is a freedom which embraces necessity; it is a freedom which can do no other than what it does.

The I is not a discovery but a creation; it is the 'regency' which provides – if only for a time – the political resolution of an ongoing process of conflict and struggle, negotiation and alliance.[51] It *is* an interpretation, but also defines the place *from which* interpretation takes place. The self-conscious I is not all there is to the self, nor does its knowledge exhaust what there is to be known about that self.[52] Nietzsche recommends that we bypass the government and communicate directly with the 'inferior parts' – especially the body – if we wish to gain better knowledge of the domain of the self.

There is no self outside this process of conflict and resolution. To become a self – and not a moral subject – is to be victorious in this process. Becoming what one is, is a task. The unity of the self is not given, nor is it discovered; it is created. To move beyond moral subjectivity is to become oneself, with full knowledge that one is one's own achievement. To be oneself is to become oneself; it is a victory over oneself, and an interpretation. It is also to accept, even to love, what one is. There can be no place here for the bad conscience: the guilty awareness of the gap between what one is and what one ought to be.

Moral subjectivity is not, however, merely a certain kind of self-awareness; it also involves a certain perspective on the world. To move beyond moral subjectivity involves changing that perspective. The moral interpretation is not just concerned to lay down how people ought to live; it also claims to locate their lives in a meaningful larger picture. It recognises that there must be some intelligible connection between acting as morality requires and making sense of one's actions in terms both of one's personal destiny and a comprehensive world order. We can make sense of the demands of individual morality only if we are able to locate it within a more encompassing narrative.[53] Where, as too often, the world does not provide much evidence of a meaningful whole, it has been the special responsibility of philosophy and religion to make up for the deficiency and display this larger order. A crucial step has been the denigration of the world as it is revealed to sense-experience. This has become the world of (mere) appearance, and thus of unreality, in contrast with the intelligible world revealed by reason. Reason discovers a cosmic order and purpose; if not the existence of God, at least of a God-like order working through history. In this grander scenario, disaster and tragedy find their larger meaning. The suffering individual is compensated, or the suffering is located in this more comprehensive story. The evil are punished, or their evil explained as necessary for some greater good.

Nietzsche's claim is that even if accounts such as these were once believable, they no longer are. In large part this was because of the development of modern science. Nietzsche was certainly sympathetic to the positivist claim that metaphysics and religion had tried to do badly what modern science did well. Indeed, he suggested that positivism was an important step on the route towards the overthrow of metaphysics.[54] However, positivism is itself a metaphysical position: it claims for science the same God's eye view of reality which had hitherto been claimed by metaphysics and religion. It does not recognise that science has not only destroyed the claims of metaphysics and religion to this status; it has destroyed the status itself. Science too is the product of a particular perspective; it is a particular kind of interpretation of the world. It has no particular epistemological privilege. However, science does not depend on its claim to a non-perspectival status; morality, on the other hand, together with its senior partners, religion and metaphysics, do. They cannot do without the claim to a truth which is absolute and unique. Truth is their own value, and one they cannot give up.

The genealogy of the moral interpretation of the world shows why it must deny its own perspectival status. It is because the man of *ressentiment* will not act on the world that he denies the need to act on it: the real word, if not the world of appearance, is as he would want it to be.

> Whoever does not know how to lay his will into things at least lays some *meaning* into them: that means, he has the faith that they already obey a will. (Principle of 'faith').[55]

The task of reason – of metaphysics, of religion – is to establish that the world already has the characteristics that a more active will would seek to create. Both *ressentiment* and the bad conscience are *re*active; strength has been turned back on itself and become thought. In the guise of reason, thought has operated to undermine the faith of the masters in their own unreflective judgement.[56] In a more positive vein, it has functioned to create the more real world which is necessary to substantiate the claims of morality. Reason can only serve these purposes if it operates behind the mask of impersonality, and if its results have the appearance of objectivity. The claim to a non-perspectival truth is essential to this enterprise.

It is this claim which is no longer available. Metaphysics and religion have long since lost the epistemological credentials to justify such large claims. The Enlightenment's faith in progress, even some versions of evolutionary theory, were attempts to provide a secular replacement to metaphysical and religious conceptions of the world. As such, they were merely lay theology: religion in disguise. Claims of this kind can now only be maintained at the price of hypocrisy, concealment – of lies. It is the task of the genealogist to turn its own values against the moral interpretation of the world. It has devalued itself. We must now give up morality for its own mendacity (and perhaps also give up the moral value of truth).

> Among the forces cultivated by morality was *truthfulness*: this eventually turned against morality, discovered its teleology, its partial perspective.[57]

The failure of the moral interpretation of the world leads directly to nihilism.[58] This is the loss of value – of meaning and purpose in life – not through the application of higher values, but through a form of self-destruction. The highest values have devaluated themselves.[59] According to Nietzsche, nihilism is the destiny of the modern world – or at least of the 'next two centuries'. Even though only some have so far glimpsed that fate, its history 'can be related even now; for necessity itself is at work here'.[60] Nietzsche draws an important distinction between two kinds of nihilism:

> A. Nihilism as a sign of increased power of the spirit: as *active* nihilism.
> B. Nihilism as decline and recession of the power of the spirit: as *passive* nihilism.[61]

Passive nihilism is one of the forms in which nihilism is first experienced: its symptom is pessimism (e.g. Schopenhauer). Passive nihilism is the recognition of the failure of morality to provide values and purposes to guide one's life. There is no world revealed by reason which provides a context for one's individual strivings;

there is no larger web of meanings with which one can identify; nor is there a final goal towards which human history is heading.[62] The pessimist – the passive nihilist – says: There are no meanings of this kind, but there ought to be. The failure of the moral interpretation is experienced as a loss.

To this Nietzsche responds: If there is no morality, there is no 'ought to be'.

> The philosophical nihilist is convinced that all that happens is meaningless and in vain; and that there ought not be anything meaningless and in vain. But whence this: there ought not to be? From where does one get *this* 'meaning', this 'standard'?[63]

While passive nihilism pretends to reject the moral interpretation of the world, it secretly accepts it. The moral interpretation lingers on in the attitude that the loss of morality and meaning *is* a loss, and that these *ought* to exist. Passive nihilism is morality's last desperate stand.

Active nihilism does not merely accept the loss of morality. It celebrates it. The self-refutation of the moral interpretation of the world is not a loss, but a triumph; an achievement of spirit, and a liberation. In place of pessimism, its attitude is one of joyfulness: it is the 'gay science'. Positive nihilism is not a return to master morality. That is no longer possible. It is a call for new values, not a reaffirmation of the old. But the values it seeks will, like those of the master, be particular and not universal; they will be created by will and not discovered by reason.

Nietzsche calls for 'new philosophers', 'free spirits' to meet the challenge of nihilism, not to overcome it, but, by pushing it beyond its limits, to turn its No into a Yes. Passive nihilism retains the perspective of morality: it continues to say No to the world, though it has not gained the confidence to say Yes to anything else. The active nihilist must say No to morality, and Yes to the world. The world, and everything in it – life, change, temporality, misery, sickness, horror, transient happiness, occasional glory – must be accepted, despite the lack of any larger meaning or cosmic purpose. Of course, the 'free spirit' will also act, and in acting strive to affirm its values. Such actions have significance, not because of what they achieve, but because of what they are. Like the world of which they are a part, they exist, and therein lies their value.

There is a limit to what can be achieved by action. In particular, it cannot change the past. This might seem to be a limitation of will: 'The will cannot will backwards; and that he cannot break time and time's covetousness, that is the will's loneliest melancholy.'[64] But if we cannot act on the past, we can reconceive it. We can 'lay our will into things', not just by changing them, but also by changing our perspective and reinterpreting them. Interpretation is a manifestation of will. To accept what one cannot change is to will that it be so.

> 'The will is a creator.' All 'it was' is a fragment, a riddle, a dreadful accident – until the creative will says to it, 'But thus I will it.' Until the creative will says to it, 'But thus I will will it; thus shall I will it.'[65]

Positive nihilism creates this new perspective on the world: one acts *as* one must, and accepts *what* one must. For the free spirit, there is no value above existence, no ought to be except what is.

To say Yes to the world is not merely to accept it; it is also to celebrate it. The reinterpretation required by Nietzsche is not just a matter of new words, but of a new life: one in which one loves what exists, even in its utmost horror or banality.

> He who has really gazed . . . into the most world-denying of all possible modes of thought – beyond good and evil and no longer, like Buddha and Schopenhauer, under the spell and illusion of morality – perhaps by that very act, and without really intending to, may have had his eyes opened to the opposite ideal: to the ideal of the most exuberant, most living and world-affirming man, who has not only learned to get on and treat with all that was and is but who wants to have it again *as it was and is* to all eternity, insatiably calling out *da capo* [i.e. again from the beginning] not only to himself but to the whole piece and play.[66]

This is the ideal of eternal recurrence; it is both the consequence and the test of positive nihilism. The free spirit must celebrate existence by willing that it recur, or – *what is the same thing* – interpreting the world as embodying such a pattern of recurrence.

The doctrine of eternal recurrence is the ultimate denial of meaning and purpose: 'Let us think this thought in its most terrible form: existence as it is, without meaning or aim, yet recurring inevitably without any finale of nothingness: "*the eternal recurrence*".'[67] But it is a denial which has become an affirmation. It is a way of saying Yes to what exists, as not needing any other validation than that which is provided by existence itself. It accepts the identity of the ought and the is; it recognises that the only universal is the particular, and it affirms – and lives – the identity of the eternal with the transient and the temporal.[68]

In a world without God, the eternal recurrence is the closest we can get to redemption:

> To redeem what is past in man and to recreate all 'it was' until the will says, 'Thus I willed it! Thus I shall will it' – this I called redemption and this alone I taught them to call redemption.[69]

But it is a redemption which is not easily earned. Zarathustra was the teacher of eternal recurrence; but he also recoiled from it. It was his 'abysmal thought', the cause of nausea and disgust; it was his destiny, but also his danger and sickness.[70] When, in *The Gay Science*, Nietzsche first proclaims the doctrine, he imagines two responses to the 'demon' who brings the news:

> Would you not throw yourself down and gnash your teeth and curse the demon who spoke thus? Or have you once experienced a tremendous moment when you would have answered him: 'You are a god and never have I heard anything more divine.' If this thought gained possession of you, it would change you as you are or perhaps crush you.[71]

To respond to the demon as a divine messenger means, not merely loving the world in all its horror and banality, but taking responsibility for it. This is to become a god oneself; to live the doctrine of the eternal recurrence is to live as if there were no world which is not one's own creation and re-creation. To respond to the demon with anguish, to receive the news he conveys as 'the greatest weight'[72] is to lose oneself in a world without meaning or purpose; it is to 'go under', not for rebirth as the near divine '*Übermensch*', but to annihilation.

The culmination of Nietzsche's genealogy of morality is to confront the moral subject with a choice between divinity and disintegration. The story of Zarathustra is largely the story of his struggle between these alternatives. Zarathustra must come to terms with the demonic or divine message of the eternal recurrence. He must recognise the world in all its meanness, emptiness and cruelty, but learn to love it – and himself – not as a duty (this would be to return to the standpoint of morality), but as a joy and a triumph.

To move beyond moral subjectivity and to become what we are, we must be able to do two things. We must create ourselves; we must assert the power and create the perspective which unifies our disparate and contradictory wills into one. We must claim sovereignty over ourselves. In this victory we must learn to accept and love ourselves, even those aspects which we might find despicable or trivial. To be what we are, we must accept the totality of what we are. Beyond moral subjectivity, there is no ground for a distinction between essence and accident, nor for one between what we are and what we ought to be. But we must also turn our attention outwards: we must create a perspective on the world which accepts and loves that also. We must will that it is as we would want it to be: the present moment and all eternity. These are not small tasks. Nietzsche has in effect ascribed to the individual the responsibilities that a previous generation had ascribed to God: creation of self and the world. To fail in these tasks is to lose oneself: to be torn apart by one's own inner conflicts or to be crushed by the world. Success is divinity; failure is disintegration.

There is in fact little to choose between the two alternatives. Eternal recurrence represents the aspiration to be at one with the totality of things. Even in the unlikely event of success in this enterprise, it would still be as much a loss of self as the disintegration it is designed to avoid. Foucault once suggested that the doctrine of eternal recurrence is identical with 'the absolute dispersion of man',[73] in that it signalled the end of the God-like status modern man had arrogated to himself as the privileged subject and object of knowledge. If the emergence of modern conceptions of rationality and knowledge had been responsible for the death of God, they were also responsible for the death of the subject who, claiming the right to speak on behalf of reason and knowledge, had excluded God from these domains. These suggestions may be taken in a more literal and material sense than Foucault intended. To step beyond moral subjectivity is to confront the choice between an absolute disintegration and an equally absolute dispersion. The individual – man as such – is lost in the essentially empty choice with which Nietzsche's philosophy came to an end.

INTERSUBJECTIVITY, EXTERNALITY AND THE SELF

What has gone wrong? Is it possible to move beyond the moral subject without the complete loss of individual identity?

I have already mentioned the tendency in Nietzsche to identify the social with the herd. This tendency emerges in a crucial way in his account of the self as the product of a Promethean act of self-creation. It is clear that the resources deployed by Nietzsche in his philosophy – and perhaps in his own life – were pitifully inadequate. Self-creation is a matter of the master will asserting its dominance over other, now subordinated, aspects of the self. There is no place in this drama for the experience of intersubjectivity, of the way in which the awareness of others is an element in the formation of the self. Though it seems likely that Nietzsche's account of master/slave morality was formulated in conscious opposition to Hegel's dialectic of master and slave, there is no glimpse in Nietzsche of the force of Hegel's argument that mastery is a defective form of human consciousness just because it does not allow for an adequate awareness of others.[74] The master gains recognition from those who have not achieved independence; but the recognition he needs can only be given by another independent self-consciousness. For Hegel, self-consciousness is formed through a complex interaction with other subjects of consciousness. It involves an awareness of others as subjects of awareness, and an awareness of ourselves as existing in the awareness of others; above all, it involves a recognition that our existence in the consciousness of others is a crucial component in our coming to exist for ourselves. On this view, we cannot form a conception of ourselves as independent centres of experience and action without at the same time forming a conception of others as independent centres of experience and action. If we are to come to have our own perspectives, both on ourselves and on the world, we must come to recognise the existenne of other perspectives. Intersubjectivity is a necessary condition for subjectivity.

There is not a hint of this in Nietzsche. This is not a mere oversight: it is an aspect of the denigration of the social which pervades his writing. If social consciousness is always herd consciousness, then there is no place for intersubjectivity, and no place for a social component in the constitution of the self. The only way to become what one is, is through one's own resources. It is to assert oneself through the repudiation of others. But this is to destroy one of the essential foundations of self-identity. The attempt to construct oneself in these circumstances can only be a futile and self-destructive gesture of megalomania.

Intersubjectivity is only one of the conditions for individual identity; the experience of externality – the awareness that we exist in a world which is not the self – is another. When we act we are aware of resistance; at one level, this may be experienced as a dimension of unfreedom. But at another and deeper level, the fact of resistance is a necessary condition for our awareness of ourselves as agents. Resistance in some form or other is a condition of agency, and thus of freedom. Nietzsche was all too aware of the world's resistance, both to his actions and to his interpretations. But he was also tempted towards the idea that the resistance was there to be overcome. The doctrine of eternal recurrence is designed to eliminate any conflict between the will and the world: if the fantasy were realised it would eliminate resistance. As a consequence, there would be no agents and no selves. Nor does this temptation surface only at the more fantastic reaches of Nietzsche's philosophy; it is also present in his perspectival account of knowledge. Perspectivism is an important corrective to those theories of knowledge which identify objectivity with a conception of the world which is not that of a particular point of view with respect to the world. It recognises that the knowledge which we have is informed by our desires, aspirations, hopes and fears. Nietzsche avoided an easy and banal relativism by recognising that our perspectives have a complexity of structure which goes beyond the particular desires which have given rise to them. Much of his own critical procedures consist in pushing forms of knowledge to their limits, showing that they have consequences which their proponents would disown. But Nietzsche does not give sufficient attention to the fact that a perspective is not just the product of a specific will: it is also directed towards an independently existing reality. In cognition we become aware of the world which our thought and beliefs must take account of. In the final analysis, it is by our experience of the world that we discover whether or not it is as we believe it to be. The adequacy of a perspective is not simply a function of it being an appropriate expression of the point of view of the knowing and willing subject; it is also a function of its appropriateness to its object, to that which it is about.

This does not mean that we can have an independent, interpretation-free access to reality in order to assess the appropriateness of a particular interpretation of it. Our knowledge of the world is always mediated by our interpretations of it. But this does not have the consequence that the world is not a crucial factor in assessing the adequacy of particular interpretations. It may be, as

Alexander Nehamas suggests, that the world is like a text, and that it makes no sense to talk of the text without assigning a particular interpretation of it. But we should not, as Nehamas and Nietzsche are both tempted to do, try to factor out the 'it'.[75] The text also places certain limits on possible interpretations. Within a given interpretation, we must constantly refer back to the text to support the interpretation, to advance it, to provide reasons for rejecting others and so on. Nehamas' suggestion that each new interpretation creates a new object (or text) ignores the role that the notion of a common object of enquiry plays, both in literary criticism and in the natural and the human sciences. It is indeed just because two or more interpretations claim to be interpretations of the same independently existing reality (or text), that we can make sense of them standing in critical relation to each other.

Nietzsche's perspectivism brings out the way in which forms of knowledge are driven, not by a desire for knowledge in its purity, but by very specific non-cognitive hopes and fears. To show that a specific form of knowledge is the product of a certain kind of will may be sufficient to destroy its epistemological credentials. If, for example, existing scientific knowledge is driven by a will to control and manipulate the world, then we have no reason to suppose that the deliverances of science are true in any strongly realist sense of truth. This, at least, is the truth in pragmatism. But this does not mean that there are not other desires which may have stronger epistemological credentials. We have, prima facie at least, better reason to accept the interpretation of a literary critic who loves and respects the work she is writing about than one who is driven by the desire for notoriety or promotion. There is no reason to suppose that there may not be desires which involve an aspiration to understand an object for its own sake; if there are such, then Nietzschean perspectivism is compatible with some quite substantial requirements of objectivity and truth.

Nietzsche was, at least some of the time, tempted to deny the significance of both intersubjectivity and externality, and this temptation informs some of his most characteristic doctrines. In these matters, Nietzsche was more a representative than a genealogist of modernity, and his philosophy was as much a symptom as a diagnosis of modern nihilism. This comes out especially with regard to the ultimate sovereignty of the self-contained individual. This claim might seem paradoxical: after all, Nietzsche is rightly celebrated for probing more deeply into the individual than anyone else before Freud. More than any of his contemporaries, Nietzsche recognised that the individual was not the indestructible atom on which society was built, but a tenuous and vulnerable construct, an uncertain and constantly fluctuating equilibrium of forces. If the modern world has created the isolated individual out of the transformation of the various constitutive links between the individual and larger social groupings, the process of transformation consistently threatens to destroy its own creation. Though Nietzsche's philosophy gives profound expression to the vulnerability of the individual, he remains at one with modernity in his faith that the individual must find his own answers to the threats that beset him.[76] Much more aware than his contemporaries of the vulnerability of the individual, he continues to assert the principle of individuality, not now as a given, but as a task. There is little confidence in this assertion, and certainly nothing of the joy that he aspired to. The tone is close to hysteria. Nietzsche's account brings out what is required to sustain the individual in a world in which individuality is both created and threatened by the experience of externality: the apparently irreducible otherness of people and of the world. Individuality can only exist by asserting itself, and it can only assert itself through the suppression of otherness. It is driven to undertake the desperate and hopeless task of destroying the necessary conditions for its own existence. Megalomania, disintegration and madness constitute the truth, not just of Nietzsche's life and philosophy, but also of the social world to which they gave exemplary expression.

7

TOWARDS MORALITY

A MORAL STATE OF NATURE

> To this war of every man, against every man, this also is consequent; that nothing can be unjust. The notions of right and wrong, justice and injustice have there no place.
>
> (Hobbes)[1]

A particular morality expresses the demands of a particular form of social life; it is the voice of society and it is addressed to the members of that society. Its function is to guide behaviour in ways which are consonant with that form of social life.

In the modern world, we are encouraged to think of ourselves as having an identity independently of the social relations in which we exist; so for us the voice of society is not our voice. It is this externality – its otherness – which is fatal to the enterprise of morality. Because morality is external, it cannot provide a reason which is a reason *for us* why we should act in the ways that it commands. We may hear its voice, but we do not know why we should obey. Even if we think of ourselves – in Kantian terms – as divided into a part which enunciates the demands of morality (a conscience, a noumenal self, a superego) and a part which resists (an empirical self, an ego), the self which resists still lacks a good reason why it should do what its other self demands of it. Morality is a demand, not a reason, and our moral life consists in a conflict between and within our selves.

If we lived in a society in which we were encouraged to think of our identities as constituted through the network of social relations within which we existed, a fuller conception of morality would be available to us. A sense of this conception is invoked by the question, not 'What ought I (here, now) do?', but rather 'What kind of life should I live?' To ask this question is not to seek information about the kind of life which is conducive to the well-being of society; it is to seek guidance on a coherent, meaningful and satisfying existence for oneself. This question is not necessarily an egocentric one: where I conceive my identity in social terms, then the life which is satisfying for me as an individual is also a life which contributes to social well-being.

This fuller conception of morality has been all but lost in the modern world. Morality has taken the form of duty; it seeks, not to guide our choices towards a meaningful life, but to restrict them. Morality has learned to limit its concern to what is right; it leaves it to us to work out what is good. Once morality has chosen to concentrate on issues of right and duty, it is ill-suited to offer guidance on the more subtle and nuanced questions as to how we might pursue our own well-being.[2] Yet if there is to be a conception of morality which is to deserve our allegiance, it will be one which we can recognise as having a place within a coherent, meaningful and satisfying way of life for us. If there is to be reason why we should do what is right, then it will be because we can recognise that so to act is conducive to, perhaps constitutive, of our own well-being. The requirements of morality must be recognised, not as external constraints, but as requirements of our own nature.

This conception of morality has been marginalised, but not completely lost in the modern world. The private realm of family life offers conceptions of identity – paradigmatically that of wife/mother – in which the individual recognises that certain activities – nurturing, caring for other family members – are both required to sustain a certain kind of social life and are also components of her own well-being. The nation too presents itself as a community whose demands are not externalities, but flow from the nature of those subject to them. Both the family and the nation provide conceptions of identity which define the individual within a framework of relations. The individual *is* Australian, or *is* a mother, and recognises that certain ways of acting are required both to express that identity and to sustain the community which provides it.

However effective these moralities are in practice, they can neither resist nor meet the demand for reason. In the rationalised modern world, the concept of reason is dominated by the requirements of efficiency, consistency and truth. Neither the private realm of emotion, expression and commitment, nor the public theatre of nationalist rhetoric and representation, can meet these requirements. Both forms of community become, not matters of reason, but of non-rational choice. Even to ask for reason is to undermine their authority. They provide a basis for morality just to the extent that they are experienced as natural and inescapable – as beyond reason. To demand reasons is to make them subject to standards which are not their own, and they must lose their claim to an overriding moral status just as surely as when they become matters of non-rational choice. In the modern world, each of us has – at least in principle - other ways in which we may identify ourselves. From the perspective of these other identities, the requirements of the family and the nation take on the form of duties. They become external demands which may coerce but which fail to be reasons.

If morality is to be possible, it will be because we are able to envisage a way of life which provides a satisfying and fulfilling existence for us as individuals, and which also contains the conditions necessary for a form of social life. Morality requires a convergence between what we can aspire to as happiness, and what is required to reproduce a form of social existence. Only then can there be adequate reason for us to do what we ought to do.[3] There can be no guarantee that this convergence is possible. It is, at best, a gamble. But it is on this gamble that the possibility of morality depends.

It may be that a form of life which satisfies the condition of convergence is immediately available, in the sense that we might now choose to live in that way. If this were the case, then we would have reason to make that choice, and the demands of the morality which is attendant on that form of social life would be our demands, and its reasons our reasons. But another – and more likely – scenario is that the way of life which we aspire to is not immediately available to us. It may be that it requires the active co-operation of other individuals, or that it requires large scale social change. It may be, for example, that honesty and co-operation are part of our desired way of life; however, we would be more than foolish if we tried to live by these values if we find ourselves in a society of cheats and thieves. To attempt to lead this way of life without the assurance that others were also leading it, would mean that we and those dependent upon us would suffer badly. In these circumstances, we would be well advised to cut our losses and live as best we can.

If the social conditions necessary for our preferred way of life are absent, its requirements do not in a direct sense count as reasons for us. We would be like the inhabitants of Hobbes' state of nature who can work out what the conditions of a peaceful life are, i.e. what the 'laws of nature' require, but have no reason to act in the ways recommended, because they have no reason to believe that others will. They hanker, however, after a form of life in which things would be different; where each would have reason to believe that others would obey the laws of nature, and so would have reason to do so as well. In a state of nature, '[t]he laws of nature oblige *in foro interno*; that is to say, they bind to a desire that they should take place: but *in foro externo*; that is, to the putting them in place, not always.'[4] We live in a moral state of nature where the requirements of morality and our own aspirations have come apart, where the right is not a component of our good. In these circumstances, the requirements of morality do not count as reasons. However, we might well have reason to leave the moral state of nature, and to live in a world in which a convergence between our aspirations and the demands of morality was possible. In this case, the requirements of morality would not oblige *in foro externo*, but they would oblige *in foro interno*, i.e. to the rational desire that we might live in the way that they prescribe.

The task of specifying a way of life which will both attract the reasoned assent of individuals and also provide the conditions of a form of social life is a daunting one. Even if we locate the preferred way of life in a possible future rather than an actual present, it must still attract the assent of people as they exist now, not as they might come to exist. At this point it is tempting to seek help from a theory of human nature. If, it might be argued, we can construct a concept of the human essence such that a certain form of human life counts as a realisation of that essence, then we will have provided a reason why all who share that essence should live that form of human life.

The more promising versions of this 'humanist' argument are of Aristotelian descent. While Aristotle himself was more concerned to celebrate a certain highly exclusive and limited form of social life than to develop a conception of human nature, attempts to construct an Aristotelian account of a less parochial kind almost inevitably call upon a theory of human nature to support a concept of human well-being ('flourishing'). Such theories will, like Aristotle's, attribute a social component to human nature, and claim that a complete human life requires that one participate in and contribute to a form of social existence. Thus, when I come to understand my nature as a social being, I will recognise that my own well-being requires that I do what is required to sustain that form of social life. Arguments of this kind often take a conservative direction: human nature is what is manifest in prevailing social conditions. However, they may also have a radical bent. The young Marx and the tradition of Marxist humanism rejected capitalism precisely because it does not allow for a satisfactory realisation of the human essence.

This is not the place to rehearse the deep epistemological problems which confront the humanist enterprise. While it is plausible to suggest that there must be some constant features which underlie and help explain the socially and historically diverse manifestations of human existence, there seems little reason to expect that these be sufficient to construct a determinate theory of human flourishing. Nor is there much reason to expect that all the characteristics which have a claim to be included in a theory of human nature are ones we would happily include in a conception of the good life. We might, for example, want to include sociability and the associated virtues of sympathy, generosity and self-sacrifice in our account of human nature; but then it would be difficult to provide a non-question begging reason why we should exclude aggression, hostility and selfishness. But an account of human nature along these lines would hardly provide the basis for an acceptable concept of morality.

Even if it were possible to provide an acceptable account of the human essence which yields interesting and acceptable conclusions about human conduct, it would not resolve the present problem. A theory of human nature will inevitably be a highly general one, and an appeal to our human nature will be an appeal to what each of us has in common with others. Now it may be that I value these common attributes more than others which I possess; but it may be that I do not. I may well, like Stirner's egoists or Nietzsche's free spirits, value more highly those characteristics which differentiate me from others; or it may be, that I value those characteristics which are unique to a particular form of social life. In these cases, the claim that a certain way of life is appropriate to human nature will not provide a reason *for me* to pursue that way of life. As Stirner argued against Feuerbach's humanistic alternative to religion, what is important for me is *my* well-being, and that is determined by what *I* am, and what *I* would like to be, not by that aspect of me which others designate as my essence.[5]

The appeal to human nature would carry more weight if it could be shown that the frustration of those needs and wants which are part of human nature inevitably spells unhappiness. If this were the case, then each of us would have a reason to pursue a way of life which is appropriate to our human nature. But this is surely too much to expect. Whatever account we provide of the essentially human, we must allow that people might find – and indeed that many have found – happiness in pursuing desires and activities which are not included in, and are even antithetical to, the favoured category. As Bernard Williams remarked:

> There is . . . the figure, rarer perhaps than Callicles supposed, but real, who is horrible enough and not miserable at all but, by any ethological standard of the bright eye and the gleaming coat, dangerously flourishing.[6]

We might even take the existence of such people as evidence of the extent to which a way of life has become dehumanised. Thus, the young Marx thought that the fact that the capitalist enjoyed a kind of happiness showed that he was even more alienated than his miserable employees.[7] But this shows that the appeal to human nature has little motivational force: it is the employees who have reason to change the situation, not the capitalist.

I do not want to reject the humanist enterprise altogether. It is not possible to go very far in thinking about moral issues without making some assumptions about what it is to be human, and about the kind of life appropriate to human beings. Still, there are moral as well as epistemological reasons for keeping these assumptions to a minimum. Whatever account we finally give of the good life, it should be sufficiently pluralistic to allow a large role for people to determine its content for themselves. Too enthusiastic an emphasis on human nature may well be incompatible with an adequate recognition of the importance of the freedom to make our own nature. If we are to go forward from liberalism, not backwards, we need to incorporate the liberal emphasis on freedom within our conception of the good life. The good life, and the kind of society which makes it possible, must be conceivable as a condition of freedom, not a restriction on it.

MODERNITY – WHY LEAVE?

If there are to be reasons which will move us to desire another way of life, then they must appeal to or provoke dissatisfaction with the way in which we live now. The humanist account proposes that the unhappiness arises out of a conflict between our human nature and our social existence. But as we have seen, this is implausible: whatever account is provided of our human nature, it is likely that many whose existence is most in conflict with this nature, will be amongst the least dissatisfied, and the least susceptible to the attractions of an alternative way of life. There is, however, another possibility: it may be that the unhappiness or dissatisfaction which gives us reason to change arises, not out of the conflict between our social existence and our human nature, but out of conflicts within our form of social existence.

Modern social life carries its own contradictions: it generates sets of incompatible desires, and desires which are incapable of satisfaction. More fundamentally, it creates a certain concept of individual identity, and it does not provide the resources necessary to sustain that identity. If the modern world revolves around the sovereign individual, it has also destroyed the conditions of its sovereignty. When we become aware that frustration is the price we pay for the proliferation of desire, that weakness is the consequence of our obsession with power, and that disintegration is the consequence of individualism, then we do have reason to hope for something else. If it emerges that the conditions which make frustration inevitable and which threaten our identity are just the conditions which make a rational practice of morality impossible, then we have reason to desire a society in which morality is possible.

It is important to emphasise that this argument is not, like its humanist counterpart, a universal one. There may be some who do not suffer the frustration, or for whom it is a minor price to pay for the powers and pleasures which the modern world provides. Their way of life may be such that the threat to their identity is weak compared with the confirmations they receive. For those people, there will be little we can provide by way of reason for them to want something else. For them, at least, there may be no path towards morality.

I have already described some of the ills of modernity. The market has placed the individual in a network of social interdependency more extensive than anything which could have been envisaged in previous forms of society. Nevertheless, it has at the same time isolated the individual from strong and constitutive relations with those others on whom he depends. In a variety of ways it has encouraged the individual to conceive of his identity as distinct from that of other individuals. He will participate effectively in market transactions just to the extent that he conceives of his relations with others instrumentally. He will have little reason to concern himself with the specific interests of those with whom he has market dealings, and every reason to be concerned with his own. Indeed, the market creates a conception of individual identity which makes it difficult to conceive of any other form of motivation than an egocentric one. Whatever the content of the desires pursued by the individual, it is always *his* desires which move him, and *his* gratification which is aimed at. It is one of the paradoxes of the market that as it has massively enlarged the extent to which individuals are dependent upon others, it has at the same time created a conception of individual identity and motivation which is overwhelmingly focussed on the self.

There is a curious emptiness to this conception of social life. Insofar as the individual conceives of himself as separate from those other individuals, relationships, and even those of his own capacities which he uses as means to pursue his goals, then his identity takes on an abstract and elusive character. In one sense, the individual is at the centre of social life: it is, after all, at the gratification of his desires that the market aims. But in another sense, the individual drops out of consideration: he is little more than the place of origin of these desires and the equally empty place of return. The ceaseless activity of the market – its 'business' – obscures the essential circularity of the path between desire and its gratification. It is not surprising, if somewhat paradoxical in a form of life concerned with the rational pursuit of ends, that it becomes the main function of the activity of the market place to conceal the emptiness of the ends pursued.

The conception of modernity as capitalism provides a more determinate content to these ends. The primary goal is power: the individual must take as an overriding end the pursuit of the means to pursue other ends. He must seek, as relentlessly and yet as unsuccessfully as those in Hobbes' state of nature, power after power. A complementary, though opposed, goal is that of consumption: capitalism cannot increase its productive capacity without a corresponding increase in the needs of consumers. The individual becomes an infinite consumer, with the gratification of each need serving only as a preliminary to the pursuit of the next. The individual is thus subject to two kinds of desire, each incompatible with the other, each incapable of satisfaction even on its own. There is no doubt that capitalism has more than kept its promise to increase social productivity, but at the cost of dissociating this from human happiness. What it has achieved is not satisfaction, but frustration; not creativity and repose, but endless repetition, punctuated with occasional satiation. It is part of the achievement of capitalism that it has succeeded in identifying this state of affairs with a concept of rationality.

It is not surprising that the identity constructed through the capitalist market is a vulnerable one. The individual is cut off from most of the resources necessary to provide coherence to his life. There is little reason to suppose that there are larger webs of meaning (e.g. of the universe, of human history). Even if there were, they would be irrelevant to the individual whose self-contained identity is the locus of all that is meaningful. But the individual may also discover that his own identity is not a given, but something improvised – a tenuous and unstable achievement which is threatened by the instrumental endeavours of those with whom he comes in contact, and by the impersonality of the social conditions in which he exists. Each individual in attempting to make his way in the capitalist market is subject to the reified laws of his own social behaviour. He is presented with the choice of succumbing to the conditions of his social life or – desperately, perilously – attempting to construct his identity for himself.

I have already made reference to Hegel's dialectic of master and slave.[8] One of the key insights in this famous passage is the idea that individual self-consciousness is acquired and sustained through interaction with and recognition by other self-consciousnesses. I do not acquire self-consciousness and then recognise (or fail to recognise) the self-consciousness of others. Rather, I become aware of myself as a centre of consciousness through the same process as that in which I become aware of the existence of other centres of consciousness. The moment of otherness is crucial: I must recognise and accept that the other has a will and a purpose, thoughts and desires, which are not mine. Ideally, the other will recognise that I too have my own distinct existence. Only through this experience of intersubjectivity – of an otherness which is not other – will I come to have an adequate awareness of myself as an independent self-consciousness. The life of the master is a defective form of self-consciousness precisely because it is not confirmed in the consciousness of an independent other.

Hegel's parable tells us something about the necessary conditions for the development of the human infant towards maturity, and also about the necessary conditions of a social life which adequately sustains the identity of its members. It is this condition which is not provided in the mainstream public life of modernity. Insofar as we are rational in the appropriately instrumental sense, we will recognise the independence of others only insofar as this is a means towards our own ends. The independent existence of others is not experienced as a necessary condition of our existence; at best, it is accepted as a constraint placed by morality or the law upon the operation of our desires. The moment of intersubjectivity is lacking.

The rationalisation of modern public life is not simply an 'iron cage' within which the individual subject finds himself imprisoned; it erodes the very basis of subjectivity itself. Insofar as the conditions within which we live are rationalised, we have little choice but to be instrumentally rational in the pursuit of our ends. But as a consequence, we must fail to reach those ends which are most crucial to our existence. Even if I were to seek the recognition of others as a means to that end, this would still be to treat others *as* means and deny the independent existence which is crucial if I am to achieve my goal. Here as elsewhere, just to the extent that we are instrumentally rational in the pursuit of our ends, we will not achieve them. In order to achieve the particular end of recognition, we must treat others, not as means, but as ends in themselves.[9] This principle is not, as Kant envisaged, a duty which must constrain our desires; it must be a component in them. As such, it is both necessary for self-identity, and also the first step towards social morality.

FRIENDSHIP, INTERSUBJECTIVITY AND MORALITY

It is of some importance that there are, even in the modern world, relationships which resist the self-destructive logic of instrumental reason. In friendship, for example, we seek and often achieve recognition from others whose independence we recognise (love is an altogether more hazardous enterprise). Insofar as we conceive, not just our having friends, but our having the particular friends that we do have, as conditions of our own well-being, then the demands of those friendships are not external: the needs of our friends are our needs, and the reason of friendship is our reason. But friendship also requires that we come to terms with otherness: we must accept our friends as they are, not as we would want them to be. Friendship involves the recognition of otherness, but of an otherness which has been integrated into our own desires, thoughts and way of life. By contrast, the demands of duty remain external, even when we have internalised them. Friendship thus provides a glimpse of a moral life in which the concept of duty plays a minimal role.

Even when we seek the pleasures which come from friendship, we must be aware that friendship involves caring for others for their own sake. If we enter into a relationship with another just in order to gain certain pleasures, the relationship is not one of friendship, and whatever we get out of it, we do not obtain the specific pleasures of friendship. Friendship challenges the dominant modern conception of reason: friendship is not, nor could be, a means towards independently specifiable goals. We thus achieve friendship just to the extent that we are able to discover or create a sphere of social life which is immune from the instrumental rationalisation of public existence. It is surely rational to desire friends, and even particular friends; we can be more or less rational both in our choice of friends and the conduct of our friendships; and we can be rational in weighing the commitments of friendship against other responsibilities. But the sense of rationality involved here is not that of instrumental rationality.

It is important not to provide too sentimentalised a picture of friendship.[10] Real life friendships involve friction and tension, even jealousy and hostility. Friendship is not a relationship of immersion, but of negotiation, in which two distinct people try – sometimes successfully, sometimes not – to come to terms with each other's separate existence. Because it is a relationship requiring freedom of choice, there is a certain fragility to the commitments that it involves, and a vulnerability to the reassurance it provides. It is, however, precisely for these reasons that it is important, not just in our lives here and now, but as a hint of how things might be. Unlike the modern family, friendship does not buy its place in the modern world through exclusion and oppression; nor does it attempt to provide guarantees of the reassurance it provides by barring one of the participants from the values of the wider public world. Whatever our final conception of an alternative form of social life, friendship – much as we conceive it now – will find a place in it.

There are other relationships which resist the hegemony of instrumental rationality. Habermas was right to identify communication as a morally significant human activity: in many cases at least, we cannot communicate without acknowledging the rights of those with whom we communicate to make up their own minds about what we are saying. However, this acknowledgement may be a very superficial one masking a deeper manipulative intent. If, on the other hand, I enter a dialogue with you in order to understand or approach the truth on some matter, then I must recognise that you will bring your own views and experiences to bear on the issue. If I am to learn from what you say, I have to be prepared to change my understanding of the issue and its bearing on my other beliefs, and even of the purposes that I was initially seeking to fulfil. These are not, however, formal commitments, still less matters of 'universal pragmatics'. If I have reason to respect your rights, it is not because my speaking to you provides me with such a reason. Rather, it is because I have reason to speak to you – or *with* you – in a way which is not manipulative, that I have reason to respect your rights. I have such reasons when I recognise that I have a need to learn from you, to be inspired or encouraged by you, or that I depend upon your independent activity. These needs cannot be tied down to specific uses of language, e.g. to Habermas' preferred category of serious, literal speech, nor even to linguistic or communicative activity as such. They may find expression in a range of different kinds of interaction. Typically, the activity will involve an openness to the judgements, opinions, feelings and actions of others. Consider, for example, the way in which practitioners of a skill listen to and observe those whose skill they respect; or the complex interaction of mutual understanding and divergence between those performing different tasks on a common project.

Our desires are intersubjective when we recognise that they cannot be satisfied except through interaction with others whose contribution is independent of ours. At a fundamental level, intersubjectivity is a necessary condition of our existence as subjects at all; at less basic, but still important levels, it is manifest in those desires which we cannot satisfy except through interaction with others whose independence we recognise. To the extent that we recognise the centrality of intersubjective desires in our lives, we will also recognise that the independence of others is a component in our conception of the good life. We will respect the rights of those others, not because it is a commitment that – as rational or communicative beings – we cannot help but make, but because it will be required by our conception of the good. Then, and perhaps only then, will we have reason, and not just a duty, to respect the rights of others.

Intersubjectivity leads a precarious and marginal existence in the modern world. Nevertheless, it is crucial for it. It is unlikely that the public morality of duty would have any purchase on those to whom it is addressed if they did not have some experience of recognition of and by others. Intersubjectivity provides some validation for the vulnerable and threatened form of subjectivity characteristic of modernity. Where the instrumental rationalisation of the modern world erodes the framework of intersubjectivity, it threatens the conditions of its own existence.

ALASDAIR MACINTYRE: THE SEDUCTION OF THE PAST

Alasdair MacIntyre has recently undertaken to rescue a concept of morality from the nihilistic tendencies of modernity.[11] There are three key elements in his account. The first is the concept of a 'practice'. He introduces this term as follows:

> By a 'practice' I am going to mean any coherent and complex form of socially established co-operative human activity through which goods internal to that form of activity are realised in the course of trying to achieve those standards of excellence which are appropriate to, and partially definitive of that form of activity, with the result that human powers to achieve excellence, and human conceptions of the ends and good involved, are systematically extended.[12]

The range of the term is wide: 'arts, sciences, games, politics in the Aristotelian sense, the making and sustaining of family life, all fall under the concept'.[13] However all practices have a certain complexity and depth; as such they express and develop significant human capacities. They are also social in that they involve participants in a relationship which is defined by the practice (as between chess players, fellow scientists, etc.), and they will often be – though MacIntyre does not use the term – intersubjective in the sense described above.

The goods of practices – the goals pursued – are 'internal', in the sense that they can only be achieved through activities of a certain sort, or – to put the point the reverse way – the practice is not just a means to, but is partially constitutive of the good pursued. (For example, learning to read texts with sensitivity and patience is not just a means to, but is partly constitutive of being a good literary critic.) Further, the goals of a practice are subject to change. 'Practices never have a goal or goals fixed for all time – painting has no such goal nor has physics – but the goals themselves are transmuted by the history of the activity.'[14] Someone will engage in a practice to pursue certain ends; however, he or she will recognise that the activities required by the practice are not merely means to those ends, but components of it. The practitioner will also be aware that the end itself is subject to change in the process of achieving it. No doubt instrumental reason will have its place in the activity; but it is essential for the character of the practice that its place be a subordinate one.

The second key concept in MacIntyre's account is that of a tradition. Someone working within a practice will be acting, more or less self-consciously, within a context of historically produced norms, conventions and standards of excellence. In this sense, a practice will always be the bearer of a tradition. However, within the practice the elements of the tradition may be subject to critical evaluation and transformation. The tradition – of portrait painting, architecture or whatever – provides the context in which current practitioners work, and also – at least when the tradition is in good order – the space in which a critical engagement with the prevailing standards, goals, etc., may take place. Through this critical engagement the practice will be – gradually or abruptly – transformed. MacIntyre explicitly rejects that notion of a tradition, which he associates with Burke, which sees it as a repository of inviolable norms and values. For MacIntyre a tradition is, or ought to be, a place of criticism, change and development.

The third component in MacIntyre's account is that of a narrative.[15] MacIntyre recognises that the nihilistic tendencies of modernity are not merely a threat to morality but also – and more fundamentally – a threat to the self, and that a solution to the moral problems of modernity must be able to explain how a concept of personal identity is to be rescued from the corrosive effects of modern life. Part of MacIntyre's explanation lies in the self's involvement in practices, and in the traditions they embody. But another and crucial part of the explanation is provided by the notion of a narrative. (MacIntyre joins the long line of philosophers who have turned to aesthetics as a way of solving their moral problems.) Just as we make sense of an action by locating it in a story, so we make sense of a life by finding its narrative structure – that which gives it sense or point as a story. For MacIntyre, in this respect at one with Nietzsche, self-identity is not something given, but a project. We succeed in that project when we are able to make a coherent story out of our lives. By providing narrative unity to our life, we give a meaning to it and – *what is the same thing* – discover what is the good for us.

> In what does the unity of an individual life consist? The answer is that its unity is the unity of a narrative embodied in a single life. To ask 'What is the good for me?' is to ask how best I might live out that unity and bring it to completion.[16]

In other words, the quest for narrative unity in our lives, something which we may or may not achieve, is the same thing as the search for our good. Where – as in modernity – we do not know what that good is, our goal must be to discover it; hence, MacIntyre's – only apparently paradoxical – conclusion that 'the good life for man is the life spent in seeking the good life for man'.[17]

MacIntyre is aware of the megalomania involved in attempting to write one's story not just *for* oneself, but *by* oneself. Our starting point – the location from which the narrative of our live takes its beginning – is our existence within certain historically constituted practices and traditions; the substantive and critical resources which will prove our initial direction are provided by those practices and traditions. We begin our search for the good as participants in already existing practices and traditions. But, as MacIntyre is also aware, there is a problem here: the main thrust of modernity is to subject practices to the demands of instrumental reason, and to isolate the individual from the commitments of tradition. The moral problem of modernity lies precisely in the fact that we confront social life *as* individuals, not as participants in practices and traditions.

MacIntyre's solution to this problem lies in an evocation of past communities which have resisted the pressures of modern life. As individuals, we must find the resources we need to begin to make sense of our lives in the various residues of the past which have not yet been completely swallowed up by modernity; in the 'fragments of the tradition . . . still found alongside characteristically modern and individualistic concepts', and more especially 'in the lives of certain communities whose historical ties with the past remain strong'.[18] There is a significant shift of emphasis in MacIntyre's own narrative at this point. His initial account of the concept of a tradition emphasises the extent that living traditions allow for critical self-development; however, the communities that he ecumenically identifies as repositories of tradition, e.g. 'some Irish Catholics, some Orthodox Greeks, and some Jews of an Orthodox persuasion', as well as 'black and white Protestant communities in the United States, especially perhaps those in or from the South',[19] are notable for their lack of this quality. And not surprisingly: it is through their rigidities and closures, not their critical openness, that they have successfully resisted the main tendencies of modern life. It is clear that their role in MacIntyre's argument is not to point to the future, but to evoke the past. The evocation of tradition is not as a place from which we can face and perhaps change the future, but as an escape route from a desperate and benighted present to a richer past.

MacIntyre's rejection of modernity is absolute: it is a complete moral catastrophe. The only hope is the rediscovery of the past. It is therefore no accident that the communities which he applauds are hierarchical and exclusive, intolerant of deviation and deeply and systematically oppressive of women. The values of equality, freedom and democracy, so conspicuously lacking in MacIntyre's preferred communities, are characteristically modern values, and are to be rejected along with the rest of modernity. It emerges that traditions and practices are important in MacIntyre's vision, not so much because they allow for creativity and change, but because they promise a way of rediscovering what has been lost.

MacIntyre's account of a narrative quest – of our living the good life through the enterprise of searching for it – is, I think, one of the most valuable parts of his account. But it needs to be removed from the gravitational field of MacIntyre's nostalgia for a past in which moral certainty was possible. The starting point of the quest is our ignorance of the good. But this ignorance may be interpreted in two ways. It may be that we do not know what our good is because we lack a certain item of knowledge. Our quest for the good life is a search in a literal sense: it aims to discover (or rediscover) something which already exists. We are like archaeologists trying to discover the plan of a city hidden beneath the rubble of history. Our good is the pre-established unity of our life; our task is to find out what it is and to live it. However, another interpretation might be that we do not know what the good life is because it has to be created. We are not like archaeologists, but more like artists attempting to bring into existence something which has never existed before. When we find our good it will not be a discovery, but a creation. Now much of what MacIntyre says in *After Virtue*, especially his rejection of an explicit teleology, and his invocation of moral agents as the authors of their own lives, suggests the second reading. However, when it comes to the point, it is clearly the first interpretation which fits MacIntyre's intention. The good life we are to discover is that good life already established in the past – by medieval Christianity on MacIntyre's not very plausible view of the matter. The role of tradition in this picture is not to enable us to create the new, but to rediscover the past. From this it is a small step to the explicit Christian apologetics of MacIntyre's later work.

What is valuable in MacIntyre needs to be rescued from the nostalgia which pervades his work. Nostalgia has its attractions as a compensation for what we feel is missing in our lives. But in everyday life we are usually aware of the fantasy element in nostalgia – that it is a kind of ideal obverse to actual life, a dream of childhood with which to escape adult realities. We imagine a past as a way of coping with modern life, not as an alternative to it. We would not choose to return to that past, even if we could: its attractions are essentially retrospective. In its more academic forms, however, nostalgia lacks this moment of self-awareness: it *believes* in the past that it creates, and even in the desire to return to it. Perhaps the life of the scholar makes the past more real, or perhaps it is the very strength of the revulsion from modernity which makes the need for this belief stronger. But whatever its cause, academic nostalgia remains an evasion of the problems of modernity, not a solution to them. Despite its many virtues, MacIntyre's project of recovery collapses into antiquarianism and eccentricity. Like all nostalgia, it provides a way of accommodating to the world, not a reason for changing it.

OPEN FUTURES

> Creation of a *thing*, and creation plus full understanding of a *correct idea* of a thing, *are very often parts of one and the same indivisible process* and cannot be separated without bringing the process to a stop. The process is not guided by a well-defined programme, and cannot be guided by such a programme, for it contains the conditions for the realisation of all possible programmes. It is guided rather by a vague urge, by a 'passion' (Kierkegaard). The passion gives rise to specific behaviour which in turn creates the circumstances and the ideas necessary for analysing and explaining the process, for making it 'rational'.
>
> (Paul Feyerabend)[20]

To do better than MacIntyre, we need to discover or create ways of life which challenge the rationalised structures of mainstream social life and also contain the elements of an alternative, movements which project a future and do not merely represent the past. To attract our allegiance, these movements must provide a way of life to which we can subscribe; to solve the moral – and perhaps the personal – problems of modernity, they must provide for a convergence between our individual well-being and the conditions necessary to sustain the way of life as a whole. There can be no guarantee that such ways of life exist. But there is reason to hope.

Above all, it is necessary that we do not conceive the future instrumentally. We do not have, except in barest outline, a concept of an alternative form of society – a goal for which we must seek means. Our position is like that of an artist: we may have a notion of what it is we are trying to create, but we will only be able to build a model of it, even in our imagination, when we have created it in reality.[21] Our project is not to reproduce what already exists, nor even to produce a new instance of an established genre; it is to create a new genre – a radically new kind of society, as different from the modern world as the modern world is from feudalism. Conceptual understanding always comes after the event, too late to guide our endeavours. If there is to be a form of social life which provides an alternative to the moral state of nature in which we exist, it will have to be created before it can be adequately understood: we cannot now write 'recipes for cook-shops of the future'.[22]

The situation is in some respects like that in a science where there are major problems within an established paradigm (e.g. a divergence between a well-established and hitherto fruitful theory and a diverse body of recalcitrant evidence), but no clear indication how to solve them. Few are willing to give up the established theory until there is at least the outline of a replacement, and many are carrying on business as usual. Those who are working on the problem have some understanding of what would count as a solution, but do not yet know what it is. This does not mean that any way forward is a step in the dark. The researchers will be aware that some attempts to resolve the problems have proved completely unsuccessful, and that others have proved fruitful, even though they have not yet resolved the basic problem. There is a direction to their work, even though there is no clearly defined end for which they are seeking means. Only when the problem is eventually solved – perhaps by a fundamentally new paradigm, or perhaps by a major modification to the old – will it become possible to indicate what would have been the most efficient means of achieving it.[23] Instrumental reasoning will only become possible when it is too late for it to be of any use.[24] It is somewhat paradoxical that a form of social life which, with some justice, prides itself on its innovation and creativity, has given priority to a concept of rationality which has no place for either.

We also need to keep in mind the truth in the conservative dictum that the end result of any process of social change is almost always different from the expectations and intentions of even the best informed protagonists. This does not mean, as conservatives have argued, that we should (or could) abstain from directing our energies towards social change. It simply means that we must plan for the future in the knowledge that the future will not be as we plan. The practice of social change must therefore be experimental and self-reflective, and open-ended and flexible in its conception of itself and the ends towards which it is directed. It must conceive itself, not just as the means to some future end, but as prefiguring that end in its own mode of activity. It will have a direction, but not a goal.

There are many possible directions of social change. I want to consider two of these which have a special pertinence to the argument of this book. The critiques of modernity which underlie these movements are very different; however, they both represent aspirations which cannot be realised without fundamental changes in the structure of modern social life.

The first of these is communism in the terms in which this was conceived by Marx, as the fulfilment of the goals of the working-class movement. The relationship implied here between the particular interests of members of a class and the goal ascribed to the class as a whole, does not (and did not) exist in any immediate sense. As Marx recognised, the initial impetus for workers to organise against capital comes from very mundane sources of dissatisfaction: poor working conditions, low wages, job insecurity and the like. At this point, the motivation of workers who form or join trade unions is not different from that of capitalists who combine in order to limit competition and raise prices. For both, the association is a means to individual ends. However, Marx suggested that workers differ from capitalists in that they would come to conceive of the association with each other as more important than the ends which had originally brought them together.

> If the first aim of resistance was merely the maintenance of wages, combinations, at first isolated, constitute themselves into groups as the capitalists in their turn unite for the purpose of repression, and in the face of always united capital, the maintenance of the association becomes more necessary to them than that of wages. This is so true that English economists are amazed to see the workers sacrifice a good part of their wages in favour of associations, which, in the eyes of the economists, are established solely in favour of wages.[25]

Marx imagined that the individual worker would in the various struggles in which he participated, come to identify his lot with that of fellow workers, not just in his own factory, but in other factories, localities and industries. He would begin to take pleasure in the successes of those others, even when they involve sacrifices on his part; more, he would begin to take pleasure in those activities which expressed and developed this shared identity. The association which had been a means would become an end. Communism, as Marx conceived it, was the ideal end point of this process.

Clearly there is much that has proved unrealistic in this scenario. Still, it illustrates one way in which individuals may come to develop new values through their own activity; values which are freely formed and freely accepted as part of a new conception of individual identity and well-being. For Marx, the proletariat was the 'universal class'. In part, this was because he believed – wrongly – that the oppression of the proletariat epitomised all human oppression, and consequently that the emancipation of the proletariat would mean human emancipation.[26] But it was also because he thought that the way of life of the proletariat, and especially collective work in the capitalist factory and collective struggle against the capitalist system, would mean that they would come to experience the 'brotherhood of man' in their individual feelings and aspirations. It would be 'no mere phrase but a fact of life'.[27] The class-conscious proletarian would no longer identify himself as an isolated individual, but as a member of his class. He would no longer conceive of the trade union merely as a means to further his own individual ends, he would not be tempted to be a free-rider on the struggles of his fellows, nor would he leave those struggles in order to achieve success for himself (perhaps by attempting to join the ranks of the bourgeoisie). His conception of his own well-being would be tied up with his contribution to the progress of his class towards emancipation.

Marx's ideal proletarian would be the subject of a new conception of morality. Its difference from bourgeois morality would reside in part in its content: it would value co-operation over competition, it would not accept or celebrate selfishness and it would not be concerned to respect private property. But, as Anthony Skillen has argued, of more significance would be that its *form* was to be different: it would not be experienced by the individual as an externally imposed duty, but as flowing from his own aspirations. As Skillen puts it, the experience of morality would be,

> not of a higher power, an authoritative voice, controlling our inclinations, but rather of the relations among our activities (dispositions, impulses, feelings, passions, values) as they are formed and expressed by our ways of life. . . . And 'socialist restraint' would be . . . the preponderance of communal, productive, loving, and communicative activities and motives over invidiously divisive (including moralistic) activities and motives.[28]

This form of morality would exist (and perhaps only exist) when each worker comes to conceive of his class membership as a fundamental component in his conception of himself, and recognises others as sharing that identity. It is then that he has reason to do what he ought to do. He will take part in the struggle, not because he thinks he will receive the benefits of a future victory, but because taking part in the struggle has itself become a benefit. Of course, the idea of a future victory remains important: the thought that others in the future will receive the fruits of his present activity is itself an aspect of the benefit he receives. The goal is necessary to give point to the activity; but is also present in it. To participate in the struggle is both to contribute to that goal and to participate in it.

The final emancipation of the proletariat as a class is only possible through the elimination of the capital/labour relationship. Marx also believed that it required the elimination of market relations. Not only would workers cease to be subject to the domination of capital, but everyone would cease to be subject to the laws of commodity exchange. Marx did not leave many hints of how a non-market communist society might work, and few of those which he did leave survive serious questioning in the light of twentieth century history. But if some conceptions of a communist alternative (e.g. state socialism) have been definitively closed off, it has become more – not less – important to develop new ones, not as blueprints for an ideal society, but as contributions to the movement towards less imperfect forms of social life. The goal of communism must be defined and redefined in the process of working towards it.

There is no reason to follow Marx in supposing that members of the working class have a special and exclusive bent towards a collective form of self-identification, and that the working class is the privileged agent of social change. Still, Marx's notion of class-consciousness contains ideas of the first importance. It suggests a way in which individuals might move from particular interests and local identifications towards a more global conception of individual identity. While it may be that the universal consciousness posited by Marx is a chimera, it is necessary that individuals make some progress towards a social conception of their identity, if social struggle towards an alternative form of society is to be either effective or worthwhile. If it is to be effective, it will be because individuals have been willing to subordinate those goods they are able to achieve as individuals to goods which they are only able to achieve through collective action. They must find their own fulfilment in participating in that action. If it is to be worthwhile, social change must be directed towards a form of society whose members confirm in their own identity the interdependent and co-operative nature of social life. Only when there is no hiatus between individual identity and social existence, will the demands of society cease to be alien to the individual, and a rational practice of morality be possible. More to the point, only then will the individual be able to live a satisfying and fulfilling life. Insofar as this goal is present in the activity designed to bring it about, individuals will be able to participate in that life as they attempt to achieve it.

The second direction of social change which I wish to consider is associated with feminism. I argued in Chapter 3 that the rationalised public world of market capitalism and bureaucratic administration presupposes a sphere of private life, that the relationship between public and private is one of exclusion, subordination and opposition, and that the distinction between masculine and feminine forms of identity is in large part constructed in terms of this structure. An assertion of the claims of women against this structure may take one of three forms. It may simply be the demand for a place for women in a more or less unchanged public world; or it may involve the assertion of the subordinated private values against those constructed in the public sphere; or finally, it may involve the demand for a fundamental reconstitution of the distinction. There is no doubt that the first two claims have been and will continue to be important; nevertheless, it is clear that they involve a less fundamental critique of modernity than the last.

It is difficult to conceive of any society – and certainly not a desirable one – which does not recognise some form of the distinction between public and private. There will always be a place for intimacy, shared confidences, special commitments and even special deceptions, which should be of no concern to the wider public world. But there is no reason why these distinctions should not be ones of gradation, emphasis and difference, rather than exclusion, subordination and opposition. Only when the public sphere has become equally available to all, and what is private has become merely a component – though an important one – of everyone's social life, will participants in both realms be in a position to relate to each other from a standpoint of equality. Only when the distinction between public and private has ceased to be one of opposition – with, for example, the self-interested individualism required by public life contrasted with the other-directed relational existence characteristic of the family – will it be possible for the two spheres to be properly continuous with each other. Only when domestic life has become a sphere of equality, will it allow for the unconcealed expression of self-directed emotions within it; only when public life has become more communal, will it encourage, not discourage, other-directed behaviour.

These are not small changes. We cannot now know what form of the public/private distinction is compatible both with egalitarian relations between men and women, and with the requirements that men, women and children have for nurture and support. Nor can we know what changes in public life are necessary to allow for men and women to participate equally, both in it and in family life. We do not know what differences must always remain in the aspirations and ways of life appropriate to men and women. Criticism of the existing form of the distinction between public and private does not of itself define an alternative. It indicates a direction for change, not a clearly defined goal. The future is – and should remain – a matter for experiment, negotiation and aspiration.

It is perhaps no accident that the dominant public form of reason – instrumental reason – has little place for this kind of open-ended movement, but requires that our goals be clearly defined before we move towards them. Reason has, as feminist critics such as Genevieve Lloyd have argued,[29] always defined itself by exclusion of those aspects of social life associated with the female. Reason in the modern world is an aspect of public life; its excluded other is the realm of the emotional, the particular and the expressive – the characteristics associated with private life and ascribed to femininity. Given this, it is not surprising that some aspects of the feminist critique have been criticised or celebrated as non-rational, insofar as they have involved the assertion of values and ways of life which have been excluded by the dominant conceptions of reason. Instrumental reason has no place for the expressive and relational activity essential for caring; impartial reason does not allow for acts of love which are of their nature particular. However, to criticise modern conceptions of reason in this way is not identical with an assertion of the non-rational. This would only be the case if we accepted the claims of modern reason to be identical with rationality itself. From a more critical and historically informed perspective, it is part of the process of constructing a more adequate conception of rationality. Indeed, as Lloyd suggests:

> Such criticisms of ideals of Reason can in fact be seen as continuous with a very old strand in the Western philosophical tradition; it has been centrally concerned with bringing to reflective awareness the deeper structures of inherited ideals of Reason.[30]

At this point, the feminist critique of the maleness of reason comes together with the criticisms of modern rationality which have been made in this book. The inadequacy of modern conceptions of reason emerge, not just from the perspective of what they exclude, but in their own terms. As we have seen, instrumental reason promises the efficient attainment of one's goals, but in central cases, guarantees failure. Juridical reason – reason as formal consistency – promises justice, but gives no weight to the special claims of particularity – of friends and family. Cognitive reason aims at objective truth, but delivers utility. It is because of its own claims for itself that we are able, indeed have no alternative, but to go beyond the bounds of modern reason.

Just as every society constructs its own form of morality, so too every society constructs its appropriate conceptions of reason. What is especially characteristic – perhaps uniquely so – of modernity is that reason and morality come apart. We do not have reason to act as morality requires; nor do we have reason to consider the claims of morality to be true. So much the worse for morality, many have concluded. Others, with equal validity, have come down on the side of morality against the claims of reason. A better alternative is to reject both. We have good reason to go beyond modern conceptions of reason, and there are moral grounds for going beyond modern conceptions of morality. But this requires that we go beyond modernity itself.

The failure of modernity to make good its own promises provides us with some reason to go beyond it. But a deeper reason is provided by the unsatisfying and imperilled nature of our own existence. In the context of the modern world, the philosopher's traditional search for self-knowledge has turned into an enterprise of self-making. There is undoubtedly something exciting in this enterprise. However, as we saw with Nietzsche, it is as likely to induce megalomania or disintegration as the repose admired or sought by philosophers. But these are not the only alternatives. If self-identity requires that we establish principles of coherence and integrity with which we can identify, we must recognise that these will not be achieved along the traditional philosophical paths of scholarship, enquiry and reflection. If the threat to our identity comes from a certain form of social existence, then identity requires social change; if the threat arises from a lack of reciprocal recognition, then identity requires the formation of communities which provide that recognition. Nietzsche was right to see the self as an achievement; but he was tragically wrong to think that it could be the achievement of the self alone.

There can be no guarantee that success in this enterprise is possible, let alone likely. But there is reason to hope that if it were possible, it would provide some of the conditions necessary for a practice of morality. Morality requires a social identity: only then will the moral subject have reason to do what is morally required. But a social identity will also provide something of the wider framework necessary for a stronger conception of one's own independent existence. We will make sense of what we are doing, even of our own existence, because of its place in a larger community. The daunting, indeed impossible, task of constructing and justifying one's own existence by oneself can be recognised for the unsustainable delusion that it is. And once we escape from the hegemony of instrumental reason, we can entertain the hope that to begin the task of building such a community is a way – and the only way – of participating in it.

NOTES

1 THE MARKET AND ITS MORALITIES: UTILITARIANISM, KANTIANISM AND THE LOSS OF VIRTUE

1 Denis Diderot, *Rameau's Nephew*, in *Rameau's Nephew and D'Alembert's Dream*, translated by Leonard Tancock, Harmondsworth, Penguin Books, 1981, p. 83.

2 Immanuel Kant, *Groundwork of the Metaphysic of Morals*, translated by H. J. Paton, New York, Harper & Row, 1964, preface, p. 56.

3 Adam Smith, *An Inquiry into the Nature and Causes of the Wealth of Nations*, edited by R. H. Campbell and A. S. Skinner, Oxford, Clarendon Press, 1976, vol. I, book I, ch. ii, pp. 26–7.

4 Smith uses the phrase 'invisible hand' in a slightly different connection in *The Wealth of Nations*, vol. I, book IV, ch. ii, p. 456.

> By preferring the support of domestic to that of foreign industry, he intends only his own security; and in directing that industry in such a manner as its produce may be of the greatest value, he intends only his own gain, and he is in this, as in many other cases, led by an invisible hand to promote an end which was no part of his intention.

The theorem about private interests and public benefits is stated particularly clearly in the passage quoted at the beginning of this section, without however the phrase 'invisible hand' being used. The invisible hand is a particular instance of the 'law of unintended consequences' which played a key role in eighteenth century social thought. See Albert O. Hirschman, *The Passions and the Interests: Political Arguments for Capitalism before Its Triumph*, Princeton, Princeton University Press, 1977; and Ronald L. Meek, *Social Science and the Ignoble Savage*, Cambridge, Cambridge University Press, 1976.

5 Jeremy Bentham, *Bentham's Political Thought*, edited by Bhikhu Parekh, London, Croom Helm, 1973, p. 123.

6 See the discussion of the rise of social science in *Social Science and the Ignoble Savage*, op. cit.

7 See the passage from Adam Smith which appears as an epigraph to this section.

8 See J. G. A. Pocock, *The Machiavellian Moment: Florentine Political*

Thought and the Atlantic Republican Tradition, Princeton and London, Princeton University Press, 1975, especially chs 13 and 14.

9 Bernard Mandeville, *The Fable of the Bees*, edited by Phillip Harth, Harmondsworth, Penguin Books, 1970, especially 'The Grumbling Hive'.

10 G. W. F. Hegel, *The Phenomenology of Spirit*, translated by A. V. Miller, Oxford, Oxford University Press, 1979, pp. 228–35. This section is entitled 'Virtue and the Way of the World'.

11 See David Hume, *A Treatise of Human Nature*, edited by L. A. Selby-Bigge, 2nd edition, revised by P. H. Nidditch, Oxford, Clarendon Press, 1983, book III, part II, section (ii), p. 492. See also the discussion in Genevieve Lloyd, 'Public Reason and Private Passion', *Politics*, 1983, vol. 18, pp. 27–37, and in *The Man of Reason*, London, Methuen, 1984, pp. 54–6. However, Hume had certainly rejected this view by the time of the *Enquiry Concerning the Principles of Morals*. See *Enquiries Concerning the Human Understanding and Concerning the Principles of Morals*, edited by L. A. Selby-Bigge, 3rd edition, revised by P. H. Nidditch, Oxford, Clarendon Press, 1988; see section V, part II, pp. 218–19 and also the discussion of the 'free-rider' (not using that term) in section IX, part II, pp. 282–3.

12 See G. W. F. Hegel, *The Philosophy of Right*, Oxford, Clarendon Press, 1965, third part, section 258, pp. 155–7, and section 323, pp. 209–10.

13 The standard modern treatment of the free-rider is Mancur Olson, *The Logic of Collective Action*, Cambridge, Mass., Harvard University Press, especially ch. 2.

14 See Hobbes, *Leviathan*, edited by Michael Oakeshott, Oxford, Blackwell, n.d., part I, ch. 14. The contemporary free-rider is a descendent of Hobbes' 'fool'.

15 See, for example, J. J. C. Smart, 'An Outline of a System of Utilitarian Ethics', in J. J. C. Smart and Bernard Williams (eds), *Utilitarianism: For and Against*, Cambridge, Cambridge University Press, 1983. This also seems to have been Hume's position in his later writings, though one should be wary of attributing to Hume the kind of systematic utilitarian position that was developed later. See *An Enquiry Concerning the Principles of Morals*, section IX, pp. 268–84.

16 See *The Wealth of Nations* op. cit., vol. II. book v, especially pp. 781–4; and Adam Ferguson, *An Essay on the History of Civil Society*, edited by Duncan Forbes, Edinburgh, Edinburgh University Press, 1966, part VI, especially section III, pp. 248–60. See also the discussion in Michael Ignatieff, *The Needs of Strangers*, London, Chatto & Windus/The Hogarth Press, 1984, ch. 4.

17 Derek Parfit has argued for the instrumental rationality of altruism on the basis that very small goods (or bads) are still goods (or bads). But the point remains that they are smaller than big ones. See Derek Parfit, 'Prudence, Morality and the Prisoner's Dilemma', in Jon Elster (ed.), *Rational Choice*, Oxford, Blackwell, 1986.

18 The major texts are the *Nicomachean Ethics*, translated by J. A. K. Thomson and revised by Hugh Tredennick, Harmondsworth, Penguin Books, 1976; and *The Politics*, translated by T. A. Sinclair, Harmondsworth, Penguin Books, 1969.

19 See the account in *The Machiavellian Moment*, op. cit., chs 13–14.
20 *The Fable of the Bees*, op. cit., 'The Grumbling Hive', p. 76.
21 ibid., 'An Enquiry into the Origin of Moral Virtue', p. 82.
22 In later additions to *The Fable of the Bees*, Mandeville distinguished between 'self-love' and 'self-liking', where self-love aims at self-preservation, while self-liking strives to increase our value in the eyes of others. On this later account, pride is not an original passion, but an effect of self-liking. See *The Fable of the Bees*, vol. II, edited by F. B. Kaye, Oxford, Clarendon Press, 1924, pp. 129–30. Rousseau's well known distinction between *amour de soi* and *amour propre* is pretty clearly derived from Mandeville. See Jean Jacques Rousseau, 'A Discourse on the Origin of Inequality', in *The Social Contract and Discourses*, London, J. M. Dent & Sons Ltd, 1975, p. 66 footnote, and the reference to Mandeville on p. 67.
23 *The Fable of the Bees*, 'An Enquiry into the Origin of Moral Virtue', op. cit., p. 87–8.
24 See the scathing and effective critique of 'government house utilitarianism', in Bernard Williams, *Ethics and the Limits of Philosophy*, London, Fontana Press/Collins, 1985, pp. 107–10.
25 Cp. Nietzsche:

> To breed an animal *with the right to make promises* – is not this the paradoxical task that nature has set itself in the case of man? Is this not the real problem concerning man?

'On the Genealogy of Morals', in *On the Genealogy of Morals; Ecce Homo*, edited by Walter Kaufmann, New York, Vintage Books, 1969, second essay, section 1, p. 57.
26 *Groundwork of the Metaphysic of Morals*, op. cit., ch. II, p. 88.
27 ibid., pp. 91–2.
28 See, for example, ibid., pp. 86–8 and ch. III, pp. 115–16.
29 See the discussion in Emile Benveniste, *Problems in General Linguistics*, Miami, University of Miami Press, 1971, ch. 28, 'Civilization: A Contribution to the History of the Word'. See also Sheldon Rothblatt, *Tradition and Change in English Liberal Education*, London, Faber & Faber, 1976, ch. 2; and Raymond Williams, *Keywords*, Glasgow, Fontana/Croom Helm, 1979, entry under 'Civilization'.
30 See *Social Science and the Ignoble Savage*, op. cit.
31 See Norbert Elias, *The Civilising Process: The History of Manners*, translated by Edmund Jephcott, Oxford, Blackwell, 1983, especially ch. 1, 'On the Sociogenesis of the Concepts "Civilization" and "Culture"'.
32 See 'A Discourse on the Origins of Inequality', op. cit., especially The First Part.
33 See, for example, 'Idea for a Universal History with a Cosmopolitan Purpose', in *Kant's Political Writings*, edited by Hans Reiss, Cambridge, Cambridge University Press, 1977.

2 CAPITALISM: THE POWER OF REASON

1 Karl Marx, Letters from *Deutsch-Französische Jahrbücher*, 1844, in Karl Marx and Friedrich Engels, *Collected Works*, vol. 3, London, Lawrence & Wishart, 1975, p. 143.

2 Fredric Jameson, 'Postmodernism, or the Cultural Logic of Late Capitalism', *New Left Review*, July/August 1984, no. 146, pp. 53–92, quoted extract on p. 86.

3 Cp. Marshall Berman, *All That is Solid Melts into Air: The Experience of Modernity*, London, Verso, 1983; see especially introduction, and the comments on Weber, pp. 27–8.

4 Marx argued that to conceive capitalism just as a market (a 'sphere of exchange' in his terminology) precluded one from explaining the phenomenon of profit. See *Capital*, vol. I, Harmondsworth, Penguin Books, 1976, especially chs 4–6.

5 Marx and Engels, *The Communist Manifesto*, in Marx and Engels, *Collected Works*, op. cit., vol. 6, 1976, p. 489.

6 Marx provides the basic argument for this in *Capital*, op. cit., vol. I, ch. 6, and provides a detailed account of the way in which the surplus is produced and appropriated in later chapters.

7 There is now a large body of literature which is concerned to define a concept of exploitation which does not depend, as Marx's own account depended, on the labour theory of value. Most of it takes as its starting point the unequal bargaining position of worker and capitalist in the labour market. See John Roemer, *A General Theory of Exploitation and Class*, Cambridge, Mass., Harvard University Press, 1982, and Jon Elster, *Making Sense of Marx*, Cambridge, Cambridge University Press, and Paris, Editions de la Maison des Sciences de l'Homme, 1985, part I, ch. 4.

8 Thus, Marx:

> Conceptually, *competition* is nothing but the *inner nature of capital*, its essential character, manifested and realised as the reciprocal action of many capitals on each other; immanent tendency realised as external necessity.

Economic Manuscripts of 1857–58 [more commonly known as the *Grundrisse*], in Marx and Engels, *Collected Works*, op. cit., vol. 28, 1986, p. 341.

9 See *Capital*, op. cit., vol. I, chs 12–15.

10 Michel Foucault, 'Two Lectures', in *Power/Knowledge*, edited by Colin Gordon, New York, Pantheon, 1980, pp. 104–5.

11 *The Communist Manifesto*, op. cit., p. 487.

12 *All That is Solid Melts into Air*, op. cit., p. 15.

13 Thomas Hobbes, *Leviathan*, edited by Michael Oakeshott, Oxford, Basil Blackwell, n.d., part 1, ch. 11, p. 64.

14 See John Rawls, *A Theory of Justice*, Cambridge, Mass., Harvard University Press, 1971, ch. I, section 5, especially his claim on p. 27 that 'utilitarianism does not take seriously the distinction between persons'.

15 For a much more detailed case against the conception of the subject implicit in utilitarianism, see Charles Taylor, *Human Agency and Language: Philosophical Papers I*, Cambridge, Cambridge University Press, 1985, essay 1, 'What is Human Agency?'

16 Easily the best discussion of changes in the capitalist labour process in the twentieth century is Harry Braverman, *Labour and Monopoly Capital*, New York and London, Monthly Review Press, 1974.

17 See *Capital*, op. cit., vol. I, ch. 6, p. 272.

18 According to G. A. Cohen's interpretation of Marx, 'history is, fundamentally, the growth of human productive power, and forms of society rise and fall according as they enable or impede that growth'. See Cohen, *Karl Marx's Theory of History: A Defence*, Oxford, Clarendon Press, 1978, p. x.

19 Quoted in Caroline Tisdall and Angelo Bozzolla, *Futurism*, London, Thames & Hudson, 1977, p. 7.

20 In the following discussion, I largely (though not completely) ignore Weber's categories of 'formal rationality' and 'substantive rationality'. Given more space, I would argue that the former is fatally ambiguous between a certain form of instrumental rationality and (what I call here) juridical rationality, and that the second is best understood as a form of instrumental reason. For more detailed accounts of Weber on rationality and rationalisation, see Donald N. Levine, 'Rationality and Freedom, Weber and Beyond', *Sociological Inquiry*, 1981, 51, pp. 5–25, and Rogers Brubaker, *The Limits of Rationality*, London, George Allen & Unwin, 1984.

21 See, for example, the editorial introduction to Jon Elster (ed.), *Rational Choice*, Oxford, Basil Blackwell, 1986.

22 Max Weber, *Economy and Society*, edited by Guenther Roth and Claus Wittich, Berkeley, University of California Press, 1978, vol. I, p. 26:

> Action is instrumentally rational when the end, the means, and the secondary result are all rationally taken into account and weighed. This involves rational consideration of alternative means to the end, of the relation of the end to secondary consequences, and finally of the relative importance of different possible ends.

23 ibid., p. 93.

24 ibid., pp. 107–9 and 150–3.

25 Weber, 'Author's Introduction' to Max Weber, *The Protestant Ethic and the Spirit of Capitalism*, London, George Allen & Unwin, 1984, p. 17.

26 See, for example, Herbert Marcuse, 'Industrialisation and Capitalism in the Work of Max Weber', in *Negations*, translated by J. J. Shapiro, Harmondsworth, Penguin Books, 1968.

27 It is not, for example, mentioned in the works by Levine and Brubacker, op. cit., note 20. See, however, the discussion in Gorän Therborn, *What the Ruling Class Does when It Rules*, London, New Left Books, 1978, pp. 51–6. Therborn has a particularly useful discussion of the tensions between the two forms of reason in the modern state.

28 See Weber, *Economy and Society*, op. cit., vol. II, pp. 665–7. Here and elsewhere I avoid the term 'formal rationality'. See note 20 above.

29 See, for example, ibid., vol. I, p. 217:

> [E]very body of law consists essentially in a consistent system of abstract rules which have normally been intentionally established. Furthermore, administration of law is held to consist in the application of these rules to particular cases.

30 ibid., vol. II, pp. 884–6.

31 Goethe, *Faust*, Part One, translated by Philip Wayne, Harmondsworth, Penguin Books, 1949, p. 87.

32 See *Leviathan*, op. cit., part I, chs 10–11.
33 As Aristotle argued; see *Nicomachean Ethics*. translated by J. A. K. Thompson and revised by Hugh Tredennick, Harmondsworth, Penguin Books, 1976, ch. 1, section 1.
34 See *Capital*, op. cit., vol. I, especially chs 13–15.
35 Karl Popper's argument against the possibility of historical prediction that we cannot predict the future growth of knowledge has special force in the modern world where social change has come to depend crucially on the results of scientific development. See Karl Popper, *The Poverty of Historicism*, London, Routlege & Kegan Paul, 1960, preface to 2nd edition, pp. v–vii.

3 THE PRIVATE SPHERE: VIRTUE REGAINED?

1 From the cover of Laurie Anderson's record *Big Science*, NY, Warner Bros Records Inc, 1982.
2 I ignore here other forms of this distinction to be found in the modern world. The most important of these is the distinction between the state and its ancillary institutions, and the rest of society. For a discussion of the relationship between the two forms of the distinction, see Carole Pateman, 'Feminist Critiques of the Public/Private Dichotomy', in S. I. Benn and G. F. Gaus (eds), *Public and Private in Social Life*, London, Croom Helm, 1983. I have attempted to provide a general characterisation of the public/private distinction in Ross Poole, 'Public Spheres', in Helen Wilson (ed.), *Australian Communications and the Public Sphere*, Melbourne, Macmillan, 1989.
3 See, for example, the discussion of Hume in Christine Battersby, 'An Enquiry Concerning the Humean Woman', *Philosophy*, 1981, vol. 56, pp. 303–12.
4 See the discussion in Michèle Barrett, 'Marxist-Feminism and the Work of Karl Marx', in Betty Matthews (ed.), *Marx: A Hundred Years On*, London, Lawrence & Wishart, 1983, especially section III, pp. 210–14.
5 Max Weber, *The Protestant Ethic and the Spirit of Capitalism*, London, George Allen & Unwin, 1976, pp. 21–2.
6 Weber, *Economy and Society*, Berkeley, University of California Press, 1978, vol. 2, ch. XI, p. 975; see also p. 957. This chapter is also available in *From Max Weber*, edited by H. H. Gerth and C. Wright Mills, London, Routledge & Kegan Paul, 1977, see pp. 215–16 and p. 197.
7 See Aristotle, *Nicomachean Ethics*, Harmondsworth, Penguin Books, 1983, Books Eight and Nine. See also the discussion in Alasdair MacIntyre, *After Virtue*, 2nd edition, Notre Dame, University of Notre Dame Press, 1984, pp. 155–9.
8 See the discussion of Locke in Teresa Brennan and Carole Pateman, '"Mere Auxiliaries to the Commonwealth": Women and the Origins of Liberalism', *Political Studies*, 1979, 27, pp. 183–200. It is, however, a central argument of Pateman's later work, *The Sexual Contract*, Cambridge, Polity, 1988, especially ch. 2, that the contractual account

which displaced *traditional* patriarchal theory did *not* displace patriarchal theory as such, but was (and is) the characteristically modern form of it.

9 See the account in Susan Moller Okin, 'Women and the Rise of the Sentimental Family', *Philosophy and Public Affairs*, 1982, vol. 11, pp. 65–88.

10 Virginia Woolf, *A Room of One's Own*, London, Collins, 1987, p. 70.

11 Carol Gilligan, *In a Different Voice*, Cambridge, Mass. and London, Harvard University Press, 1982, p. 1.

12 See Michael Stocker's discussion of friendship in 'The Schizophrenia of Modern Ethical Theories', *Journal of Philosophy*, 1976, vol. 72, pp. 453–66, especially pp. 459–60. See also Stocker, 'Values and Purposes: The Limits of Teleology and the Ends of Friendship', *Journal of Philosophy*, 1981, vol. 78, pp. 747–65.

13 See 'The Schizophrenia of Modern Ethical Theories', op. cit., especially p. 462; see also Lawrence A. Blum, *Friendship, Altruism, and Morality*, London, Routledge & Kegan Paul, 1980.

14 Probably *In a Different Voice*, op. cit., is mostly reponsible for the idea that a morality of care is characteristic of women, though Gilligan herself is wary of claiming more than a rough empirical correlation between her 'different voice' and the moral beliefs of actual women. Given the slender statistical basis for her work, and her lack of attention to the different social environments in which moral development takes place, her caution is well justified. For a survey of the literature and some critical remarks, see Joan C. Tronto, 'Beyond Gender Difference to a Theory of Care', *Signs*, 1986–7, vol. 12, pp. 644–63.

15 For discussions and references, see Carole Pateman, '"The Disorder of Women": Women, Love, and the Sense of Justice', *Ethics*, 1980, vol. 91, pp. 20–34; see also Genevieve Lloyd, 'Public Reason and Private Passion', *Politics*, 1983, vol. 18, pp. 27–37; 'Rousseau on Reason, Nature and Women', *Metaphilosophy*, vol. 14, 1983, pp. 308–26; and *The Man of Reason*, London, Methuen, 1984, ch. V.

16 For Kant, for example, virtue is expressed by obedience to the moral law solely out of respect for it without any influence by other motives. It receives some attention in the *Groundwork of the Metaphysic of Morals*, translated by H. J. Paton, New York, Harper Torchbook, 1964, see especially, ch. II, pp. 93–4; and a full treatment in part II of *The Metaphysic of Morals* entitled *The Doctrine of Virtue*, translated by Mary J. Gregor, Philadelphia, University of Pennsylvania Press, 1964. For John Rawls, 'The virtues ... are sentiments and habitual attitudes leading us to act on certain principles of right.' See *A Theory of Justice*, Cambridge, Mass., Harvard University Press, 1972, p. 437.

17 The canonical text is *Nicomachean Ethics*. A conception of morality centring around the virtues has been strongly argued for over the past twenty or thirty years by Philippa Foot. See the essays collected in *Virtues and Vices and Other Essays in Moral Philosophy*, Oxford, Basil Blackwell, 1981. Unfortunately, Foot writes with almost complete disregard for the social context involved in (if not necessary for) a virtue ethic. *After Virtue*, op. cit., shows a much greater awareness of this issue. This book provides a wide ranging and insightful if

tendentious survey of the virtue tradition from Homer to the present. I take up some of MacIntyre's account in ch. 7.

18 See *Nicomachean Ethics*, op. cit., book one, ch. iii, pp. 64–5.

19 See Nancy Chodorow, *The Reproduction of Mothering*, Berkeley, University of California Press, 1979.

20 See Quentin Skinner, *Machiavelli*, Oxford, Oxford University Press, 1981, pp. 24–6.

21 See J. G. A. Pocock, *The Machiavellian Moment*, Princeton and London, Princeton University Press, 1975, chs 13 and 14.

4 LIBERALISM AND NIHILISM

1 Max Weber, 'Science as a Vocation', in *From Max Weber*, edited by H. H. Gerth and C. Wright Mills, London, Routledge & Kegan Paul, 1977, p. 155.

2 See Max Weber, 'The Social Psychology of World Religions', in ibid., p. 293. The terms are mine, not Weber's.

3 'Science as a Vocation', op. cit., p. 142.

4 J. L. Mackie, *Ethics: Inventing Right and Wrong*, Harmondsworth, Penguin Books, 1977, pp. 38–42.

5 See, however, the articles in Geoffrey Sayre-McCord (ed.), *Essays on Moral Realism*, Ithaca and London, Cornell University Press, 1988.

6 See 'Science as a Vocation', op. cit., pp. 150–1. But see also 'The Social Psychology of World Religions', op. cit., p. 293, where Weber notes that the two 'types of rationalism are very different in spite of the fact that they ultimately belong together'.

7 See, for example, the 'Introduction' to Jon Elster (ed.), *Rational Choice*, Oxford, Blackwell, 1986, p. 1.

8 'Science as a Vocation', op. cit., p. 144.

9 Nietzsche, *Beyond Good and Evil*, translated by R. J. Hollingdale, Harmondsworth, Penguin Books, 1983, para. 207.

10 Nietszche, *The Will to Power*, translated by Walter Kaufmann and R. J. Hollingdale, New York, Vintage Books, 1968, book one, I, para. 2, p. 9.

11 ibid., para. 5, p. 10.

12 John Rawls, 'Fairness to Goodness', *Philosophical Review*, 1975, vol. 8, pp. 536–54, quoted extract on p. 537.

13 This is more or less the account of 'primary goods' given in John Rawls, *A Theory of Justice*, Cambridge, Mass., Harvard University Press, 1971. Rawls provides a slightly different account in his later writings.

14 Alan Gewirth, *Reason and Morality*, Chicago and London, Chicago University Press, 1978, p. 48. For recent discussions of Gewirth's argument, see Bernard Williams, *Ethics and the Limits of Philosophy*, London, Fontana, 1985, ch. 4, pp. 54–64, and Alasdair MacIntyre, *After Virtue*, 2nd Edition, Notre Dame, University of Notre Dame Press, 1984, pp. 66–9.

15 *Reason and Morality*, op. cit., p. 105.

16 ibid., p. 105, p. x.

17 ibid., pp. 89–90.

18 See *A Theory of Justice*, op. cit. Rawls has published a number of articles since then modifying and defending his theory. The most important of these are 'Fairness to Goodness' (see note 12); 'The Basic Structure as Subject', in *Values and Morals*, edited by A. I. Goldman and Jaegwon Kim, Dordrecht, Reidel, 1978; 'A Well-Ordered Society' in *Philosophy, Politics and Society*, P. Laslett and J. Fishkin, 5th Series, Oxford, Oxford University Press, 1979; 'Kantian Constructivism in Moral Theory', *Journal of Philosophy*, 1979, vol. 77, pp. 515–72; 'Social Unity and Primary Goods', in *Utilitarianism and Beyond*, edited by Amartya Sen and Bernard Williams, Cambridge and Paris, Cambridge University Press and Editions de la Maison des Sciences de l'Homme, 1982; 'Justice as Fairness: Political not Metaphysical', *Philosophy and Public Affairs*, 1985, vol. 14, pp. 239–51; and 'The Priority of Right and Ideas of the Good', *Philosophy and Public Affairs*, 1988, vol. 17, pp. 251–76.

19 See *A Theory of Justice*, op. cit., p. 143. 'The concept of rationality invoked here, with the exception of one essential feature, is the standard one familiar in economic theory.' The 'exception' is the assumption that 'a rational individual does not suffer from envy'.

20 ibid., p. 62.

21 ibid., p. 60. This is Rawls' initial formulation of the two principles. He makes various modifications, both later in the book and in subsequent writings, but none of these effect the points I make here. See *A Theory of Justice*, pp. 302–3 for the final version there, and 'Justice as Fairness: Political not Metaphysical', op. cit., pp. 227–8 for the final version to date.

22 See *Reason and Morality*, op. cit., p. 108; also pp. 19–20.

23 *A Theory of Justice*, op. cit., pp. 252–3; see also p. 574.

24 On the affinities between Rawls and Hegel, see Carole Pateman, *The Problem of Political Obligation*, Chichester, John Wiley & Sons, 1979, pp. 111–12.

25 'Justice as Fairness: Political not Metaphysical', op. cit., pp. 225–6 and p. 231.

26 On the 'reflective equilibrium', see *A Theory of Justice*, op. cit., pp. 17–22 and 46–53; see also 'Justice as Fairness: Political not Metaphysical', op. cit., especially pp. 226–31.

27 'Kantian Constructivism in Moral Theory', op. cit., p. 547.

28 Jürgen Habermas, 'What is Universal Pragmatics?', *Communication and the Evolution of Society*, translated by Thomas McCarthy, London, Heinemann, 1979, p. 3.

29 Charles Baudelaire, *Fusées*, section 77, *The Essence of Laughter and Other Essays, Journals and Letters*, edited by Peter Quennell, New York, Meridian Books, 1956, p. 194.

30 Jürgen Habermas, *Autonomy and Solidarity: Interviews*, edited by Peter Dews, London, Verso, 1986, pp. 170–1.

31 ibid., p. 160.

32 ibid., p. 174.

33 Habermas has developed his theory in a number of writings. In what follows I have mostly drawn on *Communication and the Evolution of*

Society, op. cit., and *The Theory of Communicative Action; vol. I: Reason and the Rationalisation of Society*, translated by Thomas McCarthy, Boston, Beacon Press, 1984.

34 See Herbert Marcuse, 'Technology and Science as Ideology', in Jürgen Habermas, *Towards a Rational Society*, translated by Jeremy J. Shapiro, Boston, Beacon Press, 1970.

35 See 'Labour and Interaction: Remarks on Hegel's Jena *Philosophy of Mind*', in *Theory and Practice*, translated by John Viertel, London, Heinemann, 1977.

36 '[S]ocial actions can be distinguished according to whether the participants adopt either a success-oriented attitude or one oriented to reaching understanding.' *Theory of Communicative Action; vol. I*, op. cit., p. 286.

37 See 'What is Universal Pragmatics', in *Communication and the Evolution of Society*, op. cit., pp. 1–5.

38 'Historical Materialism and the Development of Normative Structures', in ibid., p. 97.

39 ibid., pp. 119–20.

40 This point is made in Jonathan Culler, 'Communicative Competence and Normative Force', *New German Critique*, Spring/Summer 1985, no. 35, pp. 133–44; see especially p. 141.

41 'A Postscript to *Knowledge and Human Interests*', translated by C. Lenhardt, *Philosophy of the Social Sciences*, 1973, vol. 3, pp. 157–89, quoted extract on p. 160; cited in John B. Thompson, 'Universal Pragmatics', John B. Thompson and David Held (eds), *Habermas: Critical Debates*, London, Macmillan, 1983, p. 120.

42 Cp. Jean-François Lyotard, *The Postmodern Condition: A Report on Knowledge*, translated by Geoff Bennington and Brian Massumi, Manchester, Manchester University Press, 1984, p. xxiv: 'Such consensus does violence to the heterogeneity of language games.'

43 Cp. Marx, 'Contribution to Critique of Hegel's Philosophy of Law, Introduction', in Karl Marx and Frederick Engels, *Collected Works*, vol. 3, London, Lawrence & Wishart, 1975, p. 182: 'The weapon of criticism cannot, of course, replace criticism by weapons.'

44 Agnes Heller, 'Habermas and Marxism', in *Habermas: Critical Debates*, edited by J. B. Thompson and D. Held, London and Basingstoke, MacMillan, 1982, p. 29.

45 'A Reply to My Critics', in *Habermas: Critical Debates*, op. cit., p. 227.

46 'Habermas and Marxism', op. cit., p. 34.

47 See Claus Offe, 'Work: The Key Sociological Category?', in *Disorganised Capitalism: Contemporary Transformation of Work and Politics*, edited by John Keane, Cambridge, Polity Press, 1985.

48 *The Will to Power*, op. cit., book one, I, para. 1, p. 6.

49 Cp. Rousseau, 'The love of others, springing from self-love, is the source of human justice.' *Emile*, translated by Barbara Foxley, London, Dent Everyman Library, 1963, book IV, p. 197. See also the discussion in Marshall Berman, *The Politics of Authenticity*, New York, Atheneum, 1980, p. 181.

50 *A Theory of Justice*, op. cit., p. 264.

51 Michael J. Sandel, *Liberalism and the Limits of Justice*, Cambridge, Cambridge University Press, 1984, ch. 2. See also Michael J. Sandel (ed.), *Liberalism and Its Critics*, Oxford, Blackwell, 1984.

52 Max Weber, *The Protestant Ethic and the Spirit of Capitalism*, London, George Allen & Unwin, 1976, p. 181.

5 THE ILLUSORY COMMUNITY: THE NATION

1 Benedict Anderson, *Imagined Communities: Reflections on the Origins and Spread of Nationalism*, London, Verso, 1983, pp. 17–18.

2 See, for example, J. S. Mill, *Considerations on Representative Government*, first published 1861, reprinted in J. S. Mill, *Utilitarianism; Liberty; Representative Government*, London, J. M. Dent, 1957, ch. 16, 'Of Nationality, as Connected with Representative Government'. See, however, John E. E. D. Acton's 1862 essay 'Nationalism', reprinted in *The History of Freedom and Other Essays*, London, Macmillan, 1922, for an early dissident voice.

3 Marx and Engels, *The Communist Manifesto*, in Marx and Engels, *Collected Works*, vol. 6, London, Lawrence & Wishart, 1976, p. 488.

4 So much, at least, is common ground to all the major theorists of nationalism. Thus, for example, Hans Kohn, 'Nationalism as we understand it is not older than the second half of the eighteenth century', *The Idea of Nationalism*, NY, Macmillan, 1969, p. 3; Elie Kedourie, 'Nationalism is a doctrine invented in Europe at the beginning of the nineteenth century', *Nationalism*, London, Hutchinson University Library, 1971, p. 9; Hugh Seton-Watson, 'The doctrine of nationalism dates from the age of the French Revolution', *Nations and States*, London, Methuen, 1982, p. 6; and Benedict Anderson dates the emergence of nationalism 'towards the end of the eighteenth century', *Imagined Communities*, op. cit., p. 14. While Ernest Gellner is not quite so precise in his dating, he still identifies nationalism as an essentially modern phenomenon, rooted 'in the distinctive structural requirements of industrial society', *Nations and Nationalism*, Oxford, Basil Blackwell, 1983, p. 35.

5 Emile Durkheim, *The Division of Labour in Society*, New York, The Free Press, 1964, especially ch. 7.

6 See Hegel, *The Philosophy of Right*, Oxford, The Clarendon Press, 1965, section 324, pp. 209–10.

7 ibid., sections 268–9, pp. 163–4.

8 ibid., see Hegel's Preface, especially the polemic against romantic nationalism, pp. 5–10. This polemic provides the context of his famous remark that 'What is rational is actual and what is actual is rational'. See also the discussion of Hegel and nationalism in J. E. Toew, *Hegelianism, The Path Towards Dialectical Humanism, 1805–1841*, Cambridge, Cambridge University Press, 1980, ch. 3.

9 Ernest Renan, 'Qu'est-ce qu'une Nation?', reprinted in part in Louis L. Snyder (ed.), *The Dynamics of Nationalism, Readings in Its Meaning and Development*, Princeton, Van Nostrand, 1964, p. 9.

10 Cp. *Imagined Communities*, op. cit., p. 31: 'The idea of a sociological organism moving calendrically through homogeneous, empty time is a precise analogue of the idea of the nation, which also is conceived as a solid community moving steadily down (or up) history.'

11 Otto Bauer makes the recognition of a common destiny a primary feature of his account of the nation. See *Die Nationalitätenfrage und die Sozialdemokratie*, 1907; extracts in Tom Bottomore and Patrick Goode (eds), *Austro-Marxism*, p. 107: 'The nation is the totality of men bound together through a common destiny into a community of character.'

12 See *Imagined Communities*, op. cit., p. 133: '[T]oday, even the most insular nations accept the principle of *naturalisation* (wonderful word!), no matter how difficult in practice they make it'.

13 *The Philosophy of Right*, op. cit., section 163, p. 112. See the discussion of this in Carole Pateman, *The Sexual Contract*, Cambridge, Polity Press, 1988, pp. 173–81.

14 According to Eugene Kamenka, 'Most frequently . . . nations have arisen on a linguistic basis; but in some cases, at least, the language has been created for them by nationalist intellectuals', in 'Political Nationalism – The Evolution of an Idea', in Eugene Kamenka (ed.), *Nationalism, The Nature and Evolution of an Idea*, Canberra, Australian National University Press, 1975, p. 13. Kamenka goes on to suggest that the Slovak and Ukrainian languages were largely created by nineteenth-century intellectuals.

15 Gellner emphasises universal literacy; see *Nations and Nationalism*, op. cit., pp. 26–9; Benedict Anderson stresses the spread of printing ('print capitalism'); see *Imagined Communities*, op. cit., ch. 3.

16 See Kedourie, *Nationalism*, op. cit., p. 9:

> [Nationalism] pretends to supply a criterion for the determination of the unit of population proper to enjoy government exclusively on its own, or the legitimate exercise of power in the state, and for the right organisation of a society of states.

See also *Nations and Nationalism*, op. cit., p. 1: 'Nationalism is primarily a political principle which holds that the political and the national unit should be congruent.'

17 For this point and others in this paragraph, see the discussion in *Nations and Nationalism*, op. cit., especially ch. 2.

18 See Evgeny B. Pashukanis, *Law and Marxism, A General Theory*, London, Ink Links, 1978, especially ch. 4.

19 These points are well made by Ernest Gellner; see *Nations and Nationalism*, op. cit., ch. 3. However, Gellner explains them in terms of industrialism, not the capitalist market.

20 See, for example, Josef Stalin, 'Marxism and the National Question', 1913, reprinted in part in Bruce Franklin (ed.), *The Essential Stalin, Major Theoretical Writings 1905–1952*, London, Croom Helm, 1973, p. 67:

> The chief problem for the young bourgeoisie is the problem of the market. Its aim is to sell its goods and to emerge victorious from competition with the bourgeoisie of a different nationality. The market is the first school in which the bourgeoisie learns its nationalism.

Lenin's view is strikingly similar. See 'The Right of Nations to Self-Determination', 1914, reprinted in V. I. Lenin, *Selected Works in Two Volumes*, vol. I, part 2, Moscow, Foreign Languages Publishing House, 1952, ch. 1, p. 318:

> Throughout the world, the period of the final victory of capitalism over feudalism has been linked up with national movements. The economic basis of these movements is the fact that in order to achieve complete victory for commodity production the bourgeoisie must capture its home market.

21 See *Imagined Communities*, op. cit., p. 131.

22 See for example Joseph Schumpeter, *Capitalism, Socialism and Democracy*, London, George Allen & Unwin, 1943; reprinted 1976, pp. 134–8.

23 This is not the whole story; those intellectuals whose institutional and disciplinary affiliation directs them towards the more abstract and general have tended to be wary of nationalism. These include, especially, philosophers.

24 Cp. Carl von Clausewitz, *On War*, abridged edition, Harmondsworth, Penguin, 1982, p. 101: 'War is an act of violence intended to compel our opponent to fulfil our will.'

25 As against Virginia Woolf's claim that women are 'outside' nationalism: '[A]s a woman, I have no country. As a woman, I want no country. As a woman, my country is the whole world.' *Three Guineas*, London, The Hogarth Press, 1968, p. 197.

26 As I remarked above, Hegel was opposed to nationalism. Nevertheless, here as elsewhere, he provided a very clear account of the moral dynamic involved. See *The Phenomenology of Spirit*, Oxford, Clarendon Press, 1977, p. 274: 'In the ethical household, it is not a question of this particular husband, this particular child, but simply of husbands and children generally; the relationships of women are based, not on feeling, but on the universal.' According to Hegel, it is only through the universalisation of their domestic situation that women achieve ethical status. See the discussion in Genevieve Lloyd, 'Masters, Slaves, and Others', in Roy Edgley and Richard Osborne (eds), *The Radical Philosophy Reader*, London, Verso, 1985.

27 Marx, *On the Jewish Question*, in Marx and Engels, *Collected Works*, op. cit., vol. 3, p. 154.

28 *Imagined Communities*, op. cit., p. 15.

29 Anderson implicitly concedes this at various points in his account. See, for example, ibid., p. 19: 'If nation states are widely conceded to be "new" and "historical", the nations to which they give political expression always loom out of an immemorial past, and, still more importantly, glide into a limitless future.' All the talk of 'imagination' in the world will not provide a reading of this which does not imply that the consciousness of nationalism involves a miscomprehension of its nature.

6 MODERNITY AND MADNESS: NIETZSCHE'S APOTHEOSIS

1 Michel Foucault, *The Order of Things*, London, Tavistock Publications, 1970, p. 385.

2 A. Alvarez, *The Savage God, A Study of Suicide*, Harmondsworth, Penguin, 1974, pp. 281–2.
3 *Beyond Good and Evil*, translated by R. J. Hollingdale, Harmondsworth, Penguin Books, 1976, para. 29.
4 ibid., para. 6.
5 Robert C. Solomon, *From Hegel to Existentialism*, New York, Oxford University Press, 1989, p. 106.
6 *Beyond Good and Evil*, op. cit., para. 196.
7 ibid., para. 258; see also *The Will to Power*, translated by Walter Kaufmann and R. J. Hollingdale, New York, Vintage Books, 1968, para. 258.
8 *Twilight of the Idols*, translated by Walter Kaufmann, in *The Portable Nietzsche*, Walter Kaufmann (ed.), London, Chatto & Windus, 1971, 'The "Improvers" of Mankind', p. 501.
9 *Will to Power*, op. cit., para. 481.
10 See, for example, *Beyond Good and Evil*, op. cit., para. 14.
11 *Twilight of the Idols*, op. cit., 'The "Improvers" of Mankind', p. 501.
12 In what follows, I am indebted to Alexander Nehamas, *Nietzsche, Life as Literature*, Cambridge, Mass. and London, Harvard University Press, 1985, especially ch. 2. For some disagreement, see the text for note 75 below. See also Paul Redding, 'Nietzschean Perspectivism and the Logic of Practical Reason', *Philosophical Forum*, 1990/91, vol. 20, pp. 72–88.
13 *Beyond Good and Evil*, op. cit., para. 6.
14 ibid., para. 872.
15 See *The Gay Science*, translated by Walter Kaufmann, New York, Vintage Books, 1974, preface, para. 2; *Beyond Good and Evil*, op. cit., para. 23, para. 196, etc.
16 See *Untimely Meditations*, translated by R. J. Hollingdale, Cambridge, Cambridge University Press, 1983, for example p. 76.
17 For a sophisticated defence of the more orthodox view that science both needs and can make good a claim to objectivity, whilst morality neither needs nor can have it, see Bernard Williams, *Ethics and the Limits of Philosophy*, London, Fontana Press/Collins, 1985, ch. 8.
18 *Beyond Good and Evil*, op. cit., para. 31.
19 ibid., para. 43.
20 ibid., para. 2.
21 *The Gay Science*, op. cit., I, para. 19.
22 ibid., I, para. 21.
23 ibid., III, para. 121.
24 *Beyond Good and Evil*, op. cit., para. 229.
25 *On the Genealogy of Morals*, I, para. 8, translated by Walter Kaufmann and R. J. Hollingdale, in *On the Genealogy of Morals; Ecce Homo*, edited by Kaufmann, New York, Vintage Books, 1969.
26 *Will to Power*, op. cit., para. 272.
27 *On the Genealogy of Morals*, op. cit., II, para. 24.
28 ibid., I, para. 13.
29 *Will to Power*, op. cit., para. 484; cp. para. 477, *Beyond Good and Evil*, op. cit., para. 17.
30 *On the Genealogy of Morals*, op. cit., I, para. 10.

31 ibid.
32 ibid., para. 6.
33 ibid., para. 10; cp. also II, para. 1.
34 There is a similar thought in Stevie Smith's poem 'I forgive you',
I forgive you, Maria,
Things can never be the same,
But I forgive you, Maria,
Though I think you were to blame.
I forgive you, Maria,
I can never forget
But I forgive you, Maria
Kindly remember that.
From *Me Again, The Uncollected Writings of Stevie Smith*, London, Virago, 1984.
35 *On the Genealogy of Morals*, op. cit., I, para. 13.
36 See the interesting discussion in Rosalyn Diprose, 'Nietzsche, Ethics and Sexual Difference', *Radical Philosophy*, Summer 1989, no. 52, pp. 27–33. However, I think that Diprose underestimates the extent to which Nietzsche remains within the liberal–individualist framework.
37 *On the Genealogy of Morals*, op. cit., II, para. 16.
38 ibid., para. 1.
39 ibid., para. 3.
40 ibid., para. 16.
41 *The Gay Science*, op. cit., V, para. 354; my emphasis.
42 *On the Genealogy of Morals*, op. cit., II, para. 19.
43 *Ecce Homo*, translated by Walter Kaufmann, in *On the Genealogy of Morals; Ecce Homo*, op. cit., p. 292.
44 See Hume, *A Treatise of Human Nature*, edited by L. A. Selby-Bigge, revised by P. H. Nidditch, Oxford, Clarendon Press, 2nd edition, 1983, book I, part IV, ch. VI, pp. 251–63.
45 *Thus Spoke Zarathustra*, translated by Walter Kaufmann, in *The Portable Nietzsche*, op. cit., I, 'On the Despisers of the Body', p. 146.
46 *The Gay Science*, op. cit., I, para. 11.
47 *Beyond Good and Evil*, op. cit., para. 191.
48 ibid., para. 213.
49 *On the Genealogy of Morals*, op. cit., I, para. 13.
50 *Ecce Homo*, op. cit., p. 290.
51 *The Will to Power*, op. cit., para. 490.
52 ibid., para. 492.
53 Despite his insistence on a non-consequentialist account of duty, even Kant recognised that there must be some intelligible connection between people obeying the moral law, and at the same time making sense of their lives in terms of their own destiny and a more comprehensive world order. This formed the basis for his famous 'proofs' of individual immortality and the existence of God in the second *Critique*, and elsewhere his arguments for a law-governed teleological conception of history. See *Critique of Practical Reason*, translated by L. W. Beck, Indianapolis, Bobbs-Merrill, 1956, book II, 'Dialectic of Pure Practical Reason', especially chs. IV and V, pp. 126–36; and 'Idea for a

Universal History with a Cosmopolitan Purpose', translated by H. B. Nisbet, in *Kant's Political Writings*, Hans Reiss (ed.), Cambridge, Cambridge University Press, 1977.

54 *Twilight of the Idols*, op. cit., 'How the "True World" finally became a Fable', pp. 485–6.

55 ibid., 'Maxims and Arrows', 18, p. 469; cp. *Will to Power*, op. cit., para. 585.

56 *Twilight of the Idols*, op. cit., 'The Problem of Socrates', pp. 473–9.

57 *Will to Power*, op. cit., para. 5.

58 ibid., para. 1, 2.

59 ibid., para. 2.

60 ibid., Preface, para. 2.

61 ibid., para. 22.

62 ibid., para. 12(A).

63 ibid., para. 36.

64 *Thus Spoke Zarathustra*, op. cit., Part II, 'On Redemption', p. 251.

65 ibid., p. 253.

66 *Beyond Good and Evil*, op. cit., para. 56.

67 *Will to Power*, op. cit., para. 55.

68 Baudelaire's definition of art is close to Nietzsche on this point,

> By 'modernity' I mean the ephemeral, the fugitive, the contingent, the half of art, whose other half is the eternal and immutable.

However, Baudelaire writes as if the ephemeral and the eternal were separable elements; for Nietzsche, they were identical. See 'The Painter of Modern Life', in *The Painter of Modern Life and Other Essays*, translated and edited by Jonathan Mayne, New York, Da Capo Press, 1986.

69 *Thus Spoke Zarathustra*, op. cit., III, 'On Old and New Tablets', 3, p. 310; cp. II, 'On Redemption', pp. 249–54.

70 ibid., III, 'The Convalescent', p. 327 and pp. 331–2.

71 *The Gay Science*, op. cit., IV, para. 341.

72 ibid.; see also *Thus Spoke Zarathustra*, op. cit., III, 'On the Vision and the Riddle', pp. 267–72.

73 *The Order of Things*, op. cit., p. 385.

74 See G. W. F. Hegel, *The Phenomenology of Spirit*, translated by A. V. Miller, Oxford, Clarendon Press, 1977, pp. 111–19.

75 Nehamas, *Nietzsche, Life as Literature*, ch. 2, especially pp. 62–3, and the various references to Nietzsche's writings provided there.

76 Alasdair MacIntyre, *After Virtue*, 2nd edition, Notre Dame, University of Notre Dame Press, 1984, ch. 9, ignores the extent to which Nietzsche sees the individual as a construct out of conflicting forces. But he is right to interpret Nietzsche's values as individualistic and to treat him as the exemplary spokesman for modernity.

7 TOWARDS MORALITY

1 Hobbes, *Leviathan*, edited by Michael Oakeshott, Oxford, Basil Blackwell, n.d., part I, ch. 13, p. 83.

2 Bernard Williams, *Ethics and the Limits of Philosophy*, London, Fontana Press/Collins, 1985, ch. 10, brings out how a morality of duty – which

Williams calls 'morality' *tout court* – distorts the nature of moral deliberation when it attempts to address ethical questions of any complexity.

3 Cp. Marx: 'If correctly understood interest is the principle of all morality, man's private interest must be made to coincide with the interest of humanity.' Marx and Engels, *The Holy Family*, in Marx and Engels, *Collected Works*, vol. 4, London, Lawrence & Wishart, 1975, pp. 130–1. Marx is here commenting on eighteenth century French materialism; still, as we shall see, there is reason to suppose that this corresponds to his own views.

4 *Leviathan*, op. cit., part I, ch. 15, p. 103.

5 See Max Stirner, *The Ego and His Own*, translated by Steven T. Byington, New York, Dover, 1973, part one, ch. 2, section B.1, pp. 31–3.

6 *Ethics and the Limits of Philosophy*, op. cit., p. 46.

7 *The Holy Family*, in *Collected Works*, op. cit., vol. 4, pp. 35–7.

8 See the discussion at the end of chapter 6. For the dialectic itself, see G. W. F. Hegel, *The Phenomenology of Spirit*, translated by A. V. Miller, Oxford, Clarendon Press, 1977, pp. 111–19.

9 For a fascinating discussion of the way in which sado-masochistic fantasies attempt to combine the logic of instrumentality with a recognition of the other, see Jessica Benjamin, 'Master and Slave: The Fantasy of Erotic Domination', in Ann Snitow *et al.* (eds), *Desire: The Politics of Sexuality*, London, Virago, 1984.

10 See Sandra M. Lynch, *Conceptions of Friendship*, unpublished MA(Hons) thesis, Macquarie University, Sydney, 1988, especially ch. 2.

11 Alasdair MacIntyre, *After Virtue*, 2nd Edition, Notre Dame, University of Notre Dame Press, 1984, see especially chs 14–15.

12 ibid., p. 187.

13 ibid., p. 188.

14 ibid., pp. 193–4.

15 ibid., especially ch. 15. It was for me one of the many disappointing features of MacIntyre's later work *Whose Justice? Which Rationality?*, London, Duckworth, 1988, that this notion drops out almost entirely.

16 *After Virtue*, op. cit., p. 218.

17 ibid., p. 219.

18 ibid., p. 252.

19 ibid.

20 Paul Feyerabend, *Against Method*, London, Verso, 1984, p. 26.

21 In a much quoted passage, Marx wrote that 'what distinguishes the worst architect from the best of bees is that the architect builds the cell in his mind before he constructs it in wax', *Capital*, vol. I, translated by Ben Fowkes, Harmondsworth, Penguin, 1976, ch. 7, p. 284. This is probably wrong even for architects. It certainly does not do justice to Marx's own account of labour as purposive activity.

22 ibid., Afterword to Second Edition, p. 99. The argument given here provides, I think, the rational kernel of Marx's strictures against 'utopianism'. Unfortunately, both with Marx and more especially Engels, this argument became mixed up with a doctrine of historical inevitability.

23 See the discussion in Thomas Kuhn, *The Structure of Scientific Revolutions*, 2nd Edition, Chicago, University of Chicago Press, 1973, especially chs VII–IX.
24 See the passage by Feyerabend quoted at the beginning of this section.
25 Marx, *The Poverty of Philosophy*, in Marx and Engels, *Collected Works*, vol. 6, London, Lawrence & Wishart, 1976, pp. 210–11.
26 Marx, *Contribution to the Critique of Hegel's Philosophy of Law. Introduction*, in Marx and Engels, *Collected Works*, vol. 3, London, Lawrence & Wishart, 1975, pp. 186–7.
27 Marx, *Economic and Philosophical Manuscripts of 1844*, in Marx and Engels, *Collected Works*, op. cit., vol. 3, p. 313.
28 See Anthony Skillen, *Ruling Illusions: Philosophy and the Social Order*, Hassocks, Sussex, The Harvester Press, 1977, especially ch. 4, pp. 168–9. See also Skillen, 'Workers' Interest and the Proletarian Ethic: Conflicting Strains in Marxian Anti-Moralism', in Kai Nielsen and Steven C. Patten (eds), *Marx and Morality, Canadian Journal of Philosophy*, 1981, supp. vol. 7. Both the interpretation of Marx and the positive conception of morality advanced in this chapter owe much to Skillen's work.
29 See Genevieve Lloyd, *The Man of Reason*, London, Methuen, 1985.
30 ibid., p. 109.

BIBLIOGRAPHICAL ESSAY

In this essay, I provide suggestions for further reading on some of the issues raised in this book. I have tried to be ecumenical in my selection (though not in my comments); inevitably, however, the list is a personal one, reflecting my own intellectual history, interests and knowledge. I have only listed work published this century, and I have emphasised recent contributions. Where the work cited contains a useful bibliography, I have indicated this with an asterisk.

If responsibility for the impoverishment of moral philosophy in the analytical tradition for most of the twentieth century had to be assigned to one work, it would be G. E. Moore's *Principia Ethica* (Cambridge, Cambridge University Press, 1903). Moore directed the attention of English-speaking philosophers away from substantive moral questions towards the analysis of moral judgements – 'meta-ethics' in the jargon of later years. He also produced an argument – the 'naturalistic fallacy' – which persuaded almost everyone (no one is now clear why) that it was impossible to define moral concepts by reference to empirical ('natural') ones. For Moore, the truth of moral judgements was to be ascertained by the intuitive apprehension of non-natural moral properties in the world. The fact that intuition provided no help in settling moral disputes within a culture, let alone for coping with moral divergence between cultures, did not prevent this doctrine from attracting the allegiance of a number of influential philosophers (e.g. H. A. Prichard, W. D. Ross). The logical positivism of the 1920s and 1930s produced an account more in line with the sceptical tenor of the times: the idea that moral judgements are merely expressions of the speaker's emotions. 'Emotivism', as this doctrine came to be called, was represented in English by C. L. Stevenson's 'The

Emotive Meaning of Ethical Terms', *Mind*, vol. 46 (1937), pp. 14–31; reprinted in Stevenson's *Facts and Values* (New Haven, Yale University Press, 1963) and A. J. Ayer's *Language, Truth and Logic* (first edition 1935, second edition 1946; New York, Dover), ch. 6. R. M. Hare's 'prescriptivism' developed in the late 1940s and early 1950s is somewhat in the spirit of emotivism, but argued that moral judgements work more like commands than expressions of emotion. What distinguishes them from ordinary commands is that they express overriding commitments which apply to everyone (including the speaker). See Hare's *The Language of Morals* (Oxford, Clarendon Press, 1952) and *Freedom and Reason* (Oxford, Clarendon Press, 1963).

For Hare and the emotivists, moral judgements are not in any ordinary sense true or false: they merely express strong emotions or commitments of the speaker. What was largely overlooked was the extent to which moral language is misleading if this analysis is correct. J. L. Mackie's *Ethics: Inventing Right and Wrong* (Harmondsworth, Penguin Books, 1977) meets this issue head on. For Mackie, moral judgements assert the existence of moral facts; given that there are no moral facts, it follows that they are straightforwardly false. Curiously enough, Mackie does not see this as a reason for rejecting morality, but argues for its retention on the grounds of its social utility. Mackie's book was largely responsible for invigorating what had been a flagging interest in meta-ethics. Since then the journals have been full of debates between 'moral realists', who argue that moral judgements are as capable of truth as judgements of any other kind, and 'anti-realists' (or 'non-cognitivists') who follow the spirit, though certainly not the letter, of Ayer, Stevenson and Hare. While participants rejoice in the increased sophistication made possible by recent developments in the philosophy of language, its cost has been an ever increasing distance from substantial issues about morality. Realism is defended by David Wiggins, 'Truth, Invention, and the Meaning of Life', *Proceedings of the British Academy*, vol. 62 (1976), pp. 331–78; reprinted in his *Needs, Values, Truth* (Oxford, Blackwell, 1987), and by John McDowell in various papers, including 'Are Moral Requirements Hypothetical Imperatives?', *Proceedings of the Aristotelian Society*, supp. vol. 52 (1978), pp. 13–29, and 'Values and Secondary Qualities', in Ted Honderich (ed.), *Morality and Objectivity* (London, Routledge & Kegan Paul, 1985). It is criticised by Bernard Williams in 'Ethical Consistency', *Proceedings of the*

Aristotelian Society, supp. vol. 39 (1965), pp. 103–24, and in 'Consistency and Realism', *Proceedings of the Aristotelian Society*, supp. vol. 40 (1966), pp. 1–22, both of which are reprinted in Williams, *Problems of the Self* (Cambridge, Cambridge University Press, 1973), and by Simon Blackburn in *Spreading the Word* (Oxford, Clarendon Press, 1984), chs 5 and 6. Some of these, and much else, are reprinted in Geoffrey Sayre-McCord (ed.), *Essays on Moral Realism** (Ithaca and London, Cornell University Press, 1988). David McNaughten, *Moral Vision** (Oxford, Blackwell, 1988) provides an overview of the basic issues.

There has been a resurgence in substantial ('first order') moral philosophy over the past twenty-five years. The discussion has been dominated by the debate between utilitarians and a variety of Kantians, with the Kantians gradually coming out on top. Which is not to say that utilitarianism has lacked defenders. J. J. C. Smart takes a tough-minded view of various unpalatable consequences of the utilitarian position in 'An Outline of a System of Utilitarian Ethics', in J. J. C. Smart and Bernard Williams, *Utilitarianism: For and Against** (Cambridge, Cambridge University Press, 1973). R. M. Hare argues that utilitarianism is the moral position most consonant with prescriptivism in 'Ethical Theory and Utilitarianism', in H. D. Lewis (ed.), *Contemporary British Philosophy* (London, Allen & Unwin, 1976). This is reprinted with a number of – mostly negative – evaluations of utilitarianism in Amartya Sen and Bernard Williams (eds), *Utilitarianism and Beyond** (Cambridge, Cambridge University Press, 1982). Derek Parfit, *Reasons and Persons* (Oxford, Clarendon Press, 1984) provides a rigorously analytic argument for the dissolution of person identity. He sees this as providing a reason for utilitarianism, not for questioning his methodology. There is a symposium devoted to Parfit's views in *Ethics*, vol. 96 (1985–6), pp. 703–871.

A variety of Kantian positions are represented in the literature. Thomas Nagel's *The Possibility of Altruism* (Oxford, Clarendon Press, 1970) is an argument along recognisably Kantian lines for its necessity. See also Nagel's later work, notably *Mortal Questions* (Cambridge, Cambridge University Press, 1979) and *The View from Nowhere* (New York and Oxford, Oxford University Press, 1986). Alan Gewirth, *Reason and Morality* (Chicago and London, Chicago University Press, 1978) attempts to deduce the fundamental principles of morality from the rational presuppositions of agency. The most influential work in moral philosophy in English in recent years has been John Rawls, *A Theory of Justice* (Cambridge, Mass., Harvard University Press, 1972). Rawls' Kantian liberalism has set the parameters for most subsequent debate. Initially, Rawls' theory was largely interpreted – and perhaps intended – as an attempt to construct a theory of justice on the basis of very general considerations of rationality, human nature and the like; but Rawls himself has retreated from this interpretation, and in recent writings he avows the more modest endeavour to articulate and defend the conception of justice already implicit in the liberal tradition. For the latest instalments, see 'Kantian Constructivism in Moral Theory', *Journal of Philosophy*, vol. 77 (1980), pp. 515–72; 'Justice as Fairness: Political not Metaphysical', *Philosophy and Public Affairs*, vol. 14 (1985), pp. 239–51; and 'The Priority of Right and Ideas of the Good', *Philosophy and Public Affairs*, vol. 17 (1988), pp. 251–76. A number of early criticisms are collected in Norman Daniels (ed.), *Reading Rawls*,* (Oxford, Basil Blackwell, 1975). A systematic critique from a 'communitarian' perspective is provided by Michael J. Sandel, *Liberalism and the Limits of Justice* (Cambridge, Cambridge University Press, 1982). Sandel has also edited a useful collection, *Liberalism and Its Critics* (Oxford, Basil Blackwell, 1984), which emphasises the communitarian response to liberalism. Charles E. Larmore, *Patterns of Moral Complexity* (Cambridge, Cambridge University Press, 1987) defends a form of liberalism from communitarian and other criticisms. There is a symposium on Rawls' more recent views on justice in *Ethics*, vol. 99 (1988–9), pp. 695–944, and a more broad ranging symposium on 'Universalism vs. Communitarianism' in *Philosophy and Social Criticism*, vol. 14 (1988), pp. 237–471.*

Robert Nozick, in *Anarchy, State, and Utopia* (New York, Basic Books, 1974) argues for a right-wing liberalism ('libertarianism'). He assumes without argument that individuals have certain natural rights, and then argues that these rights can only be secured by a capitalist market economy with a laissez-faire state. The flair with which the deduction was carried out obscured for a time the essential emptiness of the enterprise. H. L. A. Hart provides an effective critique in 'Between Utility and Rights', in Alan Ryan (ed.), *The Idea of Freedom* (Oxford, Oxford University Press, 1979). Jeffrey Paul (ed.), *Reading Nozick** (Oxford, Blackwell, 1981) contains a number of responses, both critical and appreciative. See also G. A. Cohen, 'Self-Ownership, World-Ownership, and Equality', in Frank S. Lukash (ed.), *Justice and Equality Here and Now** (Ithaca and London, Cornell University Press, 1986). David Gauthier's *Morals by Agreement* (Oxford, Clarendon Press, 1986) uses the resources of rational choice theory to arrive at the constraints that self-interested individuals would accept as governing their interaction. There are symposia on Gauthier in *Canadian Journal of Philosophy*, vol. 18 (1988), pp. 315–85 and in *Ethics*, vol. 97 (1986–7), pp. 715–64. In *Contingency, Irony, and Solidarity* (Cambridge, Cambridge University Press, 1989), Richard Rorty defends a form of liberalism which avows that there is no non-circular defence of fundamental liberal positions. For criticism, see Thomas McCarthy, 'Private Irony and Public Decency: Richard Rorty's New Pragmatism', *Critical Inquiry*, vol. 16 (1990), pp. 355–70.

A significant minority voice has called for a return to an Aristotelian conception of ethics in which the concept of virtue is central. G. E. M. Anscombe, 'Modern Moral Philosophy', *Philosophy*, vol. 33 (1958), pp. 1–29; reprinted in Anscombe, *Collected Philosophical Papers Vol. III: Ethics, Religion, and Politics* (Oxford, Basil Blackwell, 1981) provides a sweeping condemnation of Kantian and utilitarian approaches. Philippa Foot has been pursuing the path of virtue since the 1950s; her most important essays are collected in *Virtues and Vices* (Oxford, Basil Blackwell, 1978). Unfortunately Foot pays very little attention to the social and historical conditions which are necessary for a life of virtue. Bernard Williams' position in *Ethics and the Limits of Philosophy* (London, Fontana Press, 1985) is not strictly an Aristotelian one, though close to it in spirit. Given his view of the limitations of philosophy when compared to the richness of concrete ethical life, it is a pity he does little more than mention the tendencies at work in the modern world to erode the kind of ethical life that he he would wish to take for granted.

One of the great virtues of Alasdair MacIntyre's *After Virtue* (Notre Dame, Indiana, University of Notre Dame Press, first edition 1981, second edition 1984) is the emphasis on the historical context of moral philosophy. MacIntyre tells an impressive story of the rise of virtue ethics (from Homer, through Aristotle, to medieval Christendom) and its subsequent fall with the Enlightenment and modernity. He also provides a sweeping but effective attack on the moral emptiness of much recent moral philosophy. However, MacIntyre does not fully confront the consequences of his own view that 'a moral philosophy . . . characteristically presupposes a sociology', and the story he tells is largely one of philosophical error, not of fundamental social change. For criticisms of *After Virtue* and replies by MacIntyre, see the symposium in *Inquiry*, vol. 26 (1983–4), pp. 387–466 and vol. 27 (1984–5), pp. 235–54; also Richard J. Bernstein, 'Nietzche or Aristotle? Reflections on *After Virtue*', *Soundings*, no. 67 (Spring 1984), reprinted in Bernstein, *Philosophical Profiles* (Cambridge, Polity Press, 1986), to which MacIntyre responded in the same issue of *Soundings*. MacIntyre and Stanley Hauerwas (ed.), *Revisions: Changing Perspectives in Moral Philosophy* (Notre Dame and London, University of Notre Dame Press, 1983), is a collection of like-minded articles expressing dissatisfaction with the current state of moral philosophy. In MacIntyre's later work, *Whose Justice? Which Rationality?* (London, Duckworth, 1988), nostalgia takes over. While it has interesting things to say about reason and tradition, the positive doctrines advanced have become increasingly reactionary (in both the literal and the political sense) and eccentric. See the review by Martha Nussbaum, 'Recoiling from Reason', *New York Review of Books* (7 December 1989), pp. 36–41.

Charles Taylor's insistence on the socially embodied nature of the self has meant that he is often treated as one of the 'communitarian' critics of liberalism. However, Taylor is more aware than most of the historical and social, as well as philosophical difficulties which need to be resolved before the notion of a community can be invoked with a good conscience. Probably the best introduction to his views is his *Hegel* (Cambridge, Cambridge University Press, 1975), Part IV, reprinted in part in Sandel (ed.), *Liberalism and Its Critics*. See also his 'What is Human Agency?' and other articles in *Human Agency and Language: Philosophical Papers 1* (Cambridge, Cambridge University Press, 1985), Part I, and *Philosophy and the Human Sciences: Philosophical Papers 2* (Cambridge, Cambridge University Press, 1985), Part II. His latest book, *Sources of the Self: The Making of Modern Identity* (Cambridge, Mass., Harvard University Press, 1989; Cambridge University Press, 1990) provides a comprehensive account of the emergence of modern notions of the self and their implications for morality.

Those influenced by the revival of Marxism in the English-speaking world in the late 1960s were properly critical of analytical philosophy for its lack of social and political self-awareness. However, the contribution of Marxism to moral philosophy has been disappointing. Allen Wood, in 'The Marxian Critique of Justice', *Philosophy and Public Affairs*, vol. 1 (1971–2), pp. 244–82, made the interesting suggestion that Marx's critique of capitalism was not a moral critique, and that Marx rejected morality altogether. Unfortunately, the ensuing discussion quickly became bogged down on the interpretation of Marx, rather than the critique of morality as such. Wood's article and various responses are collected in Marshall Cohen *et al.* (eds), *Marx, Justice, and History* (Princeton, Princeton University Press, 1980). Wood's view are developed in his *Karl Marx** (London, Routledge & Kegan Paul, 1981), especially Part 3. Norman Geras, 'The Controversy about Marx and Justice',* *New Left Review*, no. 150 (March/April 1985), pp. 47–85, provides a comprehensive overview of the debate. Steven Lukes, *Marxism and Morality** (Oxford, Oxford University Press, 1985), effectively criticises the Marxist tradition for its lack of attention to questions of morality. Largely overlooked in these debates has been Anthony Skillen's seminal development of some of Marx's ideas. Skillen draws a distinction between morality and moralism, and argues that Marx rejected moralism but not morality as such; he then goes on to develop a positive notion of morality only hinted at by Marx. See Anthony J. Skillen, *Ruling Illusions* (Hassocks, Sussex, The Harvester Press, 1977), especially ch. 4, and 'Workers' Interest and the Proletarian Ethic: Conflicting Strains in Marxian Anti-Moralism', in Kai Nielsen and Steven C. Patten (eds), *Marx and Morality*,* *Canadian Journal of Philosophy*, supp. vol. 7 (1981), pp. 155–70. Skillen's views are influenced by the account of a non-prescriptive morality developed in Australia by John Anderson in the 1930s and 1940s; see Anderson, *Studies in Empirical Philosophy* (Sydney, Angus & Robertson, 1962). For exposition, see A. J. Baker, *Anderson's Social Philosopy* (Sydney, Angus & Robertson, 1979), especially Part I.

Of contemporary European philosophers, Jürgen Habermas has received most attention from Anglo-American philosophers, perhaps because he himself has been open to the influence of analytical philosophy, and perhaps too because he has arrived at a form of Kantian liberalism with some similarities to that advocated by Rawls. The great strength of Habermas' approach as compared with analytical philosophy is that he advances his conception of morality together with a philosophy of social science and an account of the dynamics of modern societies. He has been working on his 'discourse ethics' over a number of years; the fullest version to date is in *The Theory of Communicative Action*, vols 1 and 2, (German ed. 1981; translated by Thomas McCarthy, Boston, Beacon Press, 1984 and 1987). Useful earlier versions are to be found in *Communication and the Evolution of Society* (German ed. 1976; translated by Thomas McCarthy, London, Heinemann, 1979). See now his *Moral Consciousness and Communication Action* (German edn 1983; translated by Christian Lenhardt and Shierry Weber Nicholsen, Cambridge, Mass., MIT Press, 1990). Habermas' polemic against post-structuralist and post-modernist currents of thought, *The Philosophical Discourse of Modernity* (German ed. 1985; translated by Frederick Lawrence, Cambridge, Mass., MIT Press, 1987), throws a lot of light on his position. Also informative are the interviews collected, with a useful editorial introduction, in *Autonomy and Solidarity* (ed. Peter Dews, London, Verso, 1986). Though Habermas' thought has developed considerably since it was written, Thomas McCarthy, *The Critical Theory of Jürgen Habermas* (Boston, Mass., MIT Press, 1978) remains the best introduction. Two excellent collections are Richard J. Bernstein (ed.), *Habermas and Modernity* (Cambridge, Polity Press, 1985) and John B. Thompson and David Held (eds), *Habermas: Critical Debates** (London, Macmillan, 1982) which contain material relevant to Habermas' conception of morality. The *New German Critique*, no. 35 (Spring/Summer 1985) is a special issue on Habermas; see especially the articles by Seyla Benhabib, Nancy Fraser and Jonathan Culler. Stephen K. White, *The Recent Work of Jürgen Habermas: Reason, Justice and Modernity** (Cambridge, Cambridge University Press, 1988) is an appreciative but critical overview. The special issue of *Philosophy and Social Criticism*, vol. 14 (1988), Universalism vs. Communitarianism has material on Habermas; see also *The Philosophical Forum*, vol. 21 (1989–90), special issue on *Hermeneutics in Ethics and Social Theory*, especially Jean Cohen, 'Discourse Ethics and Civil Society'.

Habermas' work is the latest – perhaps the last – episode in the tradition of Critical Theory. Perhaps the key work in this tradition is Theodor Adorno and Max Horkheimer, *The Dialectic of Enlightenment* (first published 1944; English translation by John Cumming, London, Verso, 1979). Adorno and Horkheimer argue that the rationality celebrated by the Enlightenment is not a vehicle for emancipation, but a mask for domination. It is a crucial part of Habermas' general position, not merely against his predecessors, but also against 'postmodernist' thinkers, that the project of the

Enlightenment is an emancipatory one. For Habermas' views on *The Dialectic of Enlightenment*, see *The Philosophical Discourse of Modernity*, especially Lecture 5. Andrew Arato and Eike Gebhardt (eds), *The Essential Frankfurt School Reader* (New York, Continuum, 1982), is a useful selecion of readings. On Critical Theory and its relationship to Habermas, see especially David Held, *Introduction to Critical Theory** (London, Hutchinson, 1983), and Seyla Benhabib, *Critique, Norm and Utopia** (New York, Columbia University Press, 1986).

A diverse range of offerings by French philosophers has been imported into Anglo-American countries over the past forty or so years. In the post-war period, Sartre's existentialism – developed in *Being and Nothingness* (first published 1943; translated by Hazel E. Barnes, London, Methuen, 1958) – was discussed by prominent English speaking philosophers; see Iris Murdoch, *Sartre: Romantic Rationalist* (London, Bowes & Bowes, 1953) and Mary Warnock, *The Philosophy of Sartre* (London, Hutchinson, 1965). Large doses of the structuralism and post-structuralism which dominated French philosophy from the 1960s to the 1980s were absorbed into Anglo-American intellectual life, though not philosophy departments. However, the 'anti-humanism' which was characteristic of both movements seemed antithetical to any notion of morality, and very few adherents bothered to concern themselves with moral issues.

Michel Foucault's work, such as *The Order of Things* (first published as *Les Mots et les choses* 1966; London, Tavistock, 1970), *Discipline and Punish* (first published 1975; translated by Alan Sheridan, New York, Pantheon, 1977) and *The History of Sexuality Vol. 1* (first published 1976; translated by Robert Hurley, London, Allen Lane, 1979), seemed to reaffirm the Nietzschean thesis that moral values were merely the masks of power, and that the discourse of liberation was a means of self- and other-deception. However, occasional remarks by Foucault on the importance of ethics, together with his own political commitments, seemed to suggest that there was a more positive conception of morality lurking in the background. Later volumes of *The History of Sexuality*, *The Use of Pleasure* (first published 1984; translated by Robert Hurley, New York, Pantheon Books, 1985) and *The Care of the Self* (first published 1984; translated by Robert Hurley, New York, Pantheon Books, 1986) reinforce that suggestion without making it clear what that conception is. Other relevant material is to be found in *The Foucault Reader*, edited by Paul Rabinow (New York, Pantheon Books, 1984), especially 'What is Enlightenment?', 'On the Genealogy of Ethics' and the interview entitled 'Polemics, Politics, and Problematisations'. Critics have argued that Foucault's theoretical writings do not provide the normative basis presupposed by his occasional comments and lifelong commitments; see Peter Dews, 'Power and Subjectivity in Foucault', *New Left Review*, 144 (March/April 1984), pp. 72–95; Charles Taylor, 'Foucault on Freedom and Truth', *Political Theory*, vol. 12 (1984), pp. 152–83; reprinted in Taylor's *Philosophical Papers 2* and in David Couzens Hoy (ed.), *Foucault: A Critical Reader* (Oxford, Basil Blackwell, 1986); Michael Walzer, 'The Politics of Michel Foucault', *Dissent*, vol. 30 (1984), pp. 481–90; reprinted in Hoy (ed.), *Foucault: A Critical Reader*. Defenders of Foucault have responded that critics have not recognised the radically new critical standards deployed by Foucault; see John Rajchman, *Michel Foucault: The Freedom of Philosophy* (New York, Cornell University Press, 1985) and 'Ethics after Foucault', *Social Text*, 13/14 (Winter/Spring 1986), pp. 165–83; Paul Patton, 'Michel Foucault: The Ethics of an Intellectual', *Thesis 11*, 10/11 (1984–5), pp. 71–80 and Taylor and Foucault on Power and Freedom', *Political Studies*, vol. 37 (1989), pp. 260–76. Charles Taylor has a response to Patton in the same issue of *Political Studies*, pp. 277–81. Foucault's death cut off a developing dialogue/polemic with Habermas. For Habermas' views on Foucault (and postmodernist thought generally), see *Philosophical Discourse on Modernity*; see also Peter Dews, *Logics of Disintegration* (London, Verso, 1987), especially chs 5–7. For responses on Foucault's behalf, see Rajchman, *Michel Foucault: The Freedom of Philosophy* and Thomas R. Flynn, 'Foucault and the Politics of Postmodernity', *Noûs*, vol. 23 (1989), pp. 187–98.

Various other French writers have been grouped with Foucault under the 'postmodernist' label. Of these, Gilles Deleuze is probably the closest to Foucault. Foucault remarked of Deleuze and Felix Guattari's *Anti-Oedipus: Capitalism and Schizophrenia* (first published 1972; translated by Robert Hurley, Mark Seem and Helen R. Lane, Minneapolis, University of Minneapolis Press, 1983), that it was 'the first book of ethics to be written in France in quite a long time'. Just why it is a contribution to ethics is somewhat obscure to a perspective informed by Anglo-American moral philosophy. The same may be said of Deleuze and Guattari's *A Thousand Plateaus* (first published 1980; translated by Brian

Massumi, Minneapolis, University of Minneapolis Press, 1980), though a sense of a Nietzschean, pluralist, anarchistic and non-prescriptive ethic does emerge. Perhaps the best entry into Deleuzian 'nomadology' is provided by Deleuze and Claire Parnet, *Dialogues* (first published 1977; translated by Hugh Tomlinson and Barbara Habberjam, New York, University of Columbia Press, 1987). Jean-François Lyotard, *The Postmodern Condition: A Report on Knowledge* (first published 1979; translated by Geoff Bennington and Brian Massumi, Manchester, Manchester University Press, 1984) defines postmodernity in terms of the displacement of unifying 'grand narratives' by a plurality of 'language games'. Habermas' attempt to specify the moral framework necessary for the co-existence of different language games is dismissed as yet another outmoded 'grand narrative'; though it is totally unclear what Lyotard offers in its place. See also Jean-François Lyotard and Jean-Loup Thébaud, *Just Gaming* (first published 1979; translated by Wlad Godzich, Manchester, Manchester University Press, 1985). For criticisms of Lyotard, see Peter Dews' 'Editor's Introduction' to Habermas, *Autonomy and Solidarity*; for mediation between Lyotard and Habermas, see Richard Rorty, 'Habermas and Lyotard on Postmodernity', in Richard J. Bernstein (ed.), *Habermas and Modernity*.

In the near background to most recent European thinking (and non-thinking) about ethical issues is the troubling figure of Martin Heidegger. For readers of this book, probably the most relevant place to start is Heidegger, *The Question Concerning Technology and other Essays* (translated by William Lovitt, New York, Harper & Row, 1977), especially the title essay and 'The Age of the World Picture'. For location of Heidegger with respect to the concept of modernity, and help on where to go next, see David Kolb, *The Critique of Pure Modernity: Hegel, Heidegger and After** (Chicago and London, University of Chicago Press, 1986), especially chs. 7–10. See also Richard J. Bernstein, *Philosophical Profiles* (Cambridge, Polity Press, 1986), ch. 7. For Rorty's views on Heidegger, see *Philosophy and the Mirror of Nature* (Oxford, Blackwell, 1980), especially ch. 8, *Consequences of Pragmatism* (Brighton, Harvester Press, 1982), ch. 3 (but use index as well), and *Contingency, Irony, and Solidarity*, especially ch. 5 (again, use index). For Habermas' views on Heidegger, see *The Philosophical Discourse of Modernity*, especially lecture 6.

A significant feminist critique of the assumptions, methods and content of moral philosophy has been going on for some years now, though it is only just beginning to have an impact on the 'mainstream' literature. Carol Gilligan's *In a Different Voice* (Cambridge, Mass. and London, Harvard University Press, 1982) argues that there is a distinct 'women's' voice on moral issues, which emphasises care, particularity and context, rather than justice, universality and principle. Gilligan's views have generated an enormous amount of debate, including symposia in *Signs*, vol 11 (1986), pp. 304–33, in *Social Research*, vol. 50 (1983), pp. 487–695 (see especially Linda J. Nicholson, 'Women, Morality, and History', pp. 514–36) and a series of articles in *Ethics* (see especially Lawrence A. Blum, 'Gilligan and Kohlberg: Implications for Moral Theory', vol. 98 (1987–8), pp. 472–91). See also Eva Feder Kitay and Diana T. Meyers (eds), *Women and Moral Theory* (Totowa, New Jersey, Rowman & Littlefield, 1987), especially Carol Gilligan, 'Moral Orientation and Moral Development' and Michael Stocker, 'Duty and Friendship: Towards a Synthesis of Gilligan's Contrastive Moral Concepts'. More general considerations of the idea of a specifically 'female ethic' are provided by Jean Grimshaw, *Feminist Philosophers* (Brighton, Wheatsheaf, 1986), chs. 7–8 and Virginia Held, 'Feminism and Moral Theory', in Kittay and Meyers (eds), *Women and Moral Theory*. Annette C. Baier has been developing as well as describing a distinctive voice in moral philosophy in a number of articles: see 'What Do Women Want in a Moral Theory', *Noûs*, vol. 19 (1985), pp. 53–64; 'Trust and Antitrust', *Ethics*, vol. 96 (1985–6), pp. 231–60 and 'Hume, the Women's Moral Theorist?' in Kittay and Meyers (eds), *Women and Moral Theory*.

There have been a number of important feminist critiques of liberalism. See especially Carole Pateman's *The Sexual Contract* (Cambridge, Polity Press, 1988), which presents a fundamental reinterpretation of one of the key elements in liberal social thought and practice. Susan Moller Okin, 'Justice and Gender', *Philosophy and Public Affairs*, vol. 16 (1987), pp. 42–71, looks both at what liberal theories of justice have to say about gender, and also at 'the effects of gender on justice'. I have not yet seen her *Justice, Gender and the Family* (New York, Basic Books, 1989). See also Deborah Kearns, 'A Theory of Justice – and Love; Rawls on the Family', *Politics*, vol. 18 (1983), pp. 36–42. Some feminists have argued that feminist values cannot be contained within the liberal agenda; see, for example, Iris Young,'Impartiality and the Civic Public', in

Seyla Benhabib and Drucilla Cornell (eds), *Feminism as Critique* (Cambridge, Polity Press, 1987). (This view has found its most influential proponents amongst French theorists of 'difference' discussed below.) There are relevant articles in Janna Thompson (ed.), *Women and Philosophy, Australasian Journal of Philosophy*, supp. to vol. 64 (1986) and Marsha Hanen and Kai Nielsen (eds), *Science, Morality and Feminist Theory, Canadian Journal of Philosophy*, supp. vol. 13 (1987).

Benhabib and Cornell (eds), *Feminism as Critique*, collect together a number of articles concerned with the feminist appropriation and critique of Habermas and Critical Theory. See especially Nancy Fraser, 'What's Critical about Critical Theory? The Case of Habermas and Gender' and Benhabib, 'The Generalised and the Concrete Other: The Kohlberg–Gilligan Controversy and Feminist Theory' (this is also in Kittay and Meyers (eds), *Women and Moral Theory*).

However, the work of a number of French feminist theorists has been more influential in the English-speaking world. Pride of place must be given to Simone de Beauvoir's *The Second Sex* (first published 1949; translated by H. M. Parshley, London, Jonathan Cape, 1953). Though she avows an existentialist ethic, the position developed is different in many ways from that presented earlier by Sartre. But not different enough for some feminist critics: it has been argued that the existentialist values of freedom and transcendence do not take into account the characteristic features of women's existence (e.g. child care). For sympathetic yet critical responses to de Beauvoir, see Genevieve Lloyd, *The Man of Reason** (London, Methuen, 1984), ch. 6; Toril Moi, 'Existentialism and Feminism', *Oxford Literary Review*, vol. 8, nos 1–2 (1986), Special Issue: *Sexual Difference*, pp. 88–95; and Catriona Mackenzie, 'Simone de Beauvoir: Philosophy and/or the Female Body', in Carole Pateman and Elizabeth Gross (eds), *Feminist Challenges* (Sydney, Allen & Unwin, 1986).

Michèle Le Doeuff, 'Operative Philosophy: Simone de Beauvoir and Existentialism', *Ideology and Consciousness*, no. 6 (Autumn 1979), pp. 47–58, provides a bridge between de Beauvoir and a later generation of French feminists. On Le Doeuff, see Meaghan Morris, 'Operative Reasoning: Reading Michèle Le Doeuff', *Ideology and Consciousness*, no. 9 (1981–2), pp. 71–101, reprinted in Morris, *The Pirates Fiancée: Feminism, Reading, Postmodernism** (London and New York, Verso, 1988). For an introduction to the work of Julia

Kristeva, Luce Irigaray, as well as Le Doeuff, see Elizabeth Grosz, *Sexual Subversions: Three French Feminists*★ (Sydney, Allen & Unwin, 1989). Useful collections are Toril Moi (ed.), *French Feminist Thought: A Reader* (Oxford, Blackwell, 1987), and Elaine Marks and Isabelle de Courtivron (eds), *New French Feminisms* (Brighton, Harvester Press, 1981). For Le Doeuff, see *The Philosophical Imaginary*, translated by Colin Gordon (London, The Athlone Press, 1989); for Kristeva, *The Kristeva Reader*, edited by Toril Moi (New York, Columbia University Press, 1986); and for Irigaray, *Speculum of the Other Woman* (first published 1972; translated by Gillian C. Gill, Ithaca, New York, Cornell University Press, 1985) and *This Sex Which Is Not One* (first published 1977; translated by Catherine Porter with Carolyn Burke, Ithaca, New York, Cornell University Press, 1985). On Kristeva and Irigaray especially, see Toril Moi, *Sexual/Textual Politics: Feminist Literary Theory*★ (London and New York, Methuen, 1985). See also *Hypatia*, vol. 3 (1989), Special Issue: *French Feminist Philosophy*. Recent work has emphasised recognisably ethical issues: see Irigaray's *Éthique de la Différence Sexuelle* (Paris, Les Éditions de Minuit, 1984). Relevant work in English includes Rosi Braidotti, 'The Problematic of the "Feminine" in Contemporary French Philosophy: Foucault and Irigaray', in Terry Threadgold and Anne Cranny-Francis (eds), *Feminine, Masculine and Representation* (Sydney, Allen & Unwin, 1990); Elizabeth Grosz, 'Notes Towards a Corporeal Feminism', in *Australian Feminist Studies*, no. 5 (1987), Special Issue: *Feminism and the Body*, pp. 1–16 and 'Inscriptions and Body-maps: Representations and the Corporeal', in Threadgold and Cranny-Francis (eds), *Feminine, Masculine and Representation*; and Moira Gatens, 'Woman and Her Double(s): Sex, Gender and Ethics', *Australian Feminist Studies*, no. 11 (Summer 1989), pp. 33–47. For more sceptical attitudes to French theory, see Drucilla Cornell and Adam Thurschwell, 'Feminism, Negativity, Intersubjectivity' in Benhabib and Cornell (eds), *Feminism as Critique*, and Pauline Johnson, 'Feminism and Difference: The Dilemmas of Luce Irigaray', *Australian Feminist Studies*, no. 6 (Summer 1988), pp. 87–97.

Intersecting with debates about female 'difference' is a complex set of controversies about the 'postmodern condition'. Proponents of the 'postmodern' celebrate the heterogeneous, the non-serious, parody, quotation, ambiguity; and set themselves against the traditional philosophical demands of unity, essence, principle and definition. Not surprisingly, the term 'postmodern' lacks a precise definition. It has one set of meanings when it is contrasted with the various cultural and aesthetic movements known as 'modernism', and another when it is contrasted with the socio-economic formation known as 'modernity'. Postmodern*ism* is probably the more defensible notion, with postmodern*ity* best thought of as an invitation to rethink the concept of modernity. However, most discussions run together these – and other – distinguishable themes. Hal Foster (ed.), *Postmodern Culture* (first published in the USA as *The Anti-Aesthetic* 1983; London and Sydney, Pluto Press, 1985), is a useful collection of essays. Andreas Huyssen, *After the Great Divide: Modernism, Mass Culture and Postmodernism* (first published in the USA 1986; London, Macmillan, 1988) and Charles Jencks, *What is Post-Modernism*? (London, Academy Editions, and New York, St. Martin's Press, 1986) are both favourably disposed. Fredric Jameson's 'Postmodernism, or the Cultural Logic of Late Capitalism', *New Left Review*, no. 146 (July/August 1984), pp. 53–92, provides a systematic account from a sympathetic but decidedly non-postmodernist perspective (there is an abbreviated verion of this essay in Foster (ed.), *Postmodern Culture*). There are criticisms of Jameson in subsequent issues of *New Left Review* and in Douglas Kellner (ed.), *Postmodernism/Jameson/Critique** (Washington, Maisonneuve Press, 1989). See also Linda Hutcheon, *The Politics of Postmodernism** (London and New York, Routledge, 1989). There are special issues of the *New German Critique*, no. 33 (Fall 1984): *Modernity and Postmodernity* and of *Theory, Culture and Society*, vol. 2 (1985): *The Fate of Modernity*. David Harvey's *The Condition of Postmodernity** (Oxford, Blackwell, 1989) is a highly informative and comprehensive work of synthesis. Both David Frisby, *Fragments of Modernity** (Cambridge, Mass., MIT Press, 1986) and Marshall Berman, *All That is Solid Melts into Air: The Experience of Modernity* (New York, Simon & Schuster, 1982) provide stimulating accounts of the ways in which the modern world has been experienced and represented in the work of some of the great modern social theorists, poets and novelists – Simmel, Kracauer and Benjamin in the case of Frisby, and Goethe, Marx and Baudelaire in the case of Berman. Not the least of the considerable virtues of these books is that they encourage a re-reading of the writers they deal with.

INDEX